Transforming Conflict and Building Peace

Conflict and Peace

Peter M. Kellett and Stacey L. Connaughton
Series Editors

Vol. 1

The Conflict and Peace series is part of the
Peter Lang Political Science, Economics, and Law list.
Every volume is peer reviewed and meets
the highest quality standards for content and production.

PETER LANG
New York • Bern • Berlin
Brussels • Vienna • Oxford • Warsaw

Transforming Conflict and Building Peace

Community Engagement Strategies for Communication Scholarship and Practice

Peter M. Kellett, Stacey L. Connaughton, and George Cheney, Editors

PETER LANG

New York • Bern • Berlin
Brussels • Vienna • Oxford • Warsaw

Library of Congress Cataloging-in-Publication Data

Names: Kellett, Peter M., editor. | Connaughton, Stacey L., editor. |
Cheney, George, editor.
Title: Transforming conflict and building peace: community engagement strategies
for communication scholarship and practice / edited by Peter M. Kellett,
Stacey L. Connaughton, and George Cheney.
Description: First Edition. | New York: Peter Lang, 2020.
Series: Conflict and peace; vol. 1
ISSN 2575-6796 (print) | ISSN 2575-680X (online)
Includes bibliographical references and index.
Identifiers: LCCN 2020004974 | ISBN 978-1-4331-7902-0 (hardback)
ISBN 978-1-4331-7903-7 (ebook pdf) | ISBN 978-1-4331-7904-4 (epub)
ISBN 978-1-4331-7905-1 (mobi)
Subjects: LCSH: Peace-building. | Communication in politics. |
Communication in community development.
Classification: LCC JZ5538 .T74 2020 | DDC 303.6/6071—dc23
LC record available at https://lccn.loc.gov/2020004974
DOI 10.3726/b17661

Bibliographic information published by **Die Deutsche Nationalbibliothek**.
Die Deutsche Nationalbibliothek lists this publication in the "Deutsche
Nationalbibliografie"; detailed bibliographic data are available
on the Internet at http://dnb.d-nb.de/.

The paper in this book meets the guidelines for permanence and durability
of the Committee on Production Guidelines for Book Longevity
of the Council of Library Resources.

Contents

PART III: Preventative, Restorative, and Systemic Engagement

PART IV: Volunteer and Citizen Scholars: Reflections and Lessons Learned

PART V: Teaching and Learning Peace and Conflict Transformation

Acknowledgements

Pete thanks all the conflict scholar-practitioners and peacebuilders contributing to this book. By investing their energy and expertise in various contexts locally, regionally, and globally, they continue to help make the world a fairer and more just place. By making the effort to write about their experiences here, they enrich our learning by showing us the lived reality of how such work gets done.

Stacey thanks all the peacebuilding scholar-practitioners and peacebuilders around the world who have inspired many to believe in, hope for, and actively pursue the possibilities of peace.

George thanks all the people in peace organizations, cooperatives, and ecologically minded communities who demonstrate the power of sound process and offer hope for the possible.

Introduction: The Promise and Reality of Engaged Scholarship and Practice

PETER M. KELLETT, STACEY L. CONNAUGHTON, AND GEORGE CHENEY

This book serves as the inaugural volume in the Peter Lang series, "Conflict and Peace," which is edited by Kellett and Connaughton. For this first book in the series, co-edited with Cheney, we wanted both to explain the orientation for the series and to presage future volumes, including those by other editors and authors, to follow the spirit of this one. To provide context for the present volume, we wish to highlight leading-edge conflict transformation and peacebuilding work that is achieved through engaged scholarship in the contemporary world. For the series, we wish to give voice to and advance research that demonstrates the relationship between conflict and systemic issues (e.g., relational, cultural, social, environmental, political, historical, and economic issues). This includes the roles of change practices and processes in broader systemic efforts to create a fairer, more just, healthier, and sustainable world, and the kinds of relationships that make that possible. This and future volumes will feature the lived experience of conflict transformation and peacebuilding of scholar-practitioners, and those affecting and affected by conflicts. In so doing, we wish to encourage books that explore novel ways of representing the spectrum of lived experiences of people involved in conflict transformation and peacebuilding. Series books will aim to show how theory and research design inform and are informed by practice, integrating diverse theories and methods from relevant disciplines through which conflicts are understood, addressed, and even prevented.

Our book series seeks to encourage work that considers and integrates a variety of modes and domains of conflict and peace interaction such as face to face, online, community, discursive, rhetorical, and others. We envision a series that has substantial appeal to scholarly audiences across relevant disciplines, and that speaks meaningfully to various audiences beyond academia (e.g., practitioners, policymakers, and donors). Clarity and accessibility of expression will be a hallmark of the books in this series. In this first volume, we believe, we have crafted a book that both exemplifies the type of work that we desire for the series as well as provides inspiration and guidance for succeeding volumes in a similar vein. In short, we believe this volume is a good beginning to what we hope is a valuable series for scholarly, educational, and practical purposes.

In this book, we bring together works that richly illustrate the creative tensions between the promise and the reality of applying communication theories, principles, and techniques to the world through the practice of conflict transformation and peacebuilding. The promise or ideal of helping to transform conflict and building lasting and sustainable positive peace, while aiming to help make the world around us a fairer and more just place, is at the heart of why scholars and practitioners apply communication to the world in this way (Anderson, Brown, & Jean, 2012; Boulding, 2002; Broome, 2002; Connaughton & Berns, 2019; Moix, 2019; Schirch & Campt, 2007). As Bridget Moix demonstrates in her 2019 book, people around the world *choose peace* despite tremendous structural, political, social, cultural, personal, and other kinds of barriers they face when doing the work of peacebuilding. Indeed, those of us committed to this line of work—researchers, practitioners, everyday citizens—want to make a difference. A well-designed conflict transformation and/or peacebuilding process that is culturally and relationally sensitive, as well as flexible and responsive, can unfold smoothly in practice. Yet, we also know that a lot goes into making a process look simple and elegant. Applications, in practice, also involve a broad range of context-based complexities, difficulties, and challenges about which change agents must be mindful and skillful (Ahmed & Bukhari, 2019; Autesserre, 2014; Firchow & Anastasiou, 2016; Lederach, 1997; Pineda Ruano, 2019). It is this nous, this practical knowhow of balancing promise and reality that we seek to bring to light here.

For this book, we sought a collection of essays which captures both the spirit of and desire for change that inspires each of the chapter authors to do their work in various places in the world, as well as the reality of what it is like to engage with conflicts and peacebuilding efforts. To get at this knowledge, we guided chapter authors to manifest a balance between process or technique description, and their experiences with designing, implementing, and reflecting on the impact of those processes and techniques in practice. We wanted them to be free to describe the ups and downs, ins and outs, joys and disappointments, false starts, and in-the-field/on-the-fly modifications to processes and techniques. We asked authors to reflect on and honestly address their learning experiences in doing the work of conflict transformation and peacebuilding. Some chapter authors found writing their personal experience into their chapters difficult and uncomfortable, even at odds with their social scientific training. Others relished the freedom to disclose and process the personal aspects of their work. Together, the authors offer valuable insights into the experience of doing engaged conflict transformation and peacebuilding work. We believe that the reader will benefit from how these authors address this dialectical tension of promise and reality as they strive to maximize the impact of their community and relationally engaged work.

We organized the volume into five parts, each of which examines an important aspect of the theory and practice of transforming conflict and building peace. Part I consists of two chapters that illustrate the opportunities and important considerations in designing, leading, and implementing transformative engagement processes so that they can have their desired impact on those settings. In Chapter 1 "Doing locally led peacebuilding: An examination of the relationally attentive approach to conducting engaged scholarship in Liberia, West Africa," Jennifer Ptacek and colleagues highlight the importance of including local voices in defining peace and its desired outcomes. They show us how transformative outcomes of peace processes are connected to *the quality of communicative collaboration*—the co-constructed reality—between the U.S.-based team members (PPP) and the local team members involved in and affected by the conflict. In Chapter 2 "Catalyzing deliberation: How engaged scholarship helped surface community values and transform conflict in local school facilities planning," Laura Black takes us inside a local community's struggle over planning discussions for school facilities amid scarce resources. Building on a similar theme to Chapter 1, Black shows us the importance of engaging with and listening carefully to local voices, and the delicate balance between helping to stimulate the dialogue between conflicting voices and ensuring that participants are focused on creating *their own peaceful solutions*—catalyzing but not colonizing, if you will. *Taken together, the two chapters speak to the careful sensitivity to local experiences and local involvement that are needed in order to effectively help people produce sustainable and meaningful change in their own worlds.*

Part II examines the central importance of the locally and culturally grounded reality of community engagement for conflict transformation and peacebuilding. In Chapter 3, "Rethinking the local turn in peace-building: Re(visiting) preventative stances in violent extremism: The Case of Likoni Subcounty, South Coast, Kenya," John Mwangi critiques the conventional liberal peacebuilding agenda as it is applied to countering violent extremism in Kenya. In so doing, he invites alternative constructions of terrorism (in addition to viewing terrorism as a state-centric concept) and encourages the incorporation of local actors in preventing violent extremism. Similarly, in Chapter 4, "Devising more effective peacebuilding tools for Africa," Gilbert Zvaita and Ibrahim Yusuf also critique the liberal peacebuilding agenda and its application in Africa, this time focusing our attention on engaging multiple disciplinary perspectives in order to privilege *local ownership* of peacebuilding and to help break the liberal peacebuilding agenda's hold on ways peacebuilding is approached and done in Africa.

Part III examines the opportunities, challenges, and learning experiences of designing and implementing preventative, restorative, and systemic change processes. In Chapter 5, "Disrupting cycles of revenge and boosting community resilience: A forgiveness and reconciliation program at Boys and Girls Clubs," Vince Waldron and colleagues provide a fascinating account of the joys and challenges of designing and implementing a program to *develop forgiveness and reconciliation competencies* by boys and girls. Focused on building competencies as long-term social and communicative capital, the authors invite us to think about how forgiveness and reconciliation can be taught/learned, and how these competencies will hopefully have long-term impacts on how these children will preventatively manage conflicted differences throughout their lives. Chapter 6, "Cultivating a space for restorative justice in Kansas: Exploring opportunities for restorative justice through dialogic deliberation," also takes us into the challenging but promising world of restorative justice that is used to help reshape how community members think about justice. In this chapter, Gregory Paul demonstrates how *dialogic deliberation* is central to implementing restorative justice programs at a local level. Chapter 7, "Fraught times: Engaging systemic issues of hate online" provides a timely and provocative account of *online conflict*. Whereas the other chapters in this section focus on reshaping how people engage with differences after the fact, and/or face to face, in this chapter, John Drew and Devin Thornburg take us into the contemporary online world where we see hateful conflict being generated and spread rapidly. The authors challenge us to consider how the sharp divisions develop, the roles of the virtual world in exacerbating conflict, and how the same technologies might be used more productively and in line with their promise of connection and unity.

Part IV engages the reader with two career-long "tales from the field." A community mediator and an international peacebuilder reflect on their long-term experiences and lessons learned in their extensive applied conflict and peacebuilding field work. Chapter 8, "Practicing mediation as an engaged scholar: A personal memoir," gives us a valuable reflection on what it is like to become and be a community mediator. Gwen Hullman confronts and modifies her academic knowledge in the face of the reality of mediation. She also reflects on her training experiences, *how the role of community mediator changed her relationship* to her community in Reno, Nevada, and positively impacted her work as a communication professor. In Chapter 9, "Walking the challenging path of peacebuilding: Reflections of an engaged scholar," Benjamin Broome reflects on twenty-five years of his involvement in helping to build dialogue-based peace between the factions in a complex historically grounded, cultural, ethnic, and political conflict in Cyprus. He invites us into the ebbs and flows in efforts to help the "sides" to come together *to create their own vision for peace in their world.* Both chapters show us the creative tension between scholarship and practice, and provide fascinating glimpses into how doing community-engaged scholarship changed them as scholars and people more broadly.

Part V explores the important question of how we can most effectively *teach* conflict transformation and peacebuilding given what we know about the theory and reality of doing such community engaged work. In Chapter 10, "Dialogic prudence: Promoting transformative conflict through Civil Dialogue®," Robert Razzante and colleagues advance a reflective framework for sensitively and carefully engaging with community conflicts through the notion of dialogic prudence. Chapter 11, "Teaching conflict transformation in the basic communication course: Narrative reflections by graduate teaching Instructors" takes us into the lived reality of engaging students in a basic communication course with the concepts and practices of conflict transformation, in ways that push them beyond the typical conflict resolution approaches of such textbooks. In this chapter, Alex Patti and collaborators reflect on the challenges and opportunities of fostering a deeper and more systemic understanding of conflict in students. Together, these chapters remind us that the knowledge and skills of doing community-engaged work can be promoted effectively through communication, and underscore how these competencies need to be shared and passed on if they are to be more widely known and used to make a difference.

The chapters of this volume provide us with rich insight into the *doing* of engaged scholarship—how it is and ought to be done communicatively—and the *being* of engaged scholarship—what it means to be an engaged scholar doing conflict transformation and peacebuilding work, and how it challenges and changes us as scholars, teachers, and people more broadly. The authors reveal the complexities and necessities of doing conflict transformation and peacebuilding. They invite us all to consider these complexities in the context of our own engaged scholarship and they encourage us to press onward with hope and resilience. And, they remind us that at the heart of conflict transformation and peacebuilding—as well as all engaged scholarship and practice—lies the communicative.

References

Ahmed, Z. S., & Bukhari, R. (2019). Madaris and peace education in Pakistan: A case study of Peace and Education Foundation. In S. L. Connaughton & J. Berns (eds.), *Locally led peacebuilding: Global case studies* (pp. 242–255). Lanham, MD: Rowman & Littlefield.

Anderson, M. B., Brown, D., & Jean, I. (2012). *Time to listen: Hearing people on the receiving end of international aid.* Cambridge, MA: CDA Collaborative Learning Projects.

Autesserre, S. (2014). *Peaceland: Conflict resolution and the everyday politics of international intervention.* New York: Cambridge University Press.

Broome, B. J. (2002). Participatory planning and design in a protracted conflict situation: Applications with citizen peace-building groups in Cyprus. *Systems Research and Behavioral Science, 19,* 313–321. doi: 10.1002/sres.434.

Boulding, E. (2002). Practice love and sustain hope. In J. P. Lederach & J. M. Jenner (eds.), *A handbook of international peacebuilding: Into the eye of the storm* (pp. 299–304). San Francisco, CA: Jossey-Bass.

Connaughton, S. L., & Berns, J. (2019). *Locally led peacebuilding: Global case studies.* Lanham, MD: Rowman & Littlefield.

Firchow, P., & Anastasiou, H. (2016). *Practical approaches to peacebuilding: Putting theory to work.* Boulder, CO: Lynne Reinner Publishers.

Lederach, J. P. (1997). *Building peace: Sustainable reconciliation in divided societies.* Washington, DC: United States Institute of Peace Press.

Moix, B. (2019). *Choosing peace: Agency and action in the midst of war.* London: Rowman & Littlefield International.

Pineda Ruano, J. D. (2019). Peacebuilding in Guatemala: The local peace network methodology. In S. L. Connaughton & J. Berns (eds.), *Locally led peacebuilding: Global case studies* (pp. 108–116). Lanham, MD: Rowman & Littlefield.

Schirch, L., & Campt, D. (2007). *The little book of dialogue for difficult subjects: Practical, hands-on guide.* New York: Good Books.

Part I: Designing and Leading/ Implementing Transformative Engagement

1 Doing Locally Led Peacebuilding: An Examination of the Relationally Attentive Approach to Engaged Scholarship in Liberia

JENNIFER K. PTACEK, DANIEL KAMAL, MEGHANA RAWAT, JASMINE R. LINABARY, AND STACEY L. CONNAUGHTON

The importance of locally led peacebuilding initiatives in fragile states is being increasingly recognized (e.g., Hughes, Öjendal, & Schierenbeck, 2015; Leonardsson & Rudd, 2015). Locally led peacebuilding places importance on local agency and the inclusion of local voices, both in defining peace and determining the priorities of such work (Hayman, 2013; Leonardsson & Rudd, 2015). Specifically, we define locally led peacebuilding as "an approach in which the people involved in, and most affected by, violent conflict work together to create and enact their own solutions to prevent, reduce, and/or transform the conflict, with the support they desire from others" (*Locally Driven Peacebuilding*, 2015, p. 2). Conflict within the Purdue Peace Project's work relates specifically to political violence which we define as "armed violence that is driven by competing interests, resources, and power among and/or between groups" (Connaughton & Berns, forthcoming). As the above definition suggests, central to these processes is the effective collaboration of both local actors and external entities supporting these efforts (in our case, external entities refer to us, engaged scholars based at a U.S. university). The social interactions between members of the two groups (in our case, local Liberians and engaged scholars based at a U.S. university) often result in co-constructed transformations, which can occur at the individual and/or collective levels. In conflict and negotiation studies, transformations are viewed as cognitive, discursive, and/or goal-related phenomena (Connaughton, Kuang, & Yakova, 2017). Examples of transformations often examined in prior work are a renewed perspective at the individual level, the (re)shaping of patterns of interactions at the group level (i.e., among members of the local peace committee), and the shifting of goals or outcomes at the group and community levels.

Due to the significantly communicative nature of transformations in conflict settings (Ellis, 2006), scholars have employed various perspectives to explicate the intricacies of such processes in the context of peacebuilding. Engaged scholarship, defined as an approach to research that "brings sustained focus to the relational, communication dynamics that define the research process" (Dempsey & Barge, 2014, p. 668), is one such approach. This approach to scholarship allows the participatory communication processes involved in collaborative relationships to be unpacked and examined, providing a platform for these transformations to be interrogated. Among the several models of engaged scholarship, the relationally attentive approach (RAA; Connaughton et al., 2017) is of specific relevance to conflict transformations, in that this model specifically seeks to illuminate the relationships between collaborators from academia, professional practice, and the broader community.

Against the backdrop of peacebuilding work undertaken by us, the Purdue Peace Project (PPP), concerning election-related violence in post-civil war Liberia, this chapter examines the relationship between the PPP's enactment of the RAA in the field and the individual- and group-level transformations experienced by members of the team as well as our local collaborators in the country. The chapter highlights the communicative choices made by the PPP and our Liberian counterparts during our engaged collaborations, and then charts their relationships to transformative outcomes.

Transformation in Existing Research Literature

Transformation has been studied in the context of conflict and negotiation studies (e.g., Greer, Jehn, & Mannix, 2008; Lederach, 1995) and has been an emerging area of study particularly within the field of communication (e.g., Connaughton, Kuang, & Yakova, 2017; Ellis, 2006; Putnam & Kolb, 2000). From a broadly social constructionist perspective, transformations are co-constructed through interaction (Connaughton, Kuang, & Yakova, 2017). Connaughton, Kuang, and Yakova (2017) explored the impact of the PPP's engaged collaborations in Liberia as they related to perceptual and discursive transformations. Prior to that, Putnam (2009) and Ellis (2006) noted that communication scholars can interrogate the emergence of transformation from conditions of conflict. Similarly, Putnam and Kolb (2000) inferred the communicative tensions in negotiations during conditions of conflict that influence the transformative outcomes. While the transformative impacts related to engaged collaborations have been previously discussed by scholars, the RAA, as a model rooted in the engaged scholarship tradition, contributes to the understanding of how these relational approaches are built over time. Going further, communication scholars can contribute toward understanding the different forms of transformations that take place, in part due to relationship building at the individual, group, and even community levels. Specifically, a communication perspective highlights how members construct these transformations through reflexive, reflective, and relational dialogues and actions in their lived experiences.

A Relationally Driven Approach to Transformation

In the RAA, the "relational" is considered the central factor that emphasizes the cultivation of "productive and meaningful collaborative relationships among ourselves over time" (Connaughton et al., 2017, p. 7). The term "attentive" implies close collaboration between practitioners (in our case, local citizens) and academics while developing these relationships in peacebuilding efforts. The RAA was developed to explicate the "doing" of engaged scholarship in the context of peacebuilding. The four components of the RAA are:

1. *Engaging in ongoing co-construction*: This key aspect of the RAA surrounds the idea of decision-making and communicative choices made while doing peacebuilding work with and between local peacebuilders to collaboratively identify problem areas, activities, and impacts which are rooted in dialogue.
2. *Embracing reciprocity between choices made in engaged scholarship and impacts*: In this aspect, the researchers and local peacebuilders practice engagement by prioritizing relationships, opting for communicative choices that build reciprocal relationships through engaged collaboration.
3. *Fostering conditions for inclusivity*: Another form of doing engaged scholarship proposed by RAA is to foster an inclusive mindset among both researchers and local peacebuilders. This act of striving for inclusivity ensures that practitioners transform their behavior to acknowledge various relations, positionalities, and multiple voices on the field.
4. *Practicing reflexivity*: This aspect alludes to the need for local peacebuilders and researchers to develop critical thinking and questioning of their communicative choices while in the field and keeping

relationships and the intended impacts of (in this case) their peace-building efforts (as agreed to with their collaborators) as the central goal during collaborations.

The RAA was proposed to address how practitioners from academia and other research settings can effectively strive to do engaged scholarship on the ground. In this chapter, mindful of our RAA lens, we further explicate trans-formations through the lived experiences of on-ground local collaborators and engaged researchers from the U.S.-based PPP team. Interrogating these transformations is valuable not only for evaluating the outcomes of our work but to further understand and contribute to literature on how participants, collaborators, and researchers are changed through engaged research. It is also necessary to include the lived experiences of both local collaborators and U.S.-based engaged researchers at Purdue because not only does reflecting upon our own experiences align with the PPP's approach to doing engaged research (Connaughton et al., 2017), but it also helps us to understand differ-ences in perspectives and positionalities and is an important part of conduct-ing ethical participatory research (Sultana, 2007). To explore this, we further the work of Connaughton, Kuang, and Yakova (2017) which links the role of communication to transformations in identity, and which they argue, is made possible by the development of ongoing relationships through dialogue and action.

Purdue Peace Project[1]

The PPP is an externally funded peacebuilding initiative with the mission to collaborate with local leaders and citizens in conflict-prone regions of the world to reduce the likelihood of political violence and contribute to sus-tainable peace. Since 2012, when developed by the fifth author, the PPP does engaged scholarship that is theoretically driven and relationally oriented, and it places emphasis on communication in its co-constructed peacebuilding efforts. To date, the project has engaged local leaders and citizens in peace-building efforts in West Africa and Central America, addressing issues related to political violence such as election violence, disputes over chieftaincy, land, and natural resources, as well as ethnic and religious conflicts. For example, we have worked with citizens in Berekum, Ghana, to establish the Berekum Peace Committee which worked to encourage the resolution of a twelve-plus year chieftaincy dispute between royal families. These efforts led to a ruling from the Judicial Committee of the Brong Ahafo Regional House of Chiefs, and no violence has since been reported related to the dispute.

Four main assumptions guide the PPP's peacebuilding work (Connaughton, Kuang, & Yakova, 2017). The first assumption is the belief that local citizens should be given the opportunity to actively participate in the transformation of their own communities by designing, leading, and implementing peacebuilding strategies. Second, the PPP approach assumes that leadership is fundamentally a communicative process and that all individuals have the capacity to demonstrate leadership in peacebuilding contexts. Third, the PPP believes in the primacy of inclusive and representative dialogue in producing effective change. The fourth and last assumption is the belief that external researchers/peacebuilders participate in the co-construction of peacebuilding strategies by working closely with the expertise that resides within the communities themselves. These four assumptions are manifested in the PPP approach through the application of strategies such as actor meetings and relationship building, which work toward facilitating dialogue between relevant stakeholders.

A central component of the RAA is the importance of interrogating our communicative choices, which Connaughton et al. (2017) identify as convening inclusively, deferring, supporting, and validating. Convening inclusively involves convening an inclusive group of local actors (i.e., police, pen-pen drivers, Ministry of Transport, market women, and other citizens) in order to co-construct desired actions and impacts in preventing violence. Deferring refers to our choices to rely on our local collaborators to help us understand what is appropriate and to communicate to community members when needed. Supporting includes regularly visiting Liberia and the LPG groups, verbally encouraging the group members and their work through conversations, and identifying impacts we noticed in our data. Finally, validating consists of being aware of power dynamics and the need to validate and lift up the efforts of our local collaborators.

Peacebuilding Work around Election Violence in Liberia

The Liberian Civil Wars (1989–2003) left a marked impact on the country as well as on the lives of its citizens. The conflicts were rooted in internal political conflict and resulted in the deaths of around 250,000 people (Liberia Country Profile, 2018). Among the most significant effects was the large number of ex-combatants, many of whom were in their youth, faced with the prospect of earning a living while undergoing disarmament, demobilization, rehabilitation, and reintegration (Pugel, 2009). As a means of sustaining their livelihoods, many of these youth became motorcycle taxi drivers, or colloquially known as "pen-pen riders" (Connaughton, Kuang, & Yakova, 2017).

However, having been exposed to the harsh realities of the battlefield and other manifestations of prolonged violent conflict, many pen-pen riders were seen by other citizens as lawless and aggressive both in their driving as well as in interactions with police and community members (F. Y., 2013). Their reputation for violence has seen them being hired by politicians and political parties to mobilize violent protests during campaign and election periods, such that former Liberian President Ellen Johnson Sirleaf once publicly proclaimed that pen-pen riders were an essential group that needed to be incorporated into efforts to achieve lasting peace in the country (Sirleaf, 2013).

Recognizing the need for initiatives to reduce the likelihood of political violence involving pen-pen riders in Liberia, the PPP facilitated the formation of the Liberia Peace Group (LPG), a community-based local peace committee consisting of representatives from the pen-pen rider unions, community members, market women, the Ministry of Transport, and the Liberia National Police. To help coordinate these efforts, the PPP also has a Liberia Country Director who is a Liberian citizen and works with the LPG groups. Four LPG groups have been formed in Bong, Margibi, Montserrado, and Nimba counties during the years leading up to the 2017 presidential elections, which were anticipated to result in violence. Through outreach activities such as town hall meetings, segments on radio talk shows, sports tournaments, and culturally driven entertainment events, the LPG undertook efforts to promote peaceful elections and improve relationships between pen-pen riders and the police and community members.

Based on what we currently know about transformation and what we seek to understand further, we developed the following research question:

> RQ: In what ways are those who participate in such an engaged scholarship initiative transformed through their work?

Next we describe our research methodology in how we approached this question, followed by our findings.

Methodology

To document the transformations that have occurred within members of the LPG and PPP, we analyzed data collected around the peaceful election projects including (1) five post-travel interviews from PPP members after returning from Liberia; (2) ten individual interviews with LPG members; and (3) four focus groups with members from each of the four LPG groups (see Table 1.1). Post-travel interviews were conducted shortly after PPP members returned from Liberia, and asked members to discuss their overarching

Table 1.1.   Data collection.

Type of Data	Participants
Five post-travel interviews	Three members of PPP
Ten individual interviews	Five members of Margibi LPG
	Five members of Montserrado LPG
Four focus group interviews	Seven members of Bong LPG
	Five members of Margibi LPG
	Five members of Montserrado LPG
	Six members of Nimba LPG

experiences, observations and outcomes, and reflect about different aspects of the visit. Representative interview questions include "Has this trip changed your understanding or perceptions of this project; if so, how?," "What ways did you see communication and peacebuilding relating to each other in the work you observed/participated in during this trip?," and "In what ways did your identity/ies become salient while being in Liberia and why?"

Post-travel interviews lasted an average of 55 minutes. Data from LPG focus group and individual interviews were collected during a May 2018 visit to Liberia where PPP members traveled to the four county LPG groups and were conducted in local community buildings in the respective counties. The ten individual interviews included five members each of the Margibi LPG and Montserrado LPG and were an average length of 15 minutes. Individual interview questions included asking members to describe their role in the organization and implementation of their peaceful election campaign, changes they have noticed as a result of their involvement in this campaign, and their vision for the group and peacebuilding in the future. The four focus group interviews included seven members from Bong, five members from Margibi, five members from Montserrado, and six members from Nimba. The average length of the focus groups was 81 minutes. Questions from the focus group interviews included describing their experiences and feelings leading up to, during, and after election day and the runoff election; discussing instances and differences in violence and peace compared to previous elections; and the work and contributions of the LPG groups pertaining to peace and peaceful elections. After transcribing interview data, transcripts consisted of 199 pages of single-spaced text.

Data were analyzed qualitatively using an inductive thematic analysis characterized by types of transformations (Braun & Clarke, 2006). We identified transformation in the data based on if participants described it as a change in themselves or the group since they began their work on the LPG or PPP and attributed this change specifically to the work on the project. Additionally, we follow Connaughton, Yakova, and Kuang's (2017) conceptualization of transformation as "a cognitive (individual), discursive (relational/processual), and/or goal-oriented (outcome) phenomenon" that can include a shifting of perspective and/or interaction with others (pp. 71–72). The first three authors separately conducted a first round of analysis, reading all the data to identify emergent themes, and then met to discuss themes using a constant-comparative method to refine codes (Charmaz, 2006). The first three authors then coded 10 percent of the data individually and met until they reached agreement on all codes surrounding individual- and group-level transformations of LPG and PPP members. Finally, they coded the remaining data separately. Preliminary findings were shared with LPG members to confirm accuracy of representation, and themes identified in the data were further refined by the first author as she completed additional readings of the data as well as shared with the other authors for resonance with the data.

Findings

Our analysis of the transcripts uncovered six themes in individual- and group-level transformations among both Liberia-based LPG and U.S.-based PPP members related to our ongoing collaboration. These six themes are: (1) sense of agency, (2) reified identity, (3) sense of recognition, (4) exposure to new people and places, (5) skill acquisition, and (6) camaraderie.

Sense of Agency

One theme that emerged as transformations among both members of the local peace committees and PPP team is agency. Many participants feel that they have transformed in that they have gained a sense of agency, which in this context we define as control over their roles in building peace. This is in part due to the PPP's communicative choices to defer to LPG members in their local work as well as validating both PPP and LPG members in their accomplishments. Members have stated that they now feel responsibility and accountability to themselves and to Liberia to build peace. For example, an LPG member from Montserrado County said her local peace committee was so determined to go out into the communities to speak to people about peace that people thought they were getting paid, which, per the PPP voluntary model, they were not. She said, "We did it in the rain, in the sun. We did not give up … We're not thinking about 'Oh you're not paying us for it.' We're just volunteering." She added, "we are just doing it because we love our country" and they knew they had to do it for the sake of peace.

For a Margibi County LPG member, his sense of responsibility to build peace overcame his previous inclinations for participating in violence. When a fight broke out in his area, he wanted to join in but realized he should remain neutral because of his role in the LPG. He said:

> I took some responsibility and decided to somehow be responsible ... and only to respond without violence ... they chose me to work with the [Liberia Peace Group] and I decided to teach [motorcyclists] how to make peace and teach how to deal with conflict, to talk to people about becom[ing] peacemakers. So [a riot] happened, I was about to go there to respond [violently], but the first thing that came to my mind was that I'm a [LPG] worker so I need to make peace.

He realized that if he responded in the way that he previously would have responded, with violence, that would make the problem worse. He found that once he went out and talked to people about making peace, they listened to him. He attributes being an LPG member to a reduction in violent behaviors in his area and in himself.

PPP team members based in the United States also noted that this work has given them a personal feeling of responsibility in certain ways. One PPP member reflected, "my experiences working with such dedicated individuals, through setbacks and triumphs, has solidified in me a commitment to cultivating ongoing, genuine, trusting relationships through which together, we can prevent political violence and contribute to lasting peace." Another PPP member talked about how working in the field promotes a higher sense of dedication and responsibility to work on peace. She said:

> The sense of responsibility that comes in when you are on the field is unmatchable. You want to ensure you get all their stories to understand the extent of the impact. You also want to ensure that these stories of impact reach out to the world and through their own stories, the participants are realizing the importance of peace in their lives.

These examples show some of the ways in which working on this project and the RAA have instilled a sense of purpose and commitment to building peace.

Furthermore, participants have said this responsibility extends to feeling the need to take action; to step in to encourage peace in situations where they may not have done so before they began their work as peacebuilders. One member of the Montserrado LPG stated, "Before, if two person having a conflict, I fear it is not my business and I will pass by. But now, I have to stop and talk to them and then tell them what the word peace means for me."

Similarly, a member of the Margibi LPG described his new calling to go out of his way to work toward peace:

> I am the kind of person that I mind my own business so when I come to this place and if there's some problem ... I would just go. But being a peacebuilder ... if a fire is lit in here and as a peace ambassador, you have to continue talking and listen to that fire. I used to feel that it wasn't my business ... but now it opened me up ... it is like if main house is on fire, if you don't go and help them to put the fire off, it could one day be you ... so you must always help to cut off the fire, then collectively we can live together.

As demonstrated in these quotations, members from each of the LPG groups spoke about their duty as peacebuilders to go to whatever place needs their help. Other participants even noted that they often responded before police arrived at a scene, for community members frequently reached out to the LPG before calling the police to resolve issues. One LPG member described this as "the precedent the LPG have set." This precedent has transformed participants to talk about peace within their regular work on the project, but has also inspired a deeper transformation that has tied peacebuilding to their agency as a citizen or researcher.

Reified Identity

A second theme in transformations among LPG and PPP members is reified identity. This refers to parts of participants' identities that have been realized or transformed because of their collaborative work and commitment to the PPP's communicative goal of convening inclusively. We conceptualize "reified identity" as making something somewhat abstract, such as being a peacebuilder, more "real." We use the term "reified" because it encapsulates participants' feelings that certain identities are more legitimate. This includes newly realized identities as peacebuilders. For example, members labeled themselves in various ways to describe their roles. A member from Nimba County described himself as a "peace agent," a member from Bong County used the word "peacemaker," while a member from Margibi County talked about being a "peace advisor." A PPP member described how she now sees herself as wanting to be an "advocate" for locally driven peacebuilding and for public universities' role in conducting engaged scholarship within the peacebuilding and political violence prevention space.

It is worth noting that we did not prompt committee members to refer to themselves in these ways and many of these labels were shared in response to questions such as "How would you describe this group to others?" Furthermore, these are new labels that the individuals did not identify with until they started working with the collaboration of peace groups. Many individuals stated that they "now" see themselves in this way because of the work they do in this group and through the support and validation of other members.

In addition to seeing oneself transform into being a peacebuilder, many participants expressed having a deeper understanding of what peace means and what is involved in the peacebuilding process when asked about their work on the LPG or PPP. A member of the Margibi local peace committee spoke about learning to make peace in his community as a way to have peace for himself. After living through Liberia's civil war, he explained, "I saw people suffering, I saw people in violence. So when you speak about peace, it's something that cause me to live … without confusion." Others similarly have grown to understand peace as "freedom," "happiness," and "living without fear," among other descriptions. Members of the PPP have also come to a greater understanding of peace and peacebuilding because of their work on this project. One member stated:

> Certainly a lack of violence is a part of [peace], but peace is much more than that. Peace means something very different if you have lived in a place that has experienced years of war than it does for someone like me living in a relatively stable environment with access to resources in the United States. This project opens your eyes to the different meanings of peace. Further, this work has emphasized to me that peace is not a one-time event but rather an ongoing process that needs continued cultivation in order to be sustained.

She added that her work with the PPP "continuously challenges and reshapes my perspectives of what peacebuilding is, who should be involved, and what we mean by peace." For example, she would have not initially thought of games and sporting events as peacebuilding activities (despite there being a literature about the relationship between sports and peacebuilding; see Cárdenas, 2013; Schnitzer, Stephenson Jr., Zanotti, & Stivachtis, 2013), but now has seen the impact they have in the communities in bringing people together to build peace.

The theme of reified identity also includes self-development, such that members have gained the ability to reflect on themselves and their work, feel they have become "better" people as a result of their work, and now have a renewed drive or motivation to continue building peace. For example, one PPP member described her experiences as leading her to reflect upon "who I am and want to be as a scholar and a teacher," and "It has encouraged me to think deeply about what it means and what it looks like in practice to incorporate more participatory practices into my research methods and classroom." She added that "I have been transformed by observing [LPG members'] resilience in their day-to-day lives and in their peacebuilding work ... Such moments also force me to confront my own privileges." Another PPP member described her transformation as "humbling" and that "the biggest thing I learned about myself is that the decisions I make can be based on my experiences or where I have lived ... But the way other people act or behave stem[s] from how they were raised too." She recounted hearing about one pen-pen rider's life being raised on violence and realizing "that we are all people, and our experiences shape us," which has taught her to try to be more understanding of others' experiences. Importantly, several LPG members talked about their work on the project teaching them "the meaning of life" and other valuable lessons. A Montserrado local peace committee member said: "I've also learned to accept my wrongs and I've learned to forgive people who wrong me, because of the sake of peace. I can't be pushing peace and in my heart I'm not feeling peace. So, I've learned to forgive." A pen-pen rider and member from the Margibi local peace committee described his transformation as follows:

> I understand the importance of life. But at the time I did not value life. I would not even know when I'm going to die because I feel that I could die anytime, I didn't care. But ... I got to understand the importance of my life. So the only way you can enjoy life is peace.

This member and others, both within the LPG committees and the PPP, have noted that exposure to this project and the work they have done on it has taught them about peace, themselves, the world, and how to become "better" people. The reified identities represent an individual-level transformation; group-level transformations in identity are included later in the findings.

Sense of Recognition

Participants have also noted that due to their roles on the LPG or PPP, they have gained recognition from others, whether it be other peacebuilders and researchers, people in the community, or government officials. People now recognize them for their work in building peace and may even reach out for help when needed because of their role as a peacebuilder or person of knowledge within the realm of peacebuilding. LPG members mentioned their "legacy" of peacebuilding in their communities and being recognized as they pass through an area, at times even being followed by community members curious to listen to their peaceful messages. This recognition and the earned support and validation from various stakeholders has had a positive impact on participants' identities because they know that others see them in a favorable way as well, gaining respect from friends and strangers alike.

An LPG member who is also a police officer noted that he gained respect from motorcyclists, as several of them told the officer regarding an LPG-hosted football tournament, "Hey bossman, I am there, the Federation of Liberia Youth is there." This is a significant change because historically the police and motorcyclists frequently clashed and had little respect for each other. Other participants found that people admire the LPG and its members and have shown eagerness in listening to what they have to say. Another participant even mentioned being considered the "go-to" person to resolve disputes in his community, stating "the community dwellers now, they have more respect for me and they complain to me to address some of their problems. So I now have respect in the community." Further, a PPP member found herself receiving similar respect during a visit to Liberia, being asked by several journalists for interviews and being asked to make speeches at the football tournament.

Another change that participants noticed due to their recognition as peacebuilders was a sense of credibility and trust from others. Members of the PPP mentioned being invited to conferences and other events to talk about their work and consult others on peacebuilding. A member of the Margibi LPG recalled a time when the group was asked to help a candidate's surrogate during a campaign event, as he was experiencing violent attacks from citizens. The LPG group was able to diffuse the situation and received appreciation from the representative. LPG members from various counties mentioned that they have received repeated requests during their radio talk show programs and community visits to expand their reach and continue preaching their messages of peace. A Montserrado LPG member quoted a caller on the radio who made the comment, "please, don't stop talking to our children." Another LPG member noted that one change he saw was community members talking more about peace and coming directly to the LPG to report criminal activity. In addition to their proven success in peacebuilding as a contributing factor of their credibility, participants pointed out that their unique composition of members—consisting of police, pen-pen riders, government workers, market people, and others—helped them to gain trust in the community. For example, the Bong County LPG members recalled several examples about how people were able to confide in the LPG because they saw a member who was representative of their position in the community and, therefore, felt that the group understood them.

With the recognition of being a peacebuilder, participants noted a great sense of pride. Participants talked about feeling proud after hearing radio segments and seeing newspaper articles where journalists commended the LPG for the positive changes they were making in Liberia. One LPG member recounted a personal feeling of pride in being able to open up to more people now and being recognized by name in the community. Another LPG member recalled an instance when she felt especially proud of her work after a football and board game tournament when a man approached her and said that he had not spoken to his friend in over two years because of an argument, but that day they sat down and played checkers together and began speaking once again. He attributed that interpersonal reconciliation to the LPG's work. PPP members also spoke about feeling proud to have others ask about their work, both among colleagues as well as when traveling to Liberia. In one example, a member spoke about feeling proud about her role in the PPP as Liberians thanked her for her work, adding, "I just thought, wow, it shows that whatever we are doing they feel we have an impact on their lives and ... they are the ones who are putting their energy and time into this, but they just acknowledged us." For LPG and PPP members alike, they felt proud of the contributions that they were able to make by being a part of this work in part due to the recognition they have received across the board.

Exposure to New People and Places

Exposure to new people and places has also been stated as a benefit and part of participants' personal- and group-level transformation because of their role on the LPG or PPP and commitment to convening inclusively with others. Members often spoke of traveling to many places, some to which they have never been, which exposed them to new areas within and/or outside of their country. One PPP member noted that traveling from the United States to Liberia "made it more real" because she stated:

> I remember before I had ever gone the first time, I didn't fully understand what exactly, I could read through the data, and I could read all the information that we have about it but you don't really understand exactly until you go there and see people living and ... hearing them tell stories.

She was able to have a greater understanding of others' situations when she could speak with them in person and see firsthand what was happening. This exposure helped her to "feel the importance" of the work and made her more excited and passionate to continue. Another PPP member talked about what she learned from her exposure on the project. She said:

> Through collaborating with individuals from multiple sectors (government, corporate, not-for-profit, community organizing, market women, religious leaders, youth groups, and more) and in countries and contexts that I had prior not been familiar with prior to PPP, I have become even more convinced that everyday citizens around the world, when given opportunities to lead, do in fact lead ...

I hope that I have learned how to work with people from multiple countries, multiple cultures, various socioeconomic backgrounds in such a way that celebrates what we all have in common—our humanity.

Other participants, including members of the various LPG groups, added that they learned new ideas from the people they met along the way.

In these travels and in their work, LPG members have met people who they would have not met otherwise, some resulting in new friendships. Several participants noted that they now have friends in the various communities to which they have traveled. The increased exposure has transformed participants not only through the formation of new friendships but also by increasing their level of comfort when interacting with new people. For example, a Montserrado LPG member stated that his life was enhanced because of his ability to travel around his county for the LPG, and meeting people to sit down together and talk. He added that this helped him to open up and talk with people.

This exposure to new people and places is a transformation because it has expanded their social networks and enhanced their experiences. Additionally, members now have access to a larger network of actors such as government officials, other peacebuilding organizations, and others. A Montserrado LPG member stated, "One of my biggest changes personally is I've gotten to know people in government, people that I could not personally [be able] to talk to." She recalled one time when she spoke with a government official about the LPG and he attended one of their programs, which made her feel happy both that he attended and that she was able to meet and converse with him in person. The impact of the opportunities to meet new people and see new places cannot be overstated by participants. For example, one PPP member said:

> I never would have imagined that I would be able to observe firsthand how groups of people come together to stop killing each other, but my research with the PPP has allowed me to speak personally with these people, listen to their stories, and watch them interact with each other in their communities while they work together toward peace. The impact is so big that there aren't sufficient words to describe the feeling, except that I feel blessed to have experienced such a meaningful thing in my life.

This sentiment was repeated by many of the LPG and PPP members, as they have recognized the positive transformations in their lives because of their work as peacebuilders.

Skill Acquisition

In addition to their increased level of comfort in going out and making new friends, a major individual- and group-level transformation among LPG and PPP members was the acquisition of new skills. These skills include aptitudes such as an enhanced ability to write, communicate with others, express themselves, and strategize about peacebuilding. One LPG member stated that at each of the LPG meetings, "we sit together and strategize and make us learn how to even write. We learn how to compose things that we see out there and then we include in our reports. Some of us, we love to do that. We learn so much." Some of these skills were learned through repeated experience but some were taught, such as in workshops at a retreat in which PPP members traveled to Liberia and met with all of the LPG groups together. Here they learned valuable skills such as how to write reports and action plans. For some LPG members, working on this peace collaboration was one of their first opportunities to learn these skills as the PPP deferred to LPG members to write their own action plans and go into the communities to speak with citizens.

For some participants, their communication skills were strengthened over time as they traveled around their respective counties to speak with citizens. One LPG member, for example, recalls that she initially felt shy when speaking with other people. But after watching other LPG members doing so, along with support from them, she began to pick up on how they were communicating and felt more comfortable doing it herself. She talked about how this has positively impacted her:

> I wanna be part of the [Liberia Peace Group] because I feel that there [are] some activities based on peace initiatives ... and have to talk to various communities ... when I be part of the [Liberia Peace Group] I feel like I will be able to do all that, talk to other people, and even to resolve cases when people are in conflict, I will be brave enough to go and talk to them ... It helps me a lot, talking to people, convincing people about peace.

Enhanced communication does not only involve the ability to speak well but also to listen well. This was also noted by a PPP member, who mentioned:

> I believe this work and these relationships have improved my listening skills. The RAA requires that we do far more listening than speaking, and not just listening in a general sense but listening with intent, with care, and with critical attention to one's own lack of understanding.

These skills have not only proven to be helpful in working to build peace, but participants agreed that they have had an overall positive impact on their lives and in interactions with other people outside of peacebuilding work.

In addition to enhanced communication skills, working on the LPG or PPP has transformed members by teaching them other professional development and job skills that they could use in the future. An LPG member who is also a business owner said, "[LPG] is very much helpful because it was where I was able to learn how to discern a vision of an organization, a mission, and the core values. It even helped me for my own personal organization." Another LPG member said that she learned how to organize activities and was eventually able to take initiative in the absence of the Liberia Country Director. The PPP members also noted the skills they have acquired from working on this project, including how to conduct better research, ask better questions, adapt ideas to best reach different groups of people, manage data, and hone reflexive skills in order to be aware of one's own positionality. Other skills they have learned are how to be flexible, patient, and manage unpredictable situations. One PPP member gave examples of travel difficulties such as lost luggage and canceled flights, going to unfamiliar communities that were difficult to get to, and being in the field when fights broke out nearby.

Many members talked about how this peacebuilding work has developed their ability to overcome challenges and adversity and how to work with other people who are different from them, as some of the above examples describe. The LPG groups are made up of members from different groups in the community, some of which have had deep-seated tensions with each other. Working together on the LPG has taught them to put aside their differences and work together for the sake of peace. Each of the LPG and PPP members noted a transformation in that they acquired skills that enhanced their lives as well as ability to perform their peacebuilding work.

Camaraderie

The theme of camaraderie describes the overall transformation of the LPG as creating a sense of togetherness tied to PPP's communicative choices to convene inclusively and offer support. This is more of a group-level transformation because the groups felt as a whole that this was a benefit from their work together. Even though this is a group-level transformation, individual members each mentioned a sense of belonging and support from their other group members. Many participants noted a feeling of unity and camaraderie after working together for a period of time and felt comfortable working as a unit and making decisions together. For example, some frequently mentioned statements among LPG members including "we are united," "we understand each other," and "we share a vision." This unity did not necessarily come easily though, as each LPG group consists of members supporting different political parties and even from groups that once opposed each other, such as police and pen-pen riders. One Nimba LPG member noted, "It's because of the [Liberia Peace Group] that we are working together ... Why should we have division among ourselves?... The group really brought us together and made differences go away, definitely. Now we are working together at this particular time." Even though they were not without challenges in bringing themselves together, participants said they constantly encouraged each other to focus on peace and work together as one.

Additionally, new friendships have formed within the group due in part to this voluntary organizational membership. For example, police and pen-pen riders who are members of the LPG group can now call each other for help because they are part of the same team. One police officer on an LPG team boasted about the positive transformation:

> It had changed because we are connected. Right now I could sit down and call [a member who is a pen-pen rider] and he will come right away. He sees me on the streets and says "oh you're there." So good relationship. So if any of us can call any of us at any time, and it makes us to be more connected because the peace we are talking about, we continue to talk about it. So the police and the cyclists, so even if I'm going somewhere and I don't have the money and see one of the cyclists I would say "help me" and it would be done. It's a smooth relationship, really.

Other members talked about their new friendships as well, even stating that there were negative relationships before. For example, two pen-pen riders in one LPG group were from opposing motorcyclist unions cited that there was a long period of time when they would see each other in town but not speak to one another. However, after working toward peace together on the LPG, when one of them graduated, the other traveled two hours with the entire team to attend his graduation ceremony. He said the unity that resulted from the team is "amazing."

The theme of camaraderie also includes group identity, which is different from the reified personal identity theme stated previously. Examples of group identity are members seeing themselves as part of the group and speaking with others together as a team because of the shared goals of the group. The importance of group identity is seen in the ways in which members describe the group to others. For example, several LPG members mentioned they feel somewhat like an NGO. Another LPG member described his group as "one of the greater upstanding groups in Liberia" because of the impact they have had in transforming the lives of citizens there. Another member notes the transformation of feeling "less marginalized" once the LPG was established. A Bong LPG member adds that when there was a problem, people just have to "refer to the group [LPG]" who serve as a sort of violence prevention team wherever there is trouble. These identities, along with the relationships built over time working together, have transformed these groups to form a strong bond between the members.

Discussion

Our findings reveal that LPG and PPP members believe they have experienced both individual- and group-level transformations associated with doing engaged collaborations related to peacebuilding. As our data reveal, these transformations are linked to communicative choices consistent with the RAA (Connaughton et al., 2017) made during the engaged collaboration. In addition to the six transformative outcomes discussed here, the four LPGs' efforts contributed to no major violent conflict being reported in these counties during the 2017 Liberian presidential elections, among other outcomes. This contribution will hopefully have an influence on the conflict culture in Liberia, as the LPG groups plan to continue their work in other areas of conflict in the country (i.e., drug use among citizens).

Theoretical Implications

Findings from this study yield three theoretical implications related to engaged scholarship and peacebuilding. First, the study contributes to conversations about the central role of the communicative in the theorizing and doing of engaged scholarship and peacebuilding. This study highlights the ways that transformations are constructed in and through communicative interactions over time in the context of engaged scholarship collaborations. In other words, it is through communication that we come to identify as peacebuilders, gain a greater sense of agency, and experience external recognition. These transformations do not occur as a one-time event but rather evolve out of our repeated interactions as part of our ongoing collaboration. Further, these transformations come into being not just in our everyday interactions in the process of doing engaged scholarship—in our case peacebuilding work—but also through our conversations *about* our process. It is through *talking about* that we reflect back on, engage in individual and collective sense-making about our experiences, and recognize and call into being the changes we experienced. For instance, we recognized as members of the PPP that we shared another commonality with LPG members when we discussed some of the transformations. Additionally, by acknowledging these changes through talking about them, we were then able to adjust future communication with LPG groups and insert additional questions into conversations with them to encourage reflexivity.

Second, the study highlights the importance of focusing on relational aspects of collaborations when doing engaged scholarship. The RAA encourages close attention to sustained and meaningful relationships in engaged scholarship collaborations; these relationships contributed in important ways to transformation. The cultivation of these relationships over time provided opportunities for exposure to new experiences and the acquisition of skills through the doing of the engaged work (e.g., peacebuilding). This could be seen when PPP researchers pointed to relationships with and observations of local collaborators as inspiring changes in their lives, and LPG members gained skills through workshops or other activities. However, it was not just relationships between local collaborators and external, U.S.-based researchers that came to matter. The most salient transformations came from relationships *among* local peace committee members—many of whom did not or would not have interacted before coming together to work toward peace. Their sense of camaraderie, developed through their ongoing collaboration to prevent violence in their communities, as well as their identification as peacebuilders speaks to their *potential* to sustain their efforts beyond this initial project and contribute to a more lasting peace.

Third, the study provides additional insight into the many facets of both individual- and group-level transformations and how they may be manifested through communicative choices made during engaged collaborations. We argue that the communicative choices that both we and our local collaborators made during our engaged collaborations have shaped our transformative outcomes (see Table 1.2). As mentioned previously, these communicative choices include convening inclusively, deferring, supporting, and validating (Connaughton et al., 2017). "Convening inclusively" transformed us and our collaborators in various ways, such as a reified identity as peacebuilders, exposure to new people and places by traveling and interacting with people who we would not have otherwise done so, and building camaraderie with those included in this work. "Deferring" was especially prevalent in transforming our confidence to speak up and take charge as peacebuilders, as well as with skill acquisition as members had to learn new skills when we relied on them to speak to others about peace. For example, our local collaborators found themselves in new roles because we deferred to them to not only know what their country needed in order to build peace but also the best ways to

Table 1.2.   Transformative outcomes shaped by communicative choices.

Transformative Outcomes	Communicative Choices in the RAA
Reified identity	Convening inclusively Supporting Validating
Sense of agency	Deferring Validating
Sense of recognition	Supporting Validating
Exposure to new people and places	Convening inclusively
Skill acquisition	Deferring Supporting
Camaraderie	Convening inclusively Supporting

communicate with other local citizens. "Supporting" has influenced transformations in ways such as through reified identity and sense of recognition, as members have come to see themselves as valuable players in the peacebuilding process and have been recognized as such by others too, in part through our support of their efforts. Members have also acquired new skills through our support for them in wanting to do well in their new roles as peacebuilders and even through our providing training in developing skills such as developing action plans for their work. Additionally, members' camaraderie as a group has transformed through the support needed in order to bring them together for this work. Lastly, "validating" has been shown to transform members' identity as they have been validated in their roles as community leaders, which has also inspired their sense of agency to take charge as leaders to initiate peace. Coincidently, they have begun to be recognized as leaders in their community by other citizens.

Practical Implications

The study yields four sets of practical implications as well. First, the study provides evidence to support the potential for local citizens to be actively involved in peacebuilding within their own communities and to achieve results. LPG members have made strides in working together to prevent violence in the places where they live—and in doing so have also experienced personal transformations. We encourage scholars and practitioners in peacebuilding to recognize and act on this potential by listening to and working with local citizens directly affected by conflict.

Second, the study highlights the importance of working closely with local peacebuilders to help equip them with the necessary skills to engage, and help build their confidence in engaging in effective peacebuilding. Skill acquisition was a key area of transformation in this study, and one that we have witnessed regularly in our collaborations. Yet, we recognize that sometimes one's perceived lack of skills can negatively impact identification as a peacebuilder and sense of agency. Thus, being intentional about finding ways to cultivate skills that collaborators identify as needed to further their efforts can not only aid in peacebuilding efforts but also contribute to the reification of local peacebuilders' identities, furthering their commitments to preventing violence in their communities.

Third, this study emphasizes the value of reflexivity for all participants as part of the engaged research process. Focus groups, interviews, and reflexive discussion all became opportunities to make sense of our experiences and call into being transformations that had taken place. In academic literature, reflexivity is often discussed as a process undertaken by researchers. Yet, following feminist and participatory scholars (e.g., Finlay, 2002; Hesse-Biber & Piatelli, 2012), we recognize that participants can also engage in reflective and reflexive practices, evaluating their experiences and perspectives individually and in dialogue with others. In designing engaged scholarship collaborations, we argue that opportunities for reflection for all participants should be incorporated throughout a project's life cycle.

Fourth and finally, there are broader lessons that using the RAA and enacting its communicative choices have taught us more about doing engaged scholarship. As researchers and as individuals, we have had to interrogate our experiences in the engaged research field in several ways. Enacting the RAA has reinforced the idea that listening to local citizens is an essential practice in doing locally led peacebuilding work and engaged scholarship (e.g., Connaughton & Ptacek, 2019). Additionally, in this chapter, we have demonstrated that engaged scholarly research requires sustained focus and long-term efforts with local citizens to bring about transformation. As engaged scholars, we continue to learn that these transformations are not static, but are constantly evolving, hence leading us to devote time to building stronger relationships between and within our local collaborators through sustained efforts in communication. We have also learned that, as engaged scholars, we should be mindful of power differentials between us and our collaborators in order to avoid privileging some voices "at the expense of others" (Deetz, 2003, p. 426). Lastly, we have learned that doing engaged scholarship matters to people. Engaged scholarship not only influences the lives of individuals in the affected areas in which we work, but it also impacts us as scholars and our collaborators in ways such as the transformations identified in this chapter.

Conclusion

In this chapter, we have illuminated the relationships between our approach to doing engaged scholarship (the RAA; Connaughton et al., 2017) and individual- and group-level transformations of those with whom we have collaborated and ourselves. As this chapter has made clear, the communicative choices both we and our local Liberian collaborators made during our engaged collaborations relate to the transformative outcomes that emerged through our work together. As an LPG member stated, "the only time you will be able to talk about peace is you must first be united," to which now she says, "we are united." We look forward to continuing our work with our Liberian collaborators and others to not only enhance what is known about the central role of the communicative in peacebuilding processes and outcomes but to also continuing to do locally driven peacebuilding that seeks to contribute to lasting peace. We hope the lessons from our work may be transferable and inspiring for individuals working in other areas of the world as well.

Note

1. The authors wish to thank Mr. Milton Lauenstein for his generous support of the Purdue Peace Project.

References

Braun, V., & Clarke, V. (2006). Using thematic analysis in psychology. *Qualitative Research in Psychology, 3,* 77–101. doi:10.1191/1478088706qp063oa.

Cárdenas, A. (2013). Peace building through sport? An introduction to sport for development and peace. *Journal of Conflictology, 4*(1): 24–33.

Charmaz, K. (2006). *Constructing grounded theory: A practical guide through qualitative analysis.* London: Sage.

Connaughton, S. L., & Berns, J. (eds., forthcoming). Locally led peacebuilding: A closer look. Lanham, MD: Rowman & Littlefield.

Connaughton, S. L., Kuang, K., & Yakova, L. (2017). Liberia's pen-pen riders: A case study of a locally-driven, dialogic approach to transformation, peacebuilding and social change. In T. G. Matyok & P. M. Kellett (eds.), *Communication and conflict transformation: Local to global engagements* (pp. 71–91). Lanham, MD: Lexington Books.

Connaughton, S. L., Linabary, J. R., Krishna, A., Kuang, K., Anaele, A., Vibber, K. S., Yakova, L., & Jones, C. (2017). Explicating the relationally attentive approach to conducting engaged scholarship. *Journal of Applied Communication Research*, *45*(5): 517–536. doi:10.1080/00909882.2017.1382707.

Connaughton, S. L., & Ptacek, J. (2019). Doing engaged scholarship: Inclusion theory meets practice in the context of a peacebuilding initiative in West Africa. In M. Doerfel & J. L. Gibbs (eds.), *Building Inclusiveness in Organizations, Institutions, and Communities: Communication Theory Perspectives*. New York, NY: Routledge.

Deetz, S. (2003). Reclaiming the legacy of the linguistic turn. *Organization*, *10*(3): 421–429.

Dempsey, S. E., & Barge, J. K. (2014). Engaged scholarship and democracy. In L. L. Putnam & D. K. Mumby (eds.), *Handbook of organizational communication: Advances in theory, research, and methods* (pp. 665–688). Thousand Oaks, CA: Sage.

Ellis, D. G. (2006). *Transforming conflict: Communication and ethnopolitical conflict*. Lanham, MA: Rowan & Littlefield Publishers.

Finlay, L. (2002). "Outing" the researcher: The provenance, process, and practice of reflexivity. *Qualitative Health Research*, *12*, 531–545. doi:10.1177/104973202129120052.

F. Y. (2013). The taxis fall silent. *The Economist*. Retrieved from https://www.economist.com/blogs/baobab/2013/11/liberia

Greer, L. L., Jehn, K. A., & Mannix, E. A. (2008). Conflict transformation: A longitudinal investigation of the relationships between different types of intragroup conflict and the moderating role of conflict resolution. *Small Group Research*, *39*(3): 278–302. doi: 10.1177/1046496408317793.

Hayman, C. (2013). Local first in peacebuilding. *Peace Review*, *25*(1): 17–23. doi: 10.1080/10402659.2013.759756.

Hesse-Biber, S. N., & Piatelli, D. (2012). The feminist practice of holistic reflexivity. In S. N. Hesse-Biber (ed.), *Handbook of feminist research: Theory and praxis* (pp. 557–582). Thousand Oaks, CA: Sage.

Hughes, C., Öjendal, J., & Schierenbeck, I. (2015). The struggle versus the song–the local turn in peacebuilding: An introduction. *Third World Quarterly*, *36*(5): 817–824. doi: 10.1080/01436597.2015.1029907.

Lederach, J. P. (1995). *Preparing for peace: Conflict transformation across cultures*. Syracuse, NY: Syracuse University Press.

Leonardsson, H., & Rudd, G. (2015). The "local turn" in peacebuilding: A literature review of effective and emancipatory local peacebuilding. *Third World Quarterly*, *36*(5): 825–839. doi: 10.1080/01436597.2015.1029905.

Liberia Country Profile (2018, January 22). *BBC News*. Retrieved from https://www.bbc.com/news/world-africa-13729504

Locally Driven Peacebuilding (2015). A report prepared by the Purdue Peace Project, Catalyst for Peace, Concordis International, American Friends Services Committee, Peace Direct, Peace Initiative Network, Gesr Center for Development, and independent consultants. Available at: https://cla.purdue.edu/ppp/documents/publications/Locally.pdf

Pugel, J. (2009). Measuring reintegration in Liberia: Assessing the gap between outputs and outcomes. In R. Muggah (ed.), *Security and post conflict reconstruction: Dealing with fighters in the aftermath of war* (pp. 70–102). New York, NY: Routledge.

Putnam, L. L (2009). Exploring the role of communication in transforming conflict situations: A social construction approach. In G. J. Galanes & W. Leeds-Hurwitz (eds.), *Socially constructing communication* (pp. 189–209). Cresskill, NJ: Hampton Press.

Putnam, L. L. & Kolb, D. M. (2000). Rethinking negotiation: Feminist views of communication and exchange. In P. M. Buzzanell (ed.), *Rethinking organizational & managerial communication from feminist perspectives* (pp. 76–104). Thousand Oaks, CA: Sage.

Schnitzer, M., Stephenson Jr., M., Zanotti, L., & Stivachtis, Y. (2013). Theorizing the role of sport for development and peacebuilding. *Sport in Society, 16*(5): 595–610. do i:10.1080/17430437.2012.690410.

Sirleaf, E. J. (2013). Annual message to the second session of the 53rd National Legislature of the Republic of Liberia: "A time for transformation." Retrieved from http://www. emansion.gov.lr/doc/2013o128_President_2013_Annual_Message_FINAL.pdf

Sultana, F. (2007). Reflexivity, positionality and participatory ethics: Negotiating fieldwork dilemmas in international research. *ACME: An International E-journal for Critical Geographies, 6*(3): 374–385.

2 Catalyzing Deliberation: How Engaged Scholarship Helped Surface Community Values and Transform Conflict in Local School Facilities Planning

LAURA W. BLACK

This chapter tells the story of a rural Appalachian community's controversial and conflicted school facilities planning process. Athens, Ohio, is a small, rural town in the Appalachian region. Home of Ohio University, Athens is politically progressive and vibrant. It is also rural, isolated, and located in one of the poorest counties in the state of Ohio. The Athens City School District (ACSD) is well supported by voters, especially compared to its neighboring districts. But, like other rural districts, Athens schools face declining enrollments and aging buildings that have become problematic in the past few years. The schools also highlight striking economic, cultural, political, and class differences among the students, which the school board believes are exacerbated by the grade configurations and locations of the current schools.

In 2016, the district created a steering committee to create a vision for future school facilities to address these concerns. As an engaged public dialogue scholar, I facilitated this group of parents, teachers, and community members who were charged with the task of drafting a recommendation for the school board. We met biweekly for six months, held community input sessions, and presented several options to the school board for consideration. The planning process and recommendations unearthed stark conflict around core values of "community" and "equity," which pervaded public discourse in local news coverage, during school board meetings, in yard signs, in classrooms, at high school sporting events, at the grocery store, and on local social media pages.

Drawing on research on public dialogue and deliberation, this chapter highlights the role of people I call "deliberative catalysts." These community members sparked thoughtful deliberation by engaging people on different sides of the conflict and promoting the kind of inclusive, reflective dialogue modeled in the planning meetings. The chapter explores the value tensions, highlights the voices of these deliberative catalysts and other community members, and reflects on my own experience as an engaged scholar, parent, neighbor, and friend of people on both sides of the conflict. It concludes with implications for engaged approaches to public dialogue and conflict transformation in rural communities.

Dialogue, Deliberation, and Ordinary Democracy

Public dialogue and deliberation are related ideas that involve normative models of communication. Both theoretical traditions are centered around the idea that difference is essential for democracy. As Young (1997) notes, difference should be seen as a resource.

> Democracy should be conceived and as far as possible institutionalized as a process of discussion, debate, and criticism that aims to solve collective problems. Political actors should promote their own interests in such a process, but must also be answerable to others to justify their proposals. This means that actors must be prepared to take the interests of others into account. (1997, p. 400)

This means that within a community, people ought to have a voice in decisions that affect their lives. Different perspectives should be voiced, listened to, and fairly considered. Silencing or marginalizing people is ethically problematic for a democracy, and public dialogue and deliberation theorists advocate for processes and institutions that acknowledge and clearly address difference (Barge & Andreas, 2013; Gastil & Black, 2018). Ideally, public dialogue and deliberation processes help communities acknowledge, honor, and ethically address difference.

However, these democratic ideals are often very far from the actual lived experiences, especially when people in communities are faced with difficult decisions that have wide-ranging economic, social, and cultural ramifications. In situations like the one described in this chapter, community members can easily experience difference as conflict. Definitions of conflict highlight interaction between people who are interdependent, yet perceive that they have incompatibilities that will interfere with the ability to reach their goals. Kellett adds that "conflict interaction typically occurs in patterns and cycles of expression" (2007, p. 7) and involves relational disputes, characterizations of others, and contestation of meanings. When communities are faced with difficult decisions, such as how to change the public schools, disagreements about policy can resurface long-standing contestations around values, meanings, and relationships, which are evident in polarized public discourse.

Dialogue and deliberation advocates are concerned about the ways that contentious and polarized public discourse can prevent people from seeing common ground, collaborating, or even coexisting peacefully. Both public dialogue and deliberation employ carefully designed processes to promote new ways of communicating (Aakhus, 2007; Barge & Andreas, 2013). Drawing inspiration from theorists such as Mikhail Bakhtin and Martin Buber, advocates of public dialogue promote group conversations that are generative and exploratory. Such conversations are designed to be "open-ended in the sense that they are focused on helping groups of people explore ideas deeply and build shared understanding of a common concern" and can be used to "transform understandings of a divisive conflict" (Black & Wiederhold, 2014). Deliberation is a similarly normative concept, but emphasizes principles of democratic decision making (Gastil & Black, 2018). Deliberation combines a social process that emphasizes respect and consideration of diverse views with an analytic process that helps groups build a solid information base, clarify key values, generate alternatives, weigh pros and cons, and make the best decisions possible (Gastil & Black, 2008). Deliberative processes are often done with mini publics, carefully selected groups that accurately represent the characteristics of the larger public from which they are drawn. More recently, though, some deliberative scholars have advocated for the idea of a systems approach, which promotes aspects of deliberation across the sectors of a community (Mansbridge et al., 2013; Young, 2012).

A key attribute of dialogue and deliberation practices is the presence of a group facilitator (Black & Wiederhold, 2014; Dillard, 2013). Facilitators use "meeting procedures to make it easier for groups to interact and exchange messages for the purposes of creating and sharing meaning. By structuring group communication in particular ways, facilitation unclogs blocked arteries and creates new veins for communication to flow smoothly among members" (Frey, 2006, p. 6). Practitioners of public dialogue and deliberation typically undergo significant training in group facilitation and learn specific methods to help groups move through disagreements to build shared understanding.

Many communication scholars who study public dialogue and deliberation do so through collaborating with practitioners. Sometimes this work involves researchers analyzing public problems or assessing processes led by practitioners, but often dialogue and deliberation research happens through engaged scholarship (e.g., see Carcasson, 2014; Carcasson & Sprain, 2016;

Pearce & Pearce, 2001; Spano, 2006). In these efforts, scholars and practitioners work together to understand public discourse about relevant issues, design processes to promote dialogue and deliberation, recruit people to engage in these processes, facilitate conversations, and report the outcomes of the conversations with the larger community and relevant public officials. Carcasson and Sprain (2016) refer to this work as *deliberative inquiry*, which emphasizes how these processes contribute to meaningful knowledge production.

Engaged scholarship is "an embodied, relational activity that necessitates bringing members of scholarly and practitioner communities into conversation with one another" (Barge & Shockley-Zalabak, 2008, p. 253). As a collaborative knowledge-production process, engaged scholarship involves commitment to both practical concerns and systematic, rigorous research practices. Collaboration between scholars and practitioners is essential throughout the engagement. My approach to this project is in line with Dempsey and Barge's (2014) description of engaged scholarship as democratic conversation.

> Here, both research and practice can be viewed as systems of knowledge production, each with its own distinct rules and modes of inquiry. The challenge of engaged scholarship is to cultivate democratic practices able to reclaim conflict and address these potentially conflicting knowledge systems. Engaged scholarship as democratic conversation involves cogenerating knowledge about how communication creates forms of organizing and the consequences of these forms. (2014, p. 677)

Dempsey and Barge describe democratic conversations as an attempt to recognize difference, design spaces for inquiry-based interactions around difference, and "enlarge participants' capacity to manage difficult conversation sin a productive manner" (p. 678). These commitments are evident in my work with the local schools, as my partners and I collaboratively designed and enacted the project.

Though I have always had a strong interest in the relationship between theory and practice, my own scholarship has increasingly become more engaged. Over the past few years, I have partnered with others in my local community who are interested in hosting dialogue and deliberation. Our efforts have been coordinated by the local community foundation and spearheaded by its executive director, Susan Urano. I met Susan through a mutual friend and she introduced me to Judy Millisen, a faculty member in Public Affairs who was a board member at the Athens Foundation. Judy, Susan, and I spearheaded efforts to train community facilitators through the "Art of Hosting," which is a practitioner group that utilizes many public dialogue processes. Over the course of three years, our community facilitation group convened and hosted conversations about a wide range of public issues in the Athens area, which put us in collaboration with city officials, several local business and nonprofit leaders, healthcare organizations, and members of the public.

I embraced this role as a community facilitator and, for the most part, did this work without conducting research. However, as time went on, I began to treat my work as ethnographic facilitation (Hartwig, 2014) as I drew on my training as a qualitative researcher to deepen our knowledge about the groups and our work. As I developed my understanding of the work as engaged scholarship, I was vigilant about maintaining a mutually beneficial and non-exploitative relationship with my co-facilitators. I drew inspiration from the writings of other engaged scholars (e.g., Barge & Shockley-Zalabak, 2008; Dempsey & Barge, 2014; Simpson & Seibold, 2008) who offered suggestions on how to collaborate with community partners to co-construct research projects and create useful practical knowledge.

In 2016, my community partners and I were approached by the superintendent, who asked us to help the school board engage the community in its facilities planning work. School boards are an example of *ordinary democracy* (Tracy, 2010) because they are localized organizations that do public, democratic work. As Asen notes, "school boards affirm the relationship between democracy and education ... [and] present opportunities for ordinary folks to engage with policymaking. They enable laypeople not only to develop opinions about governance, as in an advisory public sphere, but also to govern themselves" (2015, p. 3). I saw working with the school board as an excellent opportunity to do engaged scholarship that could promote tangible, meaningful social benefit in my community. In the course of the work, we encountered many of the ethical dialectics posed by Cheney (2008), such as openness versus protection, privilege versus equality, and distance versus empathy.

Deliberating the Future of Athens City Schools

Case Background

Before discussing the particulars of the school facilities planning, it is important to understand the local community. Athens, Ohio, is a place of contradictions. It is a small, progressive university town, with a vibrant local food system, active music and arts community, many outdoor recreation opportunities, and numerous local restaurants and brew pubs (Athens County Visitors Bureau, 2014). Athens also has a strong activist community and commitment to diversity and inclusion that spans both the university and the city (City of Athens, n.d., Ohio University Office of the President, 2018). It is the kind of town that has solar panels on the public library, and it boasts one of the best farmers markets in the state. Athens routinely shows up on lists of "best small towns in America" and many local leaders are people who came to Ohio University, fell in love with the place, and either stayed in Athens after college or returned to Athens later to raise a family, start a small business, or work at the university. During the academic year, the city of Athens has about 30,000 residents (City-Data, 2018), most of whom are affiliated with the university. In summer, when most students leave and many faculty families travel, the town has closer to 10,000 residents.

Athens is also extremely rural and is also located in the poorest county in the state, with 31% of the population living in poverty (Larrick, 2018). Athens County is in Southeast Ohio and is part of the Appalachian region. Indeed, Athens is closer to the West Virginia border than it is to any major Ohio city. The Southeast Ohio region's history is one of resource extraction, and deep, enduring poverty, with many of the counties surrounding Athens having poverty rates of 20% or higher (Larrick, 2018). The region has been hit hard by the opioid crisis. Unemployment rates are high and many towns in the region struggle to maintain well-functioning infrastructure.

For many in these rural communities, there is a strong commitment to take care of each other, be resilient, and promote asset-based development (Smart & Russell, 2018). But given the region's history of exploitation by outsiders—such as companies who offer employment then eventually leave the region, politicians who make promises during election cycles then ignore the region after they are elected, or academics who study community problems and then disappear—these community-based efforts are often localized and inward-facing. There are many lingering suspicions about people who are from somewhere else. In Athens, for example, there are tangible cultural differences between "university people" and "townies" (Aden, Pearson, & Sell, 2010).

These social, economic, and cultural contradictions play out in the local public schools. The ACSD includes students from the city of Athens and also some neighboring towns, such as The Plains and Chauncey, which are very small, not closely related to the university, and more economically distressed than the city of Athens. ACSD has four elementary schools (three in Athens and one in The Plains), one middle school, and one high school with graduating classes of approximately 200 students (Athens City School District, n.d.). There are no private or charter schools in the local area, so with the exception of some children who are home schooled, everybody goes to the public schools.

The four elementary schools are located in different places in the district and primarily enroll children who live in specific neighborhoods. In Athens, some neighborhoods have an extremely high concentration of families with post-graduate degrees where at least one adult in the household is affiliated with the university. A subset of these neighborhoods that are located the closest to the university, like the one I live in, have a high concentration of international families. Other neighborhoods have predominantly white, working-class families not associated with the university. This means that the four elementary schools have substantial differences in their student populations, and these students are relatively isolated from each other until they enter middle school in seventh grade. This segregation is exacerbated by the state of Ohio's open enrollment laws, which allow families to apply to have their child attend a school outside of their assigned district. Given the liberal politics in Athens and the history of passing school levies, Athens schools tend to be more financially supported than neighboring districts (Beard, 2018), and there are some students who enroll at ACSD from outside districts. The law also allows families within the district to enroll their child in an elementary school within the district that is different from the school assigned to their area of the city.

Enrollment trends have led to four very distinct elementary schools. The schools in neighborhoods with wealthier, more highly educated residents have high levels of intra-district enrollment (40–50% of the students) and present some stark contrasts from the most rural elementary in ASCD. For example, the elementary school my children attended, which has the highest rate of intra-district enrollment, has the most racial diversity (31% of students are non-white, most of these are from countries of origin outside of the United States) and the lowest poverty level (only 21% of the students are eligible for free or reduced lunch rates) of all the schools in the district. Additionally, over half of the students who participate in the district's gifted and talented program attend my kids' school. In contrast, the most rural elementary school in ACSD has a predominantly white student population (91%), an extremely high rate of economic disadvantage (77% of students are eligible for free and reduced lunch), 22% chronic absenteeism, and 2.5 times more students identified with disabilities than other schools in the district (ASCD Facilities steering committee, 2017).

The school board finds this disparity between schools to be highly problematic. Additionally, ACSD has seen decreasing enrollments over the past two decades, which means the schools are bigger than necessary for the actual number of students attending. Moreover, having four separate K-6 buildings means that some services like cafeterias, building administration, and gymnasium facilities are duplicated across buildings while others, such as art and music classes, special education, and nursing are stretched thin as either students or staff have to travel between buildings throughout the week. Most of the buildings themselves are quite old and in need of major repairs including new roofs, HVAC systems, electrical wiring, and so forth. As the buildings have aged and succumbed to varying levels of disrepair, the school district decided to look critically at the facilities in light of these changing enrollment trends. ACSD also became eligible for additional state funding to supplement repairing or replacing buildings throughout the district, so the school board began to work on a facilities master plan for the district.

At this time, ASCD had relatively new leadership. The superintendent, Tom Gibbs, had only been in his position for a year. He had been superintendent of a neighboring district, but was hired to be assistant superintendent of ASCD as the current leader was nearing retirement age. Gibbs was promoted early after a major scandal involving sexual impropriety from a high school teacher led to the early, perhaps forced, retirement of the ACSD superintendent (Morris, 2015). When Gibbs assumed leadership and came to understand the district's financial situation, facilities problems, enrollment trends, and cultural divisions, he made efforts to promote some major administrative and budgetary changes. The facilities planning was part of those changes, as were reductions in administrative staff and changing of some school principals.

Not surprisingly, the scandal and subsequent changes in the district were highly controversial and led many community members to distrust ACSD leadership. Additionally, given the active political life in Athens, it is also unsurprising that the community generally has a vibrant public sphere. Public meetings tend to be well attended; there are frequent political rallies involving university students and community members; and the local papers always have news coverage of local politics and numerous letters to the editor about local issues. This vibrant public sphere extends into the space of everyday interaction (Mansbridge, 2012). Saturday grocery shopping trips take hours because people stop and chat in the aisles, or linger at the local farmers market to discuss community and political issues. Recently, I was grocery shopping with my kid, wearing an "Athens Soccer" sweatshirt, and an older woman I had not met before stopped me in the aisle. She said she was preparing to write a letter to the editor "about this school stuff" and asked me for my opinion. My thirteen-year-old regaled the woman with dramatic stories about a water-damaged ceiling tile falling off during chorus class, and said students knew not to stand underneath it, since the tile needed to be routinely replaced. As we had this conversation, the morning host for our local NPR station glanced over at me and smiled as he pushed his grocery cart down the aisle. This kind of interaction is typical for Athens.

Athens' public sphere extends to social media. There are several neighborhood associations who have active Facebook pages where people post messages about topics ranging from missing pets and garage sales to questions about local politics, petitions for various causes, invitations to political rallies, and opinions about local and national news. These neighborhood Facebook pages often serve as a space to discuss the local schools. Each school also has a Parent-Teacher Organization with its own social media presence. Additionally, there is a Facebook group called "Parents for Participation" that serves as a centralized discussion space for families who want to talk about issues that face the district as a whole. This vibrant public sphere was very active during the facilities planning process. When the superintendent announced changes in staffing at the high school, the school board meeting had 300 people in attendance, many of whom gave prepared speeches protesting the changes (DeWitt, 2016). When the facilities planning began, it seemed like everyone was talking about it; online, in the grocery store, in the newspaper, at school drop off, and on neighborhood sidewalks. The public discourse surrounding the schools was rancorous and unavoidable.

School Facilities Steering Committee

After facing significant public pushback about proposed changes, the ACSD school board decided to create a steering committee to analyze data related to the district facilities and make a proposal for school board consideration. They charged superintendent Gibbs with comprising and overseeing the committee. Gibbs had participated in some community dialogues about other issues that Susan, Judy, and I had facilitated, so he contracted us to design and lead the steering committee process. Initially, the school board proposed a list of people they wanted to appoint to the committee consisting of representatives from the city, the university, the chamber of commerce, the teacher's union, and numerous school board member appointees. As facilitators who are committed to public deliberation and dialogue, we balked at this list and persuaded ASCD to include more parental and school involvement. The committee ended up with sixteen members: one representative from each school (six total), three teachers (appointed by the teacher union), one school administrator, one city representative, one university representative, and four people appointed by school board members. The school representatives were elected by the PTOs, and most of them were parents who had no previous school administration experience.

We designed the meetings to use dialogic methods such as circle practice, world café, and open space discussions. We stressed principles of respect, openness, creativity, and consideration of diverse views, which are hallmarks of public dialogue processes (Black & Wiederhold, 2014). The room we met in was set up with tables in a U so committee members could see each other and still have space for presenters in the front of the room. There were white boards on the walls, and committee members had big sheets of paper, markers, and post-it notes to use for various activities. We used small round tables in the next room for small group discussions as needed. We planned out a general sequence for the meetings to follow deliberative principles. Early work involved clarifying committee values and goals, and gathering and analyzing relevant information including ASCD budget, enrollment statistics, building assessments, state funding availability, and information about best practices in school design. The work also involved gathering input from community members, teachers, and students in the schools. The committee was charged with generating and considering a wide range of options, developing a proposal, and providing that proposal to the school board for consideration. This process closely mirrors the analytic and social dimensions of deliberative discussions (Gastil & Black, 2008).

Because this committee was appointed by the school board, all of the meetings were public. The steering committee was acutely aware of the public nature of their work. Our meetings were designed to maintain an open, transparent, and public process. We set up chairs in the back of the room for audience members, and community members attended every meeting. School board members were also in the audience at every meeting, as they were invited to listen and watch the committee's discussions. As facilitators, we took detailed notes about the discussions, including much more information than typical meeting minutes would provide, and made these notes available to the public. ACSD created a page on its website for the steering committee work, and we used this space to post the meeting dates and times, notes from our discussions, and all material that the committee viewed or created.

Pivotal Moments and Tensions

Early disagreements about the process. Throughout the process, there were some pivotal moments that highlighted tensions between different values at play. Initially, many steering committee members came in as stakeholders and representatives who acted as advocates for their own groups. While this is understandable, taking an adversarial stance against other committee members and the district leadership could stymie dialogue and deliberation in the group. In the first meeting, we worked to set the tone for collaborative, creative, and rigorous group processes. We challenged committee members to be open to learning, consider the best interest of the district as a whole, and to consider their role as collaborative problem solvers rather than interest group advocates. We also asked them to refrain from talking to the press individually, which creates potentially conflicting information in the public, and instead to appoint one member as the voice of the committee and to direct community members to the materials posted on the ACSD website. Several committee members pushed back against these comments and resisted the process during this first meeting. In these early meetings, we also negotiated a tension between treating the committee meetings as a safe container for dialogue and a public process that is open to community input. Although we periodically engaged the audience in our activities, the meetings largely served as a workspace for the committee where audience members observed without asking questions.

These early tensions placed me and other facilitators in the public eye. Resistance from committee members was aimed at us, with some committee members refusing to participate in the more creative and generative tasks. People I knew who were in the audience during our early meetings tended to avoid me in the community, and I witnessed at least one person glaring at me as I was walking my dog around our neighborhood. Given how small Athens is, these were frustrating and difficult things to experience in my daily life and it heightened my awareness of the communicative and emotional labor involved in this work. As facilitators, we met regularly to support each other, plan meetings, and decide how to respond.

Identifying key values. The group began to shift when they articulated some of their core values and learned more about the facilities throughout the district. A key part of deliberative inquiry is articulating the tensions between different values (Carcasson & Sprain, 2016), so getting the group to talk through what mattered to them was really important for our design. We dedicated time in some of the earlier meetings to talking through what the group was holding valuable and what those values meant. The committee articulated four values, which they described as "priorities" in their work. These were *equity, high-quality education, financial responsibility,* and *teachers' professional development* (ACSD Facilities Steering Committee, 2017). The committee referred to these values throughout their work and these became a key component of the public conversations regarding the school facilities plans.

All of these values informed the committee's work, but equity was the one that prompted the most conversation. The committee coalesced around the value of equity after learning about the discrepancies among the four elementary schools, which are also evident in student experiences in middle and high school. The committee poured over enrollment data and district lines to understand the populations at the different elementary schools. They looked at high school student leaders to get an understanding of what elementary school these students had attended. A committee member who teaches at the high school asked sophomores to place a pin on a map of the city showing where they live. He gave students different colored pins depending on what level of social studies classes they were taking (basic level, advanced, honors, and AP). The map showed visible trends supporting the idea that students living in wealthier areas had higher levels of academic achievement. Although this was clearly not a rigorous academic study, the visual representation was influential on the steering committee's discussions.

The committee's commitment to equity was evident in the information they crafted to share with the public. They defined an equitable education as "one that supports students in overcoming challenges due to a variety of circumstances (economics, gender, disability, race, sexuality, etc.) to help students reach their full potential as learners as well as to achieve a basic level of skills." As part of the commitment to equity, the committee stated, "We aspire to create an inclusive learning environment that embraces, acknowledges, and respects that Athens City Schools consists of learners from diverse socio-economic backgrounds, faith systems, races, cultures, abilities, and sexual orientations/identities. We celebrate the idea that every student's background tells a different story; stories that our students should be able to share with dignity as they grow together, learning to thrive in a multicultural society" (ASCD Facilities Steering Committee, 2017). This commitment to equity was instrumental in the committee's decisions to promote a facilities plan that integrated children from different areas into the same school much earlier in their education than our current facilities allow.

Facilitating this process was challenging in a different way. At this point, I was feeling less resistance from committee members, and I was excited to see committee members doing difficult work and being moved by one another's stories. But hearing discussions about equity confronted me with my own privilege as a parent of two students in ACSD. I remembered moving to Athens to work at the university in 2007, when my children were in preschool. Coming from Seattle, Washington, I knew very little about Athens, and virtually nothing about school districting policies. But, I wanted to make sure my kids had the best life I could make for them in this new town. Before my husband and I even met with a relator to look at houses, we visited the elementary schools to see what they were like. We loved the in-town elementary school with a lot of international students and a walkable neighborhood. We restricted our house hunting and found a home one block away from the school, in a neighborhood with old houses, lots of academic families, and a very safe and welcoming environment. In retrospect, I realized that I never even considered the more rural school as a possibility for my children (we only visited the three schools located within city limits) and that my story reflects ACSD's problems related to privilege. This realization was humbling. **Generating options and engaging the public.** Throughout the process, steering committee members engaged in a variety of activities to gather information about the schools. Representatives from the schools attended their PTO meetings to report about steering committee process and solicit parents' concerns. When concerns about the middle school's proximity to college student housing came up as a concern, committee members surveyed middle and high school students about their experiences. Several students commented that they had been teased by partying college students, or cat-called on their way to gym class, cross country, or soccer practice. These concerns were shared with the committee, and were visibly upsetting to the superintendent and school board members in the audience. The committee included these stories from students in their considerations along with the information about facilities, budget, and educational best practices.

After three months of gathering and considering information, the committee was ready to develop ideas for different grade configurations in the schools. They divided into six small groups and each group developed a proposal for what they thought would be ACSD's best facilities plan. Groups wrote their proposals on large pieces of paper, including some key points about what attributes they thought were most important. They brought these proposals back to the committee as a whole, and we displayed all the proposals around the room. The committee discussed each proposal, analyzing the strengths and drawbacks of each, and developed a seventh proposal in their discussion process. All of these proposals were displayed around the room, and we had graduate students helping keep track of the discussion of each proposal by writing on the white boards. Using our understanding of dialogue processes moving between divergent and convergent ideas (Spano, 2006), we helped the committee engage in rigorous and difficult analysis of each of the proposals. Committee members frequently used the core values of the group to help their analysis. They identified overlaps among the different proposals and eventually narrowed the options to three distinct proposals.

The committee decided that they wanted to share these three options with the public to get more detailed community feedback before making a proposal to the school board. I was active in this decision as I prompted the group to be sure that the options they presented were all ones that they could stand behind and also were clearly distinct from one another. As facilitators, we helped them write up a document that summarized each option, described the values that were guiding that option, and presented both the strengths and trade-offs of that option. The document began with a page that summarized the steering committee's charge, its work to date, and the core values that guided their discussions. The structure of this document was very similar to materials that deliberative organizations such as National Issues Forums use to inform participants about issues and frame options for deliberation.

We shared this full document with the public via a press release and by posting it on the ACSD website. We invited community members to attend open public meetings, which we held at the high school library. We designed these meetings to promote deliberation of the options, which meant that after an initial welcome to all participants we split people into smaller groups and sent them into nearby classrooms for discussions that were facilitated by members of the steering committee. Before the meetings, I had given steering committee members some basic training in group facilitation and given them discussion prompts, questions, and guidelines to share with the group. Over 300 people attended our meetings and we got quite a bit of local press coverage. Materials we posted on the ACSD website were frequently quoted in news stories, shared on social media, and used as evidence in arguments for and against the different proposals. I was particularly struck by this because in my role as the facilitator I had written up most of the meeting notes and had been instrumental in writing the document proposing the three options. I was startled by my own power to shape the public discourse by how I took notes or summarized the committee's ideas. I was also a bit amused by the idea that it was possible that these documents were the most closely scrutinized writing I had ever done—far more than my Ph.D. dissertation or any of the scholarly articles I have written. This realization weighed heavily on me as I worked with the committee, and I was mindful about our language use.

Managing community resistance. At the first community meeting, it was abundantly clear that some members of the public were angry about the proposed changes and there was some organized resistance in the meeting itself. For example, the committee's proposals involved closing the middle school, which is located right in the center of town, and building a new facility closer to the high school. This was not a popular proposal and people like the former middle school principal, a high-profile local judge, and business owners with property near the school came to the meeting and loudly expressed their displeasure. This group interrupted the superintendent during his introductory remarks to interrogate him about details in the plans. They also refused to split up and go into the smaller group discussions. My co-facilitators Susan and Judy stayed in the school library to work with this group, as did the superintendent, while everyone else went into classrooms for small group discussions. I observed these break-out discussions and I was impressed with how well members of my community articulated their questions and concerns, shared their stories, and listened to others in their group. For the most part, I thought these conversations were great examples of rigorous and reflective public dialogue. School board members who observed these discussions were similarly impressed and made many positive comments to me and the steering committee members after the meetings.

But these meetings also sowed the seeds of resistance in the community. It became clear that some groups of people affiliated with the different elementary schools were unhappy about some of the proposals. Because of the steering committee's commitment to equity, most of the proposals involved reconfiguring the elementary schools to be more inclusive and less neighborhood-specific. One of the options proposed that ACSD build completely new K-6 facilities, which would consist of grade-level buildings that would all be housed on a single campus. This kind of single campus school facility is common in our region, but represented a stark departure from the current ACSD school building configurations. Community members who did not like this plan referred to it as a "mega school" and argued that the steering committee and school board wanted to create a corporate education system that went against the clearly positive value of "community" that was central to life in Athens. This group made yard signs declaring "No to Mega School!" and distributed them to interested families throughout the district.

My neighborhood had a strong concentration of these signs, which seemed to suddenly appear *en masse* as part of an organized campaign. I could not leave my house without seeing these signs in almost every yard. When I walked my dog, I was sometimes stopped by neighbors who asked, "when do we get to vote against the mega school?" despite the fact that the committee had not yet made a proposal to the school board and there would not be anything on the ballot for well over a year. These signs immediately became the source of controversy and public attention. Local social network pages and letters to the editor were filled with accusations about mega schools or NIMBYism. The steering committee saw the signs as a direct attack on their work. I personally felt angry because the signs could be seen as an attempt to hijack the deliberative process and move the public discourse into a false dichotomy that would prevent meaningful dialogue and social change.

At the time I was emotionally overwhelmed by these signs and the conflict that they surfaced. But in retrospect, I recognize that the "mega school" discourse helped articulate the tension between "equity" and "community" as core values that were inherent in the school deliberations. Eventually the group behind the campaign changed their language. The "mega school" signs came down and were replaced with signs saying "We love our small schools." The group began calling itself "community-centered schools of Athens" and promoted options as an alternative to the steering committee's proposals. To this group, community seemed to indicate positive relationships, a focus on local assets, and a feeling of connection among students and teachers. In contrast, those who advocated for equity emphasized fairness, reducing disparities and cultural barriers, and helping all students reach their full potential. In abstract terms, these two ideas do not necessarily preclude one another. But, in the local public discourse related to schools, "community" and "equity" became clearly distinct terms with different groups of advocates backing different proposals. These groups also characterized the other in negative light. "Equity" was cast as an unreflective effort to make all students the same and strip the schools of their local character. "Community" was stereotyped as a thinly veiled preference for keeping a status quo and maintained the privilege of dominant groups.

Final proposal to school board. In the midst of all this public controversy, the steering committee continued to do its work. Members held smaller, local meetings at all of the different schools in the district. They weighed the feedback from community members at all of these sessions and they discussed news coverage and local social media messages. During this time, it was clear that the committee members were stressed, and they had disagreements about what to propose to the school board. Some members wanted to only promote the single campus option. Others wanted to propose a range of options. At one point, a committee member noted that as a group they had done everything "by consensus" so far and that she did not think it was right for the group to make this important final decision by vote. This comment seemed to resonate with the group, and they decided to make some adjustments to their initial ideas and propose three distinct options to the school board. Members of the committee created a "Frequently Asked Questions" document, which summarized relevant information about their process and the proposals. They prepared a presentation for the school board and elected two of their members to present this information to the school board. This allowed the committee to speak as a group and all stand behind the work.

I was immensely proud of the committee members for negotiating this consensus and presenting a nuanced and well-informed set of materials to the school board. The FAQ document that they created was visually engaging, informative, and used widely after their presentation to the school board. The proposal they made was supported by the teacher's union and even people who were critical of the school district expressed appreciation for the steering committee members and their work. Over time the school board analyzed the proposals, investigated the possibility of a single campus option and found there was not an appropriate space in the city limits. Based on more community input, the school board adopted a plan that is a slight variation from one of the options proposed by the steering committee. Over the subsequent year, the school board developed more detailed plans, engaged in more research and community conversations, and built funding into a school levy. Public discourse around the levy remained contentious, but there were continued efforts to promote deliberative discussions in community forums and localized online spaces throughout the year. The levy narrowly passed in November 2018, providing funding for the new school facilities.

Deliberative Catalysts

Even after the school board decided on a plan, the public discourse swirled with the language of "community versus equity." Soon after the steering committee completed their work, ACSD had a hotly contested school board election that included candidates from both camps. During the school board elections and the levy vote, the Athens public sphere was alive with arguments for and against the school plan, and these arguments were anchored in the competing values of community and equity.

But the interdependence that is inherent to living in a small town makes it difficult to maintain such firm stereotypes. Through this planning process, many people found themselves at odds with friends and neighbors. For instance, I have close friends and colleagues on both sides of this debate, and I found myself defending these people and their positions from attacks by the "other" side. I also found myself tacking between the positions in my own conversations in my everyday life. I was moved by the discussions of equity and came to strongly support proposals for socioeconomic integration. Still, I held a lingering concern that the move for equity could dilute the inclusive and welcoming culture that I saw at my children's elementary school. I worried about what more integrated schools would be like for international students and people of color. I tried to engage people in conversations that moved beyond the false dichotomy of equity versus community and really entertained questions about what our schools could do to manage these issues through facilities design and curricular practices. I witnessed other people in the community also negotiating this tension and becoming what I have come to think of as "deliberative catalysts."

Deliberative catalysts are *people who participate in a deliberative process and then take on deliberative habits or engage in communication practices that promote deliberation in other community spaces.* This happens when people embody deliberative tasks such as sharing high-quality information, posing analytic questions, articulating values tensions, listening to and considering diverse views, and promoting respectful interaction. Deliberative scholars argue that deliberation can have tangible impacts on community capacity-building effort (Kinney, 2012). Moreover, research provides some evidence that engaging in high-quality deliberation can increase people's sense of civic agency, trust in their fellow citizens, and participation in civic life (Gastil, black, Deess, & Leighter, 2008). But it is not clear whether and how deliberative participants might transfer what they've learned into these other contexts. In this case, people who acted as deliberative catalysts created opportunities for deliberative talk outside of the steering committee meetings, thereby helping to promote a more robust deliberative system in Athens. This deserves deeper investigation, but to support my claim here I offer three examples.

The first example comes from the "Parents for Participation" Facebook group, which was created many years ago to promote conversations among families throughout the district. It originated out of frustration about the high volume of snow days in the district but grew into a much broader platform for local discussion about school issues. The group is organized by four volunteers who provide basic discussion guidelines and moderate the conversations. One of these volunteers served as a member of the steering committee, another attended all the meetings as an observer. They frequently posted information from the steering committee webpage and encouraged people to attend meetings, read documents, and make efforts to communicate their ideas to the committee. Moderators also prompted participants to engage in "civil" discussion and reminded them of group guidelines like "no personal attacks." This meant that they frequently participated in group discussions to manage conflicts and ask people to tone down or reframe their comments.

Moderators told me that they will occasionally delete a post if it clearly violates the group guidelines, but before they do so they reach out to the person who posted it to try to explain their concern and encourage the person to revise their post. One time I saw this happen was when a neighbor of mine, a staunch social justice advocate, posted a photo of the "We love our small schools" sign with the words "small schools" crossed out and replaced by "privilege and status quo." This photo garnered many responses, most of which were angry and divisive. Moderators took down the photo and made a separate post that framed the question about privilege in less polarizing way to prompt discussion of the issues. Behind the scenes, moderators also reached out to my neighbor to explain why they found his post to be problematic and to encourage him to continue to participate, but in less inflammatory ways.

In this way, the moderators enacted many of the behaviors that a facilitator might engage in during deliberative discussions (Dillard, 2013).

Another example from this same Facebook group came from a faculty member in the college of education who had observed many of the steering committee meetings. He made two nearly identical posts to this group: one post about the single campus option and one about maintaining community-based schools. In each post he asked people to provide their thoughts on the proposal, articulate their concerns about it, and reflect on what they thought would need to happen to address their concerns if this proposal was selected by the school board. These two posts prompted deliberative discussion by soliciting thoughtful feedback and asking people to weigh trade-offs of the proposals. The person who made these posts also responded to comments to thank people for their perspective and to answer questions if prompted.

Finally, I saw members of the steering committee engage in informal conversations throughout the community, especially during school events. They talked about the proposals with people sitting near them during high school football games or standing in line at the grocery store. They chatted about the steering committee work during pickup and drop off at the elementary schools. They encouraged friends to go to school board meetings or to read materials posted on ACSD website. This kind of everyday talk embodied the deliberative work and catalyzed further discussion. One extreme example of this comes from Sean, a steering committee member who fully embraced the task of sharing relevant information in an accessible way. He was instrumental in creating the steering committee's FAQ and presenting the proposals to the school board. After the steering committee's work was complete, he began making informational videos about the school board's work with the proposals. Sean posted these videos on social media and became a trusted source of information about the schools. He eventually won a seat on the school board after running on a campaign of clear communication and thoughtful consideration of community input.

I theorize these people's actions as deliberative catalysts because they help move the dialogic and deliberative norms into more spheres of interaction. By promoting respectful discussion, asking analytic questions, providing clear information, and encouraging thoughtful discussion, these people have emerged as informal community leaders who bring dialogue and deliberation into more spaces of ordinary democracy and everyday life. Their actions help create and support a local deliberative system.

Unconcluded

It has been several years since the steering committee began its work. The levy proposing a tax increase to support the facilities improvements was supported by the voters, and school construction is currently underway. Our elementary schools will be reconfigured to encourage socioeconomic integration at an earlier age, and our district will have more up-to-date facilities. Simultaneously, ACSD is managing the cultural shifts that come with engaging with difference. The facilities planning process occurred within a larger context in which students, families, community members, and school employees are confronted with substantial cultural and socioeconomic differences. Since 2016, these differences have been even more visible in political discourse, including both national and localized conversations about topics like race, immigration, inequality, and sexual assault. Currently ACSD leaders are promoting a variety of curricular and policy changes to decrease bias, discrimination, and bullying in the schools. These conversations are not directly related to school facilities planning, but they are based on the same value tensions and involve many of the same people.

Some of the public discourse about our schools remains contentious and polarizing. But the conversations prompted by deliberative catalysts continue on and can be seen in letters to the editor and local social media pages. As I write this chapter, I am heartened by the deliberative character of much of the public discourse; I would like to think that my engaged scholarship has been meaningful in shaping that discourse. But, I believe that public dialogue and deliberation are fragile and need to be carefully tended over time. I wonder how much conflict transformation is possible around these issues. As a community, can we carry a dialogic spirit forward through the course of building and reconstruction? Can we also bring this spirit to our current discussions of bias and discrimination in the schools?

This case offers some implications for others doing engaged scholarship on similarly public issues. First, it is clear that stakeholder processes like this one need to include careful design, transparency, articulation of key values, openness to feedback, and commitment to the process. But even with carefully designed processes, conflict and dissent seem inevitable. As facilitators, we continuously reflected on how to respond to these conflicts in ways that were consistent with our commitment to public dialogue and deliberation. For us, it was essential to be reflective and flexible enough to respond to concerns. Second, this process heightened my awareness that facilitating dialogue and deliberation involves difficult emotional and communicative labor. As a facilitator, I often found myself managing other people's emotions both in the steering committee meetings and also in other settings. This emotional labor was stressful and at times exhausting. It was even more difficult because I am a member of the community. As a facilitator, I felt obligated to be even-keeled and civil even when I myself felt angry or sad. Working on this project illuminated for me that it can be easy to overlook the emotional toll that engaged scholarship can have, especially when engaging in one's home community.

However, this project has also shown me that deliberative participation can spread throughout a community and have meaningful, positive impact on public discourse. The deliberative catalysts I saw in this work demonstrate Mansbridge's (2012) claim that the informal conversations of everyday talk have the potential to meaningfully contribute to a deliberative system. As Dempsey and Barge (2014) note, engaged scholarship as democratic conversation helps construct new knowledge about how to address public problems. "If engaged scholars are inviting and attempting to model more democratic forms of conversation in these activities, participants build their capacity to create democratic futures" (p. 680). Engaged communication scholars have the potential, then, to help communities transform conflicts and go through meaningful change. This insight motivates me to continue with my work and hopefully can inspire others to engage deliberatively in their own communities.

References

Aakhus, M. (2007). Communication as design. *Communication Monographs, 74*, 112–117. doi: 1 0.1080/03637750701196383.

Aden, R. C., Pearson, P., & Sell, R. (2010). Placing townies: The symbolic work of naming. *Communication Quarterly, 58*, 279–296. doi: 0.1080/01463373.2010.503157.

Asen, R. (2015). *Democracy, deliberation, and education*. University Park, PA: Penn State University Press.

ASCD Facilities Steering Committee (2017, March 16). *FAQ Report*. Retrieved from: http://www.athenscsd.org/docs/district/steering_committee

Athens City School District (n.d.) Retrieved from: http://www.athenscsd.org/

Athens County Visitor's Bureau (2014). *Athens County Ohio*. Retrieved from http://athensohio.com/

Barge, J. K., & Andreas, D. (2013). Communication, conflict, and the design of dialogic conversations. In J. Oetzel & S. Ting-Toomey (eds.), *The SAGE handbook of conflict management* (pp. 609–634, 2nd ed.). Thousand Oaks, CA: Sage.

Barge, J. K., & Shockley-Zalabak, P. (2008). Engaged scholarship and the creation of useful organizational knowledge. *Journal of Applied Communication Research, 36*, 251–265. doi: 10.1080/00909880802172277.

Beard, K. (2018, May 9). Alex schools run into brick wall as levy fails for fourth time. *Athens News*. Retrieved from https://www.athensnews.com/news/

Black, L. W., & Wiederhold, A. (2014). Discursive strategies of civil disagreement in public dialogue groups. *Journal of Applied Communication Research, 42*, 285–306. doi: 10.1080/00909882.2014.911938.

Carcasson, M. (2014). The critical role of local centers and institutes in advancing deliberative democracy. *Journal of Public Deliberation, 10*, Article 11. Retrieved from: http://www.publicdeliberation.net/jpd/vol10/iss1/art11.

Carcasson, M., & Sprain, L. (2016). Beyond problem solving: Reconceptualizing the work of public deliberation as Deliberative Inquiry. *Communication Theory, 26*, 41–63. doi: 10.1111/comt.12055.

Cheney, G. (2008). Encountering the ethics of engaged scholarship. *Journal of Applied Communication Research, 36*, 281–288. doi: 10.1080/00909880802172293.

City of Athens. (n.d.) *Community Relations Commission*. Retrieved from: https://www.ci.athens.oh.us/419/Community-Relations-Commission

City-Data. (2018) *Athens, Ohio*. Retrieved from http://www.city-data.com/city/Athens-Ohio.html

Dempsey, S. E., & Barge, J. K. (2014). Engaged scholarship and democracy. In L. L. Putnam & D. K. Mumby (eds.), *The SAGE Handbook of Organizational Communication: Advances in Theory, Research, and Methods* (pp. 665–688). Thousand Oaks, CA: Sage.

DeWitt, D. (2016). Athens school officials refute reports of substantial teacher layoffs, school closing. *Athens News*. Retrieved from: https://www.athensnews.com/news/local/athens-school-officials-refute-reports-of-substantial-teacher-layoffs-school/article_d892371c-0c98-11e6-8eb3-5fb8d5412682.html

Dillard, K. (2013). Envisioning the role of facilitation in public deliberation. *Journal of Applied Communication Research, 41*, 217–235. doi: 10.1080/00909882.2013.82 6813.

Frey, L. R. (2006). *Facilitating group communication in context: Innovations and applications with natural groups. Volume 1: Facilitating group creation, conflict, and conversation*. Creskill, NJ: Hampton Press.

Gastil, J., & Black, L. W. (2008). Public deliberation as an organizing principle for political communication research. *Journal of Public Deliberation, 4*, Article 3. Available at: https://www.publicdeliberation.net/jpd/vol4/iss1/art3/

Gastil, J., & Black, L. W. (2018). Deliberation in communication studies. In A. Baechtiger, J. Dryzek, J. Mansbridge, & M. Warren (eds.), *Oxford Handbook of Deliberative Democracy* (pp. 502–517). New York: Oxford University Press.

Gastil, J., Black, L. W., Deess, P., & Leighter, J. (2008). From group member to democratic citizen: How deliberating with fellow jurors reshapes civic attitudes. *Human Communication Research, 35*, 137–169.

Hartwig, R. T. (2014). Ethnographic facilitation as a complementary methodology for conducting applied communication scholarship. *Journal of Applied Communication Research, 42*, 60–84. doi: 10.1080/00909882.2013.874567.

Kellett, P. M. (2007). *Conflict dialogue: Working with layers of meaning for productive relationships.* Thousand Oaks, CA: Sage.

Kinney, B. (2012). Deliberation's contribution to community capacity building. In T. Nabatchi, J. Gastil, G. M. Weiksner, & M. Leighninger (eds.), *Democracy in motion: Evaluating the practice and impact of deliberative civic engagement* (pp. 163–180). New York: Oxford University Press.

Larrick, D. (2018). *The Ohio poverty report.* Ohio Development Services Agency Research Office: A state affiliate of the U.S. Census Bureau. Retrieved from: https://www.development.ohio.gov/files/research/p7005.pdf

Mansbridge, J. (2012). Everyday talk in the deliberative system. In D. W. M. Barker, N. McAfee, & D. McIvor (eds.), *Democratizing deliberation: A political theory anthology* (pp. 85–112). Dayton, OH: Kettering Foundation Press.

Mansbridge, J., Bohman, J., Chambers, S., Christiano, T., Fung, A., Parkinson, J., Thompson, D. F., & Warren, M. (2013). A systemic approach to deliberative democracy. In J. Parkinson & J. Mansbridge (eds.), *Deliberative systems: Deliberative democracy at the large scale* (pp. 1–26). New York: Cambridge University Press.

Morris, C. (2015, May 21). Athens school supe to retire; no action taken in connection with imprisoned teacher. *Athens News.* Retrieved from: https://www.athensnews.com/news/local/athens-school-supe-to-retire-no-action-taken-in-connection/article_4e359fec-2fb0-597b-a1d7-173f7bdf093f.html

Ohio University Office of the President. (2018). *Strategic Pathways for Ohio University's Future.* Retrieved from: https://www.ohio.edu/president/initiatives/strategic-pathways.cfm

Pearce, K. A., & Pearce, W. B. (2001). The public dialogue consortium's school-wide dialogue process: A communicative approach to develop citizenship skills and enhance school climate. *Communication Theory, 11*, 105–123.

Simpson, J. L, & Seibold, D. R. (2008) Practical engagements and co-created research. *Journal of Applied Communication Research, 36*, 266–280. doi: 10.1080/00909880802172285.

Spano, S. (2006). Theory and practice in public dialogue: A case study in facilitating community transformation. In L. Frey (ed.), *Facilitating group communication in context: Innovations and applications with natural groups* (pp. 271–289). Creskill, NJ: Hampton Press.

Smart, A. J., & Russell, B. (2018, August 21). What rural America can teach us about civil society. *Stanford Social Innovation Review.* Retrieved from: https://ssir.org/articles/entry/what_rural_america_can_teach_us_about_civil_society

Tracy, K. (2010). *Challenges of ordinary democracy: A case study in deliberation and dissent.* University Park, PA: Penn State University Press.

Young, I. M. (1997). Difference as a resource for democratic communication. In J. Bohman & W. Rehg (eds.), *Deliberative democracy: Essays on reason and politics* (pp. 383–406). Cambridge, MA: MIT Press.

Young, I. M. (2012). De-centering deliberative democracy. In D. W. M. Barker, N. McAfee, & D. McIvor (eds.), *Democratizing deliberation: A political theory anthology* (pp. 113–125). Dayton, OH: Kettering Foundation Press.

Part II: Locally and Culturally Grounded Engagement

3 Rethinking the Local Turn in Peacebuilding: Re(visiting) Preventative Stances in Violent Extremism: The Case of Likoni Subcounty, South Coast, Kenya

JOHN MWANGI GITHIGARO

This chapter examines the value of local agency in peacebuilding with a focus on countering violent extremism. It examines local-level peacebuilding initiatives that are being used in Likoni, Mombasa, Kenya. Peacebuilding is applied here to mean the development of a social, political, and economic infrastructure to prevent future violence and lay the foundations for a durable peace (Butler, 2009) This study is drawn from empirical work, interrogating the working of local-level initiatives in preventing violent extremism and their potential in the field of peacebuilding at Kenya's South Coast. The empirical work was collected qualitatively through key informant interviews, focus group discussions, and participant observation. The study uses the framework of the "local turn" in peacebuilding and interrogates its potential in countering violent extremism. In doing so, the study critiques the often-formulated liberal peacebuilding agenda applied to the counter-terrorism agenda (Richmond & Tellidis, 2012). The liberal peacebuilding agenda in terrorism discourses places primacy on state-centric approaches of governing to bring "peace and security" to a polity. For liberal peace, the understanding of security is from a state-centric position where security is constructed from a national interest point of view. For liberal peace, therefore, terrorism threats are constructed from a "nationalist" position and for which the securitization process begins. Terrorism is thus constructed as a security threat that requires the response of the liberal state and to the neglect of other actors such as grassroots and civil society actors (Richmond & Tellidis, 2012).

As a direct critique of the liberal peacebuilding models as applied to counter-terrorism discourses, this study argues for the value of local agency in peacebuilding. The value of local-level initiatives is itself a shift in security governance mechanisms. While not discounting the role of the state in security provision and broadly too in peacebuilding, this study examines the value of local-level initiatives and their potential in the security governance framework (Solomon, 2017). Local-level initiatives are applied in this study to mean the involvement of non-state actors in security provision in contexts where the state is weak or absent. The local is contested in scholarship but would require context and a range of peace interventions by grassroots agencies, for instance. By incorporating local actors in the process, a form of "security from below" is then made possible (Solomon, 2017). Community actors by themselves and in situations where the state has "contracted" can be relied upon for community safety (Solomon, 2017). Community actors in this chapter's context include religious leaders, community elders, civil society organizations (CSOs), and community-based organizations (CBOs).

These kinds of local-level initiatives that incorporate local political actors have worked in Somalia in the Halmadug state largely dominated by the Hawiye clan. Arising out of the state collapse in Somalia (post-1991), the local community convened a public meeting where they (clan members) deliberated on community safety and appointed 325 officers that worked under the authority of clan elders on crime safety. These police officers were, however, not subject to the authorities in Mogadishu and instead offered allegiance to their clans. Given that the process was community owned and transparent, this security model achieved legitimacy at the community level (Solomon, 2017). This Somalia example demonstrates the changing nature of security governance emphasizing the value of local actors in guaranteeing peace in their locales. In addition, this example calls for a need to reconceptualize the state-centric notions of security provision that have hitherto been framed from state lenses (Solomon, 2017). What this example and others are calling for is a hybrid form of peace that would bring on board the positive peace notions of liberal peace while remaining engaged with localized processes that are locally owned and reflective of the particularities of local contexts (Richmond & Tellidis, 2012). Positive peace in the context of peace studies refers to a just and equitable society that would include happiness and justice. It refers to a society devoid of social exploitation and structural violence broadly (Barash & Webel, 2014).

In the current context of countering violent extremism, the youth in uncritical ways have been securitized as security threats locally, nationally, and globally in the current discourses on the global war on terror (Sukarieh &

Tannock, 2017). Securitization is a concept applied to refer to the speech acts of influential state officials who label from a social constructivist lens a particular phenomenon as a security threat and which requires extra-legal interventions (Buzan & Waever, 2009; Williams, 2003). In this case, the youth are securitized as threats due to their perceived linkages with violent extremism. This discourse has been on account of a global surge in population vis-à-vis minimal economic opportunities. The challenge with these kinds of discourses is their tendency to blame the youth for global insecurity, yet they remain muted on grievances that may predispose individuals to acts of violence. Instead, states have been keen on youth surveillance while underappreciating their peacebuilding potential (Sukarieh & Tannock, 2017).

Governments globally have securitized the youth identity making it possible for increased surveillance, while similarly mounting anti-radicalization and countering violent extremism strategies. In mounting these counter-radicalization strategies, there is less appreciation for the legitimate grievances that may create opportunities for terrorist acts of violence. Counter-radicalization approaches often assume that violence is rooted in psychology, ideology, and individual actions or extremist groups (Sukarieh & Tannock, 2017).

Notwithstanding the global securitization of youth, there has been a paradigmatic shift at the level of the United Nations through Resolution 2250 ratified in December 2015 that underscores the need for youth involvement in peacebuilding efforts. This document acknowledges the youth bulge (a large portion of the population is comprised of children and youth) globally and points to the need for inclusive participation of youth in decision making in local, regional, and international institutions including their involvement in conflict prevention. The document acknowledges the overall rise of youth radicalization and violent extremism, with calls to counter conditions that may make terrorism thrive (United Nations, 2015).

In contextualizing the "local" and critiquing liberal peacebuilding, this study adopts MacGinty and Richmond's (2013) perspective as they note: "By 'local' we mean the range of locally based agencies present within a conflict and post-conflict environment, some of which are aimed at identifying and creating the necessary processes for peace, perhaps with or without international help, and framed in a way in which legitimacy in local and international terms converges" (p. 769). Local actors can often be discriminatory or partisan in their peace roles. The conceptualization of local is elastic. What is not in contention is its identification of a particular theme within a geographical space. What is termed as "local" is often socially negotiated. In that respect the local approach to peace takes both localized ideas but also adopts non-localized ideas, practices, and norms. Local agency here needs to be seen in light of small scale, yet tactical, pursuits for peace and which could be hidden from public view (MacGinty & Richmond, 2013). While the local holds potential for peacebuilding, its working is also hampered by international orthodox approaches to peacebuilding. Local agency may be co-opted into the practices and norms of international peacebuilding approaches. The co-optation of the local into the orthodox often is made possible by the latter's access to material power such as resources and legitimacy (MacGinty & Richmond, 2013). The next section of this chapter contextualizes Likoni, Mombasa, and its linkages to violent extremism.

Contextualizing Likoni, the Coastal Strip of Kenya and Links to Violent Extremism

The context of this study is Likoni subcounty, in the South Coast of Kenya. It is part of Mombasa County which has had an uneasy relationship with the Kenyan state since Kenya's independence from Great Britain in 1963. Mombasa generally is inhabited by a predominantly Muslim population and has held grievances against the Kenyan state since the 1990s. It would be through the return of multi-party democracy in 1991 that a window through which to channel Muslim grievances would be re-opened (Oded, 1996). Through a constitutional amendment in 1982, Kenya had become a one-party state with the then ruling party—the Kenya African National Union (KANU)—as the sole political party.

For clarity, the coastal strip of Kenya has been contested between the coastal residents and the national government. As early as the 1950s, the coastal strip (a 10-mile strip) was then administered by the Sultan of Zanzibar following an 1885 agreement with the British. As independence neared, the coastal movement (the *Mwambao*—Kiswahili for the coastline) began to agitate for its own autonomy and independence from mainland Kenya. The push for the *Mwambao* (c. 1953–1963) was led by the Swahili and Arab residents of the coast who prior to independence were expressing their fears of domination by the "Up-Country Immigrants" (Brennan, 2008).

Pushing for their coastal autonomy was a protective mechanism to cushion several privileges. These included local land control, the staffing of bureaucratic positions, the introduction of Sharia law, some of which had been guaranteed under the nominal sovereignty of the Sultan. The *Mwambao* call faded following the lowering of the Sultan Flag in 1961 and the return of the 10-mile strip to Kenyan territory (Brennan, 2008). While the *Mwambao* debate thrived with a focus on the 10-mile coastal strip, competing claims of various political territories also came up. These included claims of the entire coastal autonomy, expressed through *Majimboism* (Kiswahili for regionalism) and which in addition was advocated by the Mijikenda. These competing claims were also reflective of the rise of faction-based political parties at the Kenyan coast. The Kenya African Democratic Union (KADU) at Kenya's independence pushed for a *Majimbo* (regionalism) structure, while the mainly Nairobi-based Kenya African National Union (KANU) with a broad membership of "up-country" people preferred a centralized state (Brennan, 2008).

These positions were themselves representative of the multiple social divisions at the coast. Whereas the 10-mile coastal strip become part of Kenya shortly before Kenya's independence, one of the unspoken fears of the *Mwambao* movement was the land question. Owing to political patronage, in the post-independence era, huge chunks of land (both urban and rural) went to "up-country" people. The result was an intensification of the land-squatting problem at the coast while creating tensions between coastal squatters and up country "immigrants" (Brennan, 2008).

Drawing on my fieldwork conducted at the Kenyan Coast (2016–2018), similar or applied grievances continue to be expressed by coastal residents and some of these that can be directly linked to violent extremism. Starting as early as 1992 following the return of multi-party democracy in Kenya, there was the rise of Islamic ideology manifested by the rise of the Islamic Party of Kenya (IPK). The IPK through the fiery and radical leader, Sheikh Khalid Balala, fermented a new wave of dissent against the Daniel Moi government (Oded, 1996). The IPK in assuming an extremist position spoke against the perceptions of coastal Muslims' discrimination by the then centralized government. The grievances which led to violent protests on the street were linked to lived realities of Muslims being treated as "second-class citizens," a theme that in addition was ever present in my fieldwork data. These realities were narrated in terms of neglect in social provisions such as schools, marginalization in government jobs among others. The mobilization of violence immediately ignited swift governmental responses. The government response was meant to counter rising secessionist demands dating back to Kenya's independence. This was not a far-fetched idea as the Kenyan Somalis on the former Northern Frontier District had attempted to secede (1963–1967, *Shifta* War) in the quest for Pan-Somalism (Oded, 1996).

Fieldwork participants in Likoni, Mombasa, linked real or perceived realities of marginalization to the rise of violent extremism. Both individual and collective interviews strongly associated with a marginalization theme at the coast. Study participants observed that grievances in the context of Islamic marginalization offered a window for extremist ideology. Similar narratives such as those documented by Oded (1996) continued to be expressed in my fieldwork.

Claims of marginalization in terms of limited to no access to jobs, being treated as terror suspects, and a poor economic outlook were particularly cited as grievances that could lead individuals to take up violence (Lind et al. 2017). A research participant in Likoni would refer to the domination of "up-country people" in business and jobs, which reinforced the feelings that Muslims were treated as second-class citizens. These discourses even in the advent of the decentralized governance structure post-2013 continued to be expressed through the categorization of the *Wabara* (Kiswahili for up-country people) who had been taking over jobs and economic opportunities from the *Wapwani* (Kiswahili for Coasterians). Kenya has since 2013 changed her governance structure from a centralized state to a decentralized unit with forty-seven county governments. This kind of discourse rekindling the politics of belonging generally has been used to categorize the so-called insiders versus outsiders. While not new, these grievances have similarly been documented by other researchers working on the coast (Kresse, 2009). Participants noted that these kind of grievances had created opportunities for violence though such groups as the Mombasa Republican Council (MRC) with their secessionist slogan, '*Pwani* si Kenya' (the Coast is not Kenya) (Willis & Gona, 2012), with occasional claims of links between the secessionist MRC and the Al-Shabaab. The links between Al-Shabaab and the MRC remain disputed. One research participant claimed that some members of the MRC had initially been joining the Shabaab as a strategy to acquire military training that they could utilize in pursuing their cause.[1]

Drawing on fieldwork findings, no single variable could explain the radicalization process. Instead, the findings suggested a multiplicity of variables to explain the process. These variables were rather complex and contextual (cf. Irwin, 2015). In the participants' perspective, it was both an individualized and contextualized process. The explanations ranged from claims of marginalization to religious identity. The radicalization process thus cannot be generalized and would need to consider the local and the contextual dynamics (Holmes, 2017, p. 86). Field findings opined the roots of youth radicalization were setup at the coast of Kenya by the late Sheikh Abdulaziz Rimo in the early 1990s. Rimo returned to Kenya's South Coast with a Ph.D. in Islamic Sharia from Saudi Arabia. He had trained in both Afghanistan and Pakistan where he lived cumulatively for over thirty years. Upon his return, he founded the Answar sect in Kwale, Kenya, which eventually found linkages with Tanzania. Study participants claimed that two of his followers' students, Sheikhs Aboud Rogo and Makaburi, would be implicated in the 2000s with radicalization at the Kenyan Coast and beyond.[2] Following a contextual analysis of the events and issues that have in part shaped the radicalization process, this study now turns to the local-level peacebuilding interventions in place in Likoni, Mombasa, to counter violent extremism.

Local-Level Interventions in Countering Violent Extremism in Likoni, Mombasa

Using a case study of Likoni, Mombasa, a number of local-level interventions to counter violent extremism are discussed in this section. These interventions include the use of counter-narratives, neighbourhood watches/community policing, harmonizing Madaris curriculum among others.

Counter-Narratives Strategies

In Likoni, Mombasa, study participants noted the use of alternative messaging to counter the messaging and narratives of radical groups. These localized counter-narratives had relied first on a process of capacity building for identified change agents. These identified change agents included religious leaders, community workers, and opinion leaders. The capacity building was focused on identifying the religious narratives that had been used by "radical" preachers in the past (cf. Leuprecht et al., 2010). It was prudent to engage with these narratives as a result of the uptake of religious ideology as a variable in the radicalization process. This had involved seeking the proper interpretation of the often-misquoted texts justifying violence. The change agents were using the religious and social spaces to counter the varied narratives of the radicalizers. These ranged from debates on identity, belonging, citizenship, and so on as a way to cement the ethos of nationalism that radicalizers had utilized.[3]

Countering ideological narratives could also predispose individuals to harm. Interviews in Mombasa linked the death of some prominent Sheikhs to radical networks that were displeased about their counter-radicalization initiatives. These included Sheikh Mohamed Idris, then chairman of the Council of Imams and Preachers of Kenya (CIPK) Coast chapter in 2014. Interviews in Mombasa also mentioned an intervention that had run across varied channels known as the Building Resilience Against Violent Extremism (BRAVE) campaign.

Participants in both focus group discussions and in-depth interviews noted that counter-narrative work had involved trainings and targeted messaging in audio-visual adverts. This chapter is based on twelve key informant interviews, and two focus groups discussions. Participants included government officials, religious leaders, members of community policing, civil society officials and residents of Likoni, Mombasa. Some key informant interviews conducted in Nairobi are also relied on in the chapter. Purposive and snow-ball-sampling approaches were employed. Each focus group had eight participants bringing to a total of sixteen participants. Qualitative data techniques were adopted through the use of semi-structured interview guides. Data were analyzed thematically with isolation of key themes from the participants' perspectives. Some of the training modules that participants had taken included early warning signs of the radicalization process. Some of the discussed signs of radicalization included sudden change in behavior, arriving home late, secluding oneself, and becoming suddenly very critical of aspects of the state's poor governance. Being critical of Western ideals such as television and education suddenly was also considered to be a warning sign. Trained participants in their reflections at the focus group discussions argued that they had been equipped with a fair grasp of the dynamics of the radicalization process in their localities. Thus, they felt they were in a better position to counter recruitment narratives.[4]

Participants spoke too about their engagement with the Building Resilience Against Violent Extremism (BRAVE) campaign as part of countering violent extremism. The BRAVE campaign countered recruitment narratives that justified violence using the concept of jihad (Bwana, 2015). Both the individual and focus group discussions indicated that the BRAVE program was useful in debating the varied usage of the jihad concept. This then had allowed respondents additional knowledge to convene community debates aimed at demystifying the misinterpretations. Debating the concept had become particularly useful for the new converts to the Islamic faith that were considered vulnerable to radicalization networks.

In Mombasa County and in the wider coastal region, the Coast Interfaith Council of Clerics-Trust (CICC), a group comprised of individuals from various faiths working on peaceful co-existence had also engaged in counter-radicalization. CICC had partnered with like-minded organizations with similar goals beyond Mombasa County. In addition to inter-faith dialogues, the trust worked on counter-narratives by seeking a proper interpretation of misused religious verses. While the organization had been working by convening conversations with religious leaders to contextualize misinterpreted verses, they also developed print materials to advance their counter-narrative work. These print materials contextualized both Christian biblical verses and narratives from the Holy Quran that had been used to encourage violence. For instance, the training materials references the Holy Quran as below to show how particular *Hadiths* were being misused:

1. Surah Al- Hajj 22- Verse 39 (22:39)

> To those against whom war is made, permission is given to (fight) because they are wronged-and verily, Allah is most powerful.

Additionally, as narrated by Prophet Mohamad ("Peace be Upon Him"; PBUH), "I have been commanded by Allah to fight with them until they submit that there is no God but Allah and Muhammad is his Messenger." The above Hadith was claimed to be misused in order to mobilize violence on non-Muslims until they embraced Islam. In contextualizing the above, the conversation discussed the meaning of jihad. The reinforced view was that jihad was not to kill or fight but rather to struggle for one's rights or to escape from prosecution (CICC, n.d.). For CICC, engaging with religious scriptures was a valuable way to promote peaceful co-existence. They not only discussed and contextualized verses that were being misinterpreted but also those that emphasized peaceful-co-existence.

Harmonizing Madaris Curriculum in Likoni, Mombasa: A Religious Response

Research participants in Likoni, Mombasa, pointed to a reviewing of the *Madaris'* (religious schools) curricula as a preventative strategy. Reviewing the curricula, they observed a counter-response to violent curricula used in some select Madaris in their neighbourhood for radicalization into violent extremism. This preventative action had been necessitated by the rise of youth radicalization in Likoni and in the wider coast region. In the view of interviewed religious leaders, a unified and a centralized curriculum would ensure control of religious schools' syllabi.

Some participants remarked that *Madaris* have been used as an entry point for youth radicalization in the coastal region and beyond.[5] In related discourses, the Kenyan state had previously securitized a section of *Madaris* as being part of the radicalization process (Mogire & Mkutu, 2011). Similarly, in neighbouring Zanzibar, the government and influential individuals within the Islamic movements have called for the introduction of a common curriculum for *Madaris* including their centralized control. Tanzania has previously expressed fears that *Madaris* may be breeding grounds for radical Islamist movements (Turner, 2009).

Religious leaders interviewed in Likoni argued that this harmonization initiative of the Madaris curriculum had the overarching goal of preventing violent extremism in their localities. The result for these religious leaders would be the proper interpretation and teaching of religion. Interviews indicated that this localized intervention began in 2009 in Kenya's South Coast as a response to the rise of radical religious leaders in the coast region. Religious leaders hoped that this curriculum would be applied beyond Kenya's South Coast. One participant emphasized a counter-radicalization theme and noted:

> Within our religious network, and in developing a unified madaris curriculum, we found it prudent to bring on board a counter-radicalization theme ... bringing on board this theme provides a proper interpretation of Islam. We want to build the attitude of a Muslim from an early age so that they are not susceptible to violence ... We want our children to be fed with the correct religious interpretation.[6]

The aforementioned quotation from a religious leader interviewed for this study speaks principally to the claimed agency between the misinterpretation of religious texts and radicalization. By seeking a proper interpretation of Islam, the said participant hoped to pre-empt radicalization vulnerabilities. By emphasizing the proper religious interpretation and by grounding children and youth at their formative stages, the expected outcome would be pious and tolerant Muslims. In deepening a counter-radicalization theme, the curricula specifically located some of the most commonly misused scriptures justifying religious violence.

As part of rolling out the unified Madaris curriculum, this religious network had worked with local *Imams* in Likoni, thus, broadening their reach and impact. This network in the participants' view had over time sought to work with like-minded mosques and religious schools for wider community outreach about their teaching content and their intentions. A section of participants observed the non-participation of some religious leaders in the revision owing to doctrinal differences.

One participant mentioned that a similar intervention plan running across Mombasa County and in partnership with the county government had been strategized. This government-planned intervention was interpreted as the state's intention to regulate the religious sphere. This arose out of the state's apprehension that failures to exercise control of the religious schools could create radicalization avenues.

Interviewed officials gave accounts of mosques spread across Mombasa, Nairobi, among other counties as sites of youth indoctrination and recruitment into violence. For example, the Masjid Musa Mosque in Majengo, Mombasa, was claimed to have been a radicalization hub in late 2013 and early 2014. This recruitment being not only for Al-Shabaab but also for Daesh (Islamic State). An interviewed security official gave an account of a group of youth intercepted by security agencies as they attempted to cross Uganda, then to Sudan and onward to Libya where they were to join Daesh. The youth were intercepted in Eldoret town, in the North Rift of Kenya on their way to Libya.[7]

While Madaris and mosques have been claimed to be sites of youth radicalization, they constituted the ever-evolving pathways to youth radicalization. Radical Madaris have been considered outside of the current context as pushing an extremist agenda. In the Indian subcontinent, for instance, some Madaris have encouraged the uptake of political violence. The persuasion to take up violence would be framed on the basis that Islam was under threat globally and, therefore, there was a call for violent response. For example, some Madaris in Pakistan are claimed to have provided short-term violence training such as bombings to foreigners including European Muslims that had expressed interest in participating in jihad (Hippel, 2010). It has been alleged, for instance, that the July 2005 London bombers had spent their time in a Pakistan Madrassa (Hippel, 2010, pp. 56–57).

Neighborhood Watches and Community Policing in Likoni, Mombasa

An analysis of fieldwork findings from Likoni, Mombasa, revealed two forms of collective community security models that had been applied in counter-radicalization work. The two models discussed are community policing and neighbourhood watches. Community policing is considered formal as it is government initiated. It works by way of community and government agencies cooperating to provide security. On the other hand, the neighbourhood watch model is largely informal. It is a home-grown solution even though it has found nodes of cooperation with the government.

The neighbourhood watch, even though now linked to the community policing forum, is a self-help model that has been working since 2010. It is adapted from neighboring Tanzania. It has clustered in each of the locations in Likoni with subsections and where credible individuals are identified to take charge of security in their neighbourhood. It then has linkages to the police and other local administrators.[8]

Community policing strategies that have been applied in ordinary crime prevention are considered valuable in the broad counter-terrorism domains. Notwithstanding their contestations around their applicability for crime prevention, they offer opportunities for collective problem-solving strategies.

This collective crime prevention strategy is dependent on trust levels between the community and the police and particularly with regards to information sharing (Huq, 2016).

Participants observed the use of neighbourhood watches and community policing initiatives as preventative strategies that they had applied. These crime prevention strategies were also influenced by the nature of community police relations at particular moments. The study participants noted that these models had not only been working in counter radicalization but also in preventing other crimes such as drug trafficking.

Using a case study of Likoni, a local community-based organization (CBO), the Likoni Community Development Program (LICODEP), had been utilizing community policing as a preventative strategy. This CBO had linked with the local government security structures such as community policing. The local community-based organization group has however maintained its neighborhood watch model. This worked through a clustering of Likoni across various areas and each with elected officials mapping various forms of crime in their respective areas including youth radicalization. Whereas community policing has been in existence since 2003, around 2013, the Kenyan government introduced a new security structure known as the *Nyumba Kumi* (ten households in Kiswahili).

Participants noted several preventative interventions made possible by the use of community policing. Overall, it has assisted the police in mapping insecurity challenges including preventative work to counter radicalization. A key contribution of the community policing initiative has been information sharing on a number of fronts. Interviews noted that this has ranged from information sharing on suspicious characters in their respective neighbourhoods for the police to open up further investigations. Information sharing by the public is considered a disruptive strategy. This shared information usually opens up a basis for investigations into further leads (Bjørgo, 2016, p. 33).

Suspected individuals with the intent to radicalize could also be identified for further police investigations. Community policing additionally was termed by participants as an input of joint problem solving in partnership with police. Reinforcing the Likoni perspective, one security official interviewed in Majengo, Nairobi, noted that:

> There is the whole shift of public participation in the security issues such as through the *Nyumba Kumi* and community policing platform. The national police service act acknowledges this public participation in security. The government has been encouraging citizens to be vigilant and report suspicious individuals or groups to them. Seeking this public participation is helpful in that it allows the public to share with their security agencies their security concerns. Criminals

stays in our courts, flats, if they become suspicious, they ought to share their concerns with the police or with the administrators.[9]

Moreover, the members of the community policing had the option of suggesting a number of policing interventions. Drawing on participant observation on a community policing session attended in Likoni, Mombasa, in August 2016, this perspective was clear. The community representatives raised names of suspicious individuals with probable links to radical groups that the police needed to investigate. In this particular meeting, names of suspects, including their locations were shared with the police. This was followed up with an additional six key informant interviews with a section of community policing members within Likoni subcounty in Mombasa County. Through two focus group discussions and key informant interviews, participants spoke at length of how they regularly mapped potential crime issues including radicalization which they transmitted for police action.

Community policing members relied on tip-offs from community members about such threats. Information sharing of this type eased policing work and thus contributed to community safety in the long term. Crime mapping as participants noted worked through community elders compiling crime incidences in their localities. This had worked through a clustering of the Likoni area into sections under the leadership of designated community policing members. In each assigned locality, a community policing member identified crime patterns and incidences. The collected information formed part of the community policing meeting discussions.

This shift in policing from state-led policing to more community-oriented policing despite presenting challenges of confidentiality and personal safety concerns indicated a slow uptake of police reforms in Kenya. Police reforms have been in place post-2003 with the support of the donor community (Omeje & Githigaro, 2012). Participants decried the lack of meaningful police reforms to enhance police accountability. This lack of accountability had yet to provide overall confidence for the public to cooperate optimally with the police. Personal safety concerns had arisen in instances where confidential information shared with the police had leaked.

The aforementioned view was expressed in Likoni by participants who had suffered reprisals from criminals they had reported to the police.[10] Notwithstanding some of these challenges, some level of success in crime prevention was being achieved. Whereas government officials emphasized a policing shift toward citizen-led policing through initiatives such as *Nyumba Kumi* and community policing, more confidence building measures were required. Citizen-led policing was being adopted incrementally in spite of some of the confidence hurdles it had been facing.

In Likoni, there existed competition between *Nyumba Kumi*, local peace committees run by local administrators versus the community policing run by the national police service. In spite of some of these challenges, a section of the community and the police continued to cooperate in information sharing. The cooperation between the police and the community in counter-radicalization demonstrates in part also the changing philosophy of policing on the section of the Kenyan police.

The gradual uptake of the public in contributing to their community safety through such platforms was laudable overall. It demonstrated that the public had begun to appreciate the value of co-delivering security with the government. This approach complemented various state counter-terrorism responses. These included hard power and legislative responses. Research interviews reiterated that community policing forums were encouraging members to raise awareness at the community level on radicalization concerns through the open and accessible *barazas* (Kiswahili for meetings) held by chiefs in their respective locations. Chiefs as local government administrators at the local level are required to convene regular *barazas* where among other responsibilities they share information on government policies.

Community policing meetings usually held at the local police station draw only a small segment of community representatives but they nevertheless represent opportunities for counter-radicalization initiatives. For their optimum working, trust levels and accountability of the police was essential as confidence-building measures.

Community Partnerships with Government Agencies

Two community-government initiatives were found to be working in Likoni, Mombasa. One was the Mombasa County Action Plan for Prevention and Countering Violent Extremism (MCAP-PCVE) (Haki Africa/GOK, 2017). The County Action Plan derives its mandate from the National Strategy for Countering Violent Extremism (NSCVE) and its accompanying Guide to Developing County Action Plans (CDCAP). Second was the Mombasa County's Strong Citizenship Framework for Public Participation.[11] This initiative according to an interview with the county commissioner in Mombasa was launched in early May 2017. This strategy was a localization of Kenya's National Counter-Terrorism Strategy launched by the national government in 2016. The latter strategy is coordinated by the Kenya's National Counter Terrorism Centre (NCTC).

The national strategy advocates for community engagement as part of counter-terrorism responses. In Mombasa, a local non-governmental organization called Haki Africa has steered the development of the County Action Plan in partnership with the national government. This was through the Mombasa County Commissioner's office.[12] Furthermore, this strategy was developed alongside other actors engaged in counter-radicalization work.[13] This community-state partnership had afforded an opportunity for joint problem solving. Providing opportunity for collective problem solving is in itself a form of a paradigm shift with regards to previous counter-terrorism responses.

The National Strategy has nine pillars and calls for multi-stakeholder engagement in both reactive and preventative actions (GOK, 2016). The civil society, community-based organizations, the private sector, organs of government including members of the research community are called upon to collectively engage in countering violent extremism. Furthermore, the National Counter Terrorism Centre (NCTC) is charged with the coordination of CVE interventions in the country (GOK, 2016). The other emerging intervention has been focused on building community-police relations. This has been through convening meetings especially between the youth and police in selected neighbourhoods in Mombasa as part of trust-building measures. By building confidence among the youth, it was hoped that it would create allies in them which would provide additional potentials for counter-radicalization initiatives.

A participant engaged in programming work for counter-radicalization in the Kenyan Coast lauded the effort of the civil society actors in Mombasa most principally led by Haki Africa but warned that care needed to be taken on two fronts. One was the need for a clear implementation plan of the CVE strategy. In the absence of a clear implementation plan, the participant noted: "It would just be a beautiful document on paper."[14] Care too was needed to ensure that the document was not "possessed" by the national government structure. In other words, while the plan had been developed through a consultative process that involved multiple actors, the credit and the implementation plan required collaboration and continuous engagement.

The Use of Drama as a Strategy for Counter-Radicalization in Likoni, Mombasa

In Likoni, a community-based organization reflected on the use of drama as a counter-radicalization strategy. This organization, Hatua Likoni, had partnered with a local organization to use film as a method to open up community discussions around the topic of radicalization and counter-radicalization. Prior to the community discussions, a drama would be shown to a particular audience. After the drama screening, an action-oriented research methodology was adopted. This involved role playing the characters shown in the drama in order to generate a conversation on this particular threat. Community-led discussions then followed. The goal for these discussions was to collectively brainstorm on the probable solutions/strategies that both community and government actors needed to adopt.

The rationale for this approach had been the rapid realization that Likoni subcounty and indeed the rest of Mombasa County had become radicalization hotspots. This intervention that ran for eight months in Likoni, Mombasa, in 2016 had been informed by the rising threats of youth radicalization. This intervention had proceeded with the production of a short drama profiling a hypothetical case of a young man planning to take a journey to Somalia to join a radical group. This hypothetical scenario which drew in local actors to dramatize the situation had formed the basis for which to open up an action-oriented discussion at the community level.

This drama screening had been organized as part of a three-day activity across public, private, primary, and secondary schools including youth groups within Likoni subcounty. For the primary schools, the focus of the program was on upper-primary school pupils as they were deemed of age to comprehend radicalization debates.

The activity had proceeded as follows. On the first day, the movie would be screened and a discussion initiated on what the community ought to have done to stop the individual from joining a radical organization. This activity was completed with facilitators guiding the discussion. On the second day of the activity, the levels of radicalization were engaged through a facilitated discussion. The rationale behind this activity was to create awareness on the radicalization trends. The third day of the activity required that participants develop an array of materials to counter radicalization messaging. Participants were thus required to prepare creative materials for countering violent extremism. These ranged from board messaging to theatre approaches (to include skits and plays) with a focus on countering violent extremism. This intervention was only rolled out after pre-testing the program curricula including stakeholders' views that were critical for the intervention's success. These stakeholders included school representatives and leaders of selected youth groups within Likoni.

An official at Hatua Likoni that was responsible for this intervention reported that the pre-testing of the drama and the related action-oriented research helped in the program's buy in. It was anticipated that it would open doors not only across the schools but also within the youth groups that were targeted for this pilot project. Before the intervention was rolled out, a ten-day training was conducted for the project facilitators. The overall goal of this intervention was to shed more light on the radicalization processes in the county including appropriate counter-interventions. Recounting the success and the potential of this project for counter-radicalization, the interviewed official of Hatua Likoni responsible for co-delivering the program put forward that "The success of this project in my view was the involvement of the community. It was a plus for the community to be involved. It is important to create ownership of the project at the community level .... There were local actors, plus the community having the opportunity to provide solutions collectively to social problems."[15]

The aforementioned quote speaks of useful lessons for counter-radicalization work in other contexts. One of the lessons would be the need for program/project interveners to seek partnerships with communities on the kind of solutions that would be required. This kind of partnership would help in terms of local-context sensitivity. The use of drama and creative arts could be tapped in other contexts for counter-radicalization interventions.

Conclusion

This study has examined the various local-level approaches in use to counter youth radicalization in Likoni, Kenya. The approaches discussed have included community conversation spaces, community policing, and counter-narratives among others. The implication to be drawn from these approaches is that given the different processes of radicalization which are context-specific, community-level initiatives need to be tailored to the specific contexts.

The existence of a neighbourhood watch in Likoni serves to deconstruct the assumption that it was the singular responsibility of the state to provide security. The community considered organizing their own security to be their responsibility as well as finding partnerships with the state. Optimum community-police relations in Likoni had faced several challenges. These included trust deficits between police and the community, in addition to heavy handedness by the police in counter-terrorism operations.

Findings derived from data collected in the field have reinforced the value of trust as an enabler of community-policing relations. In engaging with the counter-radicalization domain from below, it would be important to cultivate trust levels between the community and the police. Community policing as a preventative option is being aided in part by this notable shift in policing that is placing the community as partners in security provision. This new shift is likely to be gradual and also to be faced with resistance as it rolls out.

These community interventions while opening opportunities for counter-radicalization have also served to limit the effectiveness of the interventions. Their effectiveness was in part limited by the blanket association of Islam and radicalization. This in part reinforces the "culture talk" perspective raised by Mamdani (2005). Mamdani (2005) argues that within the global war on terror discourses there has been the tendency to make binary distinctions between "good" and "bad" Muslims. It is the "bad" Muslims that then are to be blamed for terrorism. Instead, Mamdani argues the need for a reading of terrorism as a modern political phenomenon and dismisses simplistic readings that say Islam is to blame for political violence.

One of the lessons learnt in this study is the value of community ownership of the preventative interventions. A collaboration with different sectors of the community has created a community peacebuilding architecture with great potential. One potential created in the process has been an understanding of the context and the dynamics of the radicalization process despite its complexity. Having a localized and a nuanced understanding of the context/issues driving the radicalization process was a plus. The implication of this has been to generate community-led solutions. Whereas some of the community-level interventions discussed in this study have had the support of the donor communities such as the Danish and the U.S. governments, sustenance lay at the level of community structures. While the study does not discount the value of donor funding for capacity building, facilitation and the like for some components of these local-level initiatives, research participants were cognizant of the short-term priorities and interventions of donor partners.

In Likoni, Mombasa, such interventions have been created by conversation spaces/dialogues, community policing, among others which would not necessary halt because of cuts or lack of donor funding. The community in Likoni was utilizing local resources (e.g., community halls, trained volunteers) to engage in their preventative interventions. Taking, in particular, the community policing platform, community representatives had opportunities to suggest which police counter-interventions they could take as part of their preventative work. Whereas community-police relations have been lukewarm, some of the local-level initiatives studied in Likoni have brought on board the value of trust with institutions raising implications for how peacebuilding interventions would proceed.

The other potential takeaway from this case study is the value of long-term engagement with communities in so far as peacebuilding was concerned. Having an enduring engagement with the community by civil society organizations (CSOs) was also helping to build a buy-in component of peacebuilding interventions. In the case of Likoni, a community-based organization known as the Likoni Development Programme (LIKODEP) had long-term connections with the community since the late 1990s in the fields of peace-building. Their point of entry into this new domain of Countering Violent Extremism had evolved based on the trust and credibility that they had developed over time. It would be useful for future studies to engage in a comparative analysis of some of the challenges and potentials in other contexts engaged in countering violent extremism from a community perspective. This could create evidence-based policy lessons on what works and does not work in community engagements countering violent extremism beyond the current study context.

Acknowledgments

I am indebted to the Next Generation Social Sciences in Africa (Next-Gen) fellowships under the Social Sciences Research Council, New York (SSRC), with funds provided by the Carnegie Corporation of New York for fieldwork support.

Notes

1. Male research participant, Likoni, Mombasa, November 23, 2016.
2. Interview with a local administrator in Mombasa, October 2016.
3. Interview with a religious leader in Likoni, Mombasa, August 24, 2016.
4. A mixed focus group discussion with youth (men, women) in Likoni, Mombasa, June 7, 2017.
5. Focus group discussions with male religious leaders in Likoni, Mombasa, March 16, 2017.
6. Interview with a religious leader in Likoni, Mombasa, March 16, 2017.
7. Interview with a senior police officer, in Nairobi, February 2, 2017.
8. Key informant interview with an official of LICODEP, in Likoni, Mombasa, August 23, 2016.
9. Interview with a police officer, in Majengo, Nairobi, July 21, 2017.
10. Findings of a focus group discussion in Likoni, Mombasa, March 16, 2017.
11. The Mombasa County Action Plan for Prevention and Countering Violent Extremism (MCAP-PCVE) (2017). Document on file with the researcher.
12. Interview with Mombasa County Commissioner, in Mombasa, June 7, 2017.
13. Interview with an official of Haki Africa, in Mombasa, March 17, 2017.
14. Interview with a project officer of an NGO in Mombasa in Nairobi, June 23, 2017.
15. Interview with a project officer of a NGO in Likoni, Mombasa, June 9, 2017.

References

Barash, D. P., & Webel, C. P. (2014). *Peace and Conflict Studies*, 3rd ed. Thousand Oaks, CA: Sage.

Bjørgo, T. (2016). Counter-terrorism as crime prevention: a holistic approach. *Behavioral Sciences of Terrorism and Political Aggression*, 8(1): 25–44.

Brennan, J. R. (2008). Lowering the sultan's flag: Sovereignty and decolonization in Coastal Kenya. *Comparative Studies in Society and History*, 50(4): 831–861.

Butler, M. J. (2009). *International conflict management*. London: Routledge.

Buzan, B., & Wæver, O. (2009). Macrosecuritisation and security constellations: reconsidering scale in securitisation theory. *Review of International Studies*. 35(2): 253–276. doi: 10.1017/S0260210509008511.

Bwana, M. Y. (2015). *Peace-building and conflict prevention training manual and resource guide for building resilience against violent extremism*. Nairobi: Center for Sustainable Conflict Resolution.

Government of Kenya. (2016). *National strategy to counter violent extremism*. Nairobi: Government of Kenya.

Hippel, K. V. (2010). The role of poverty in radicalization and terrorism. In S. Gottlieb (ed.), *Debating Terrorism and Counter Terrorism* (pp. 51–66). Washington, DC: CQ Press.

Holmes, M. (2017). Preventing violent extremism through peacebuilding: Current perspectives from the field. *Journal of Peacebuilding and Development*, 12(2): 85–89.

Huq, A. Z. (2016). Community-led counter terrorism. *Studies in Conflict and Terrorism*. doi: 10.1080/1057610X.2016.1253988 (advance publication October), 1–31.

Irwin, N. (2015). The complexity of responding to home-grown terrorism: Radicalization, de-radicalization and disengagement. *Journal of Policing, Intelligence and Counter terrorism*, 10(2): 166–175.

Kresse, K. (2009). Muslim politics in postcolonial Kenya: Negotiating knowledge on the double-periphery. *The Journal of the Royal Anthropological Institute*, 15, S76–S94.

Leuprecht, C., Hataley, T., Moskalenko, S., & Mccauley, C. (2010). (2010). Containing the narrative: Strategy and tactics in countering the storyline of global jihad. *Journal of Policing, Intelligence and Counter Terrorism*, 5(1): 42–57.

Lind, J. et al. (2017). "Killing a mosquito with a hammer": Al-Shabaab violence and state securitty responses in Kenya. *Peacebuilding*. doi: 10.1080/21647259.2016.1277010, 1-19.

MacGinty, R., & Richmond, O. P. (2013). The local turn in peace building: A critical agenda for peace. *Third World Quarterly*, 34(5): 763–783.

Mamdani, M. (2005). Good Muslim, bad Muslim: America, the Cold War and the origins of terror. *India International Centre Quarterly*, 32(1): 1–10.

Ministry of Interior and Coordination of National Government Kenya. (2016). Kenya to Launch a National Counter Violent Extremism Policy. Available at www. Interior. go.ke=2937 (accessed April 12, 2016).

Mogire, E., & Mkutu, K. (2011). Counter-terrorism in Kenya. *Journal of Contemporary African Studies, 29*(2): 473–491.

Oded, A. (1996). Islamic extremism in Kenya: The rise and fall of Sheikh Khalid Balala. *Journal of Religion in Africa, 26*(4): 406–415.

Omeje, K., & Githigaro, J. (2012). The challenges of state policing in Kenya. *The Peace and Conflict Review, 7*(1): 64–87.

Solomon, H. (2017). Beyond the state: Reconceptualising African security in the 21st century. *African Security Review, 26*(1): 62–76.

Tannock, S., & Sukarieh, M. (2017). The global securitisation of youth. *Third World Quarterly.* doi: 10.1080/01436597.2017.1369038.

Tellidis, I., & Richmond, O. P. (2012). The complex relationship between peacebuilding and terrorism approaches: Towards post-terrorism and a post-liberal peace? *Terrorism and Political Violence, 24*(1): 121–143.

Turner, S. (2009). "These young men show no respect for local customs"—Globalisation and Islamic revival in Zanzibar. *Journal of Religion in Africa, 39*(3): 237–261.

Williams, M. (2003). Words, images, enemies: Securitization and international politics. *International Studies Quarterly, 47,* 511–531.

Willis, J., & Gona, G. (2012). Pwani C Kenya? Memory, documents and seccessionist politics in Coastal Kenya. *African Affairs, 112*(446): 48–71.

4 Devising More Effective Peacebuilding Tools for Africa

GILBERT T. ZVAITA AND IBRAHIM YUSUF

The myriad of conflicts confronting the African continent are surging on a daily basis. Efforts made to nip them in the bud appear to be failing consistently. Careful analysis examining the reasons for these continuous failings becomes necessary so that adequate and effective mechanisms and policies can be put together to arrest the menace. In this chapter, we critically examine the liberal peacebuilding approach and the role it has played in shaping peace initiatives across Africa. In so doing, we illuminate the impact of a liberal peacebuilding framework in the African context bedeviled by intractable and protracted social conflicts. We argue that the enacting of different multi-dimensional peace approaches developed through the lens of liberal peace remains ineffective in Africa. We draw attention to the importance of engaging integrative multi-disciplinary perspectives that are grounded in local peace ownership in devising initiatives that help to deliver sustainable peace in the continent. As Keen (2012) observed, most conflicts experienced in Africa seem to be endless situations and involve different armed groups that have consistently proliferated into additional conflicts.

The literature on conflict resolution, conflict management, and conflict transformation points out various foundational causes of continuous relapse into violent conflict and "underscores the need for new instruments and approaches to support sustainable peace in complex emergencies and intra-state conflicts" (Tschirgi, 2015, p. 477). This work gives further credence to the need to re-examine the mechanisms and approaches the international community employs in the pursuits of peacebuilding in Africa. Tracing the various trends of peacebuilding interventions since the 1990s, it is evident they have been run as ad hoc, piecemeal and highly fragmented programs that disguised themselves under the mantra of local ownership; they are in fact dominated by external driving factors and introduce foreign principles to local elements (Tschirgi, 2015). Given these circumstances, and the consequences of relapses into violent conflict in countries like Somalia, the Democratic Republic of the Congo (DRC), and South Sudan, it is evident that alternative strategies for peacebuilding are required.

Liberal peacebuilding processes have dominated approaches to peacebuilding in Africa (Yamashita, 2014; Zaum, 2012). The idea of liberal peacebuilding is guided by the democratic peace theory which seeks to establish democratic principles and structures as the basis for building lasting peace (Newman, 2009; Oneal & Russet, 1999; Russet & Oneal, 2001). Hence, liberal peace gives an idea that "certain kinds of society will tend to be more peaceful, both in their domestic affairs and in their international relations, than 'illiberal' states" (Lemay-Hébert, 2013, p. 242). Zaum (2012) outlines that the processes that characterize liberal peacebuilding across the literature include:

> external peacebuilding interventions that share several characteristics: first, they are conducted by liberal, Western states; second, they are motivated by liberal objectives such as responding to large-scale human rights violations or being conducted under an international responsibility to protect; and third, these interventions promote liberal-democratic political institutions, human rights, effective and good governance, and economic liberalization as a means to bring peace and prosperity to war-torn countries. (pp. 121–122)

The aforementioned notions give an assumption that the emergence and continuity of conflict is problematized on the failure to adhere to liberal principles such as democratization and free market economies. This study opposes the liberal perspective of peacebuilding in Africa as much of their proposals lack the content required for lasting peace within the continent. Liberal peacebuilding processes are monolithic and imposing. They lack contextual insight and relevance on the different basic traditional, societal, cultural, moral, and religious values that exist in most African communities. Linabary, Krishna, and Connaughton (2016) reflect that "lack of cultural relevance and ownership" among those (communities) peacebuilding processes seek to impact is problematic because it may result in "lack of acceptance or outright rejection" (p. 2). Indeed, there is a need to deliberate about the conceptual framework that currently defines our approaches. Building durable peace should be guided by approaches that are fluid to reflect more on local challenges and opportunities that can be harnessed to promote ideas and practices toward sustainable peace in the given specific context (Zvaita & Mbara, 2019). To find new constructive peace mechanisms would be of tremendous significance in Africa's conflict predicament. Therefore, the need to devise more peace approaches in the African context.

Koko (2009) argued that the transformation processes of building peace are always "a recipe for competition, heightened contestations and, if not well managed, violent confrontations" (p. 55). This assessment poses interesting rhetoric to revisit all the African conflict transformation processes that may include services such as security sector reform, disarmament, demobilization, the rule of law, and reintegration that may have been properly engaged. The essence of doing this is to deduce the liberal theoretical functions which (might) have weakened and alienated management and transformation strategies for peace in a given conflict environment. This allows the identification of holistic and pragmatic approaches to peace through local initiatives and empowerment of civil societies and edifies the role they may play in building the capacity for sustainable local peace.

Re-tracing such steps helps in outlining the important roles that can be played by both international actors and local actors; and in gleaning the relevant ideas, strategies, or new insights that can be utilized from both internal and external facilitators of peace. This may allow for proper consideration of the informal political rules and power networks that command social influence into developing local strategies to peace ownership as well as allowing international actors to view the different patterns of relationships and understand the reactions required in the conflict context to bring in the necessary urgency and mobility for effective outcomes (Hendrick, 2009). Of course, various consequences in history and this present day are the benchmarks that inform research and inspire new thinking on the effectiveness of specific practices in addressing the long-standing problem of conflict relapse in post-conflict states.

According to Muruthi (2006), "large chunks of resources have been spent to craft peace agreements most of which have often collapsed under the weight of competing interests" (p. 9). This chapter unravels a vehement argument on the setbacks of liberal peace perspective and the limitations of its paternal approaches in institutional relations as well as its weaknesses when it comes to supporting local ownership in peacebuilding. This chapter outlines the incompatibility of liberal peace in ensuring sustainable peace in Africa because it lacks the value-added elements of "local cultural assumptions, norms and values as well as traditional and grassroots notions of justice and community-based political dialogue" (Murithi, 2008, p. 28). This chapter deliberates on the shortfalls of liberal peace using case studies and reflects on possible locally driven alternatives for the future.

Lessons from Three Conflict Haunted Houses

From the background presented earlier, the issues surrounding the cases examined in this chapter are vast and have a lot of historical qualifications and analysis. These facts give much credence in relating theory to practice in the building of effective peace in Africa. They give an essential means to identify some of the aspects that are of note in reflecting the blindside of most liberal peace approaches in African peacebuilding processes. The experienced challenges in these countries are immensely contributing to conflict relapse not because state actors or non-state actors are not acting enough to address the conflict problem, but because there is poor or no incorporation of local factors in solutions. Indeed, often local factors are rendered irrelevant in mainstream peacebuilding approaches which are dominantly liberal (Bräuchler & Naucke, 2017). The DRC, South Sudan, and Somalia have a history of conflict that goes back more than two decades. Despite the involvement of non-governmental organizations (NGOs) and various regional and international actors in trying to build peace in these conflict zones, their efforts have been in contempt. Different factors demonstrate the challenges that have and may continue to hinder the sustainable peace if not engaged holistically. Therefore, the plight of civil society in Somalia, the United Nations peace mission in the DRC, and the United Nations-African Union (UN-AU) mission in South Sudan as highlighted later in the chapter clarify the problems that are promoting conflict relapse and continuity. The argument is that even if multi-dimensional approaches are developed with a purely liberal perspective in mind, they will remain ineffective in an African setting. On the contrary, there is a need for integrative multi-disciplinary approaches that value local ownership of peace if any meaningful and sustainable peace is to be achieved in most of the intractable conflicts in Africa.

The Civil Society and the Hurdles to State Functionality in Somalia

The demise of Siad Barre's authoritarian rule in Somalia witnessed the reinforcement of clans[1] "as central providers of public goods to their members" (Lake, 2015, p. 303). It immediately pushed clans from egalitarian societies into hierarchical structures allowing warlords to gain political control. The warlords would manipulate and dominate communities as they had access to weapons and stolen food that they used to stamp their authority. This scenario alone has fought and blocked the re-emergence of the state while allowing the increase of terrorist organizations and criminal activities. With this in mind, it remains an interesting phenomenon that despite challenges and setbacks, Somalia established a functional state; the private authorities (i.e., local and international NGOs, UN agencies, foreign and regional donors) and clan networks, however, remain major players in service provision and as such remain the major unifying factor among citizens (Abdulle, 2008; Osman, 2018).

The meaning of "civil society" in Somalia is contested. While there is a common agreement about "civil society" as the representation of citizen interests, Somalians engage the concept differently. Osman (2018) explains that some castigate civil society as a Western idea, while others connect it to the traditional system where clan elders played a critical role as leaders of civil society mediating between society and authorities during colonization. There is disparity between the Western expectation of civil society and the interests of Somalians in civil society organizations (CSOs). While the former expects the execution of targeted and perceived human development goals, the latter has traditional and local interests which might not necessarily fall within the donor framework.

Civil society in Somalia has demonstrated a distinct cultural context which emanates from a strong background of social engagements within communities (Somalia Corruption Report, 2019). In other words, it is the only civil society in history, which has taken or shouldered state duties of service delivery and which engages in day-to-day governance of stately issues before the establishment of a functioning central government in 2012 (e.g., social security, service delivery and other public service provision including health). The role of the state has been overtaken and overshadowed. Lake (2015) captured this idea succinctly when he said that:

> Although Somalia, through its decentralized structure, may be one of the sovereign polities best able to cope with the absence of a state, the larger point is that the continued vibrancy of private authorities and their further entrenchment into society continues to prevent the consolidation of the Somali state. (p. 304)

Civil society actors in Somalia have taken an active role in channeling resources provided by donors. However, the active role of civil society, in this case, has been more of distributing resources rather than mobilizing the public to participate in building an effective governance system or working on channels to end the conflict. Osman (2018) notes that CSOs in Somalia lack unity and have been involved in causing divisive political and clan conflicts. Thus, the role of civil society in Somalia is restricted to service delivery only, not educating people on peace initiatives that can be used as basic platforms for building tolerance and consolidating the state. Hence the very existence of civil society has hindered the state's re-establishment. These are some of the barriers which have distorted the role and the position of civil society in rebuilding the state and building sustainable peace in the country. The major destabilizing challenges to the effectiveness of Somali civil society are its overdependence on external support and a lack of coherent and coordinated strategy.

International and regional donors have increasingly demonstrated trust in civil society service delivery despite the establishment of a functional state in 2012. Ibrahim (2011) outlines how the international community has tried to re-build the state through a two-track method in Somalia. He argued that the first track is a top-down process, which intends to build a transitional government through a power-sharing agreement between the political elites and warlords, a situation that has resulted in consequential failures. The second track is a bottom-up approach, which focused on funding civil societies for local project initiatives. This track received various support and funding from the World Bank, European Union, and USAID just to mention a few. Most of these institutions favored the idea of engaging state building through civil society arguing that it is a pillar of democratic values and will eventually lead to effective governance. These efforts have made civil society "more powerful and reliable in delivering goods and services than the institutions of national government that exist in Somalia" (Ibrahim, 2011, p. 9). It is important to understand that the existence of such a strong civil society has weakened the consolidation of the state. Scholars agree that the existence of powerful private authorities outside the national structures in a state-building process may lead to various competitions and destabilize the legitimization processes of service provision (Lake, 2015; Ibrahim, 2011).

The development of different private authorities has created various challenges such that there is no distinction between profit-driven organizations and civil societies in Somalia. This environment has become a problem in creating more divisions that distort peacebuilding and state-building processes. A stateless society has not only incentivized civil societies but also warlords and criminals who have attained public support through the provision of basic services such that it weakens the advocacy for a strong central government.

From MONUC to MONUSCO[2]: Traces of a Haunted Peace Process in the DRC

In 2010, *Mission de l'Organisation des Nations Uniesen République démocratique du Cong* (MONUC) was renamed the UN Stabilization Organization Mission in the Congo (MONUSCO). By 2013, it was further expanded following the introduction of Force Intervention Brigade (FIB), which some also called "the UN's first-ever offensive combat force". Unfortunately, the UN's "Islands of stability" strategy, patterned after the U.S. counterinsurgency theory, attracted serious criticisms especially, that this so-called "Island of stability" was a failure as it left the majority of the poor population vulnerable to more instability, lack of access to government services, and other humanitarian assistance. From this incident, it is much clearer that the liberal-centered pattern of peacebuilding cannot be relied on without understanding the values of the indigenous people and their contributions to any proposed peace initiatives.

The presence of the UN in the Congo (formally, Republic of the Congo), and now-Democratic Republic of Congo (DRC) can be traced to its first peacekeeping mission from 1960 to 1964 (United Nations Operation in the Congo [Opération des Nations Unies au Congo], ONUC). Since then, the UN's presence in Africa has stretched to "promote democratic institutions, supporting economic and social development, establishing peace between aggressive nations and promoting and protection of human rights" (Global Issues, 2014). The aftermath of the First Congo War (1996–1997) witnessed the toppling of President Mobutu Sese Seko[3] from power through a coup by a coalition named Alliance des Forces Démocratiques Pour la Libération du Congo-Zaïre[4] (AFDL) which was led by Laurent Kabila.[5] The conflict left the country that had already been plighted with weak security and governance institutions in a devastating state.

In 1999, the UN made its second mark in the DRC through its mission known in French as the *Mission de l'Organisation des Nations Uniesen République démocratique du Cong* (MUNOC). MUNOC's main mandate was to protect civilians who were under imminent threats of violence. Following the Lusaka Peace Agreement, the first initial role of MONUC, when it was launched by Résolution 1279, meant to only monitor the terms of the ceasefire, disarm and disengage forces, and ensure the maintenance of communication involved stakeholders. However, with later resolutions, the Council went from just monitoring to adopting other related tasks, slowly expanding the mandate of MUNOC. In spite of all these measures meant to curtail and bring about peace, peace has remained very elusive. Majorly because the peace framework lacks the local content of the people it is meant for, partly because not much commitment has been shown by the West toward genuine peace in Africa.

Democratization and the Loopholes of Crisis
In trying to fulfil its mandate, MUNOC focused on establishing a democratic government through elections, and disarmament, demobilization, repatriation, reintegration, and resettlement (DDRRR). Scholars agree that the main challenge that has haunted the DRC peace process since 1999 is the

extensive democratization of the process. The structures of building peace in the country neglected the different social dynamics, which include ethnicity, cultural, and traditional values, as well as social hierarchies that make up the backbone of the communities (Autesserre, 2011; Matagne, 2011). It is important to clarify here that the DRC is characterized by various polarities, which are mainly ethnic. The bedrock of both the First and Second Congo Wars was mainly driven by various ethnic forces, which support and promote their agenda. Dijkzeul (2008) contends that the establishment of an election mechanism often marks the end of the peacebuilding process and the establishment of a package for economic recovery. The DRC, however, has proven to be a unique case. Menodji (2013) notes that "after ceasefires, peacebuilding organisations placed precedence on creating a stable electoral process. However, in the DRC, elections increased instability in a fragmented society which had not yet solved antagonisms" (p. 1). For instance, Laurent Nkunda[6] unleashed violence portraying himself as the defender of the Tutsi minority from the FDRL rebels whom he declared intended to perpetrate genocide against the Tutsis. Even though millions of people in Eastern Congo had voted for Kabila for promising them peace, it is clear that the promise alone was not enough, as it required a strong institution to back up the promise. The lack of strong institutions that control and secure the rule of law created much room for violent perpetrators. Therefore, it is evident that through the election, the process was regarded as a success and peaceful; it was not the end of the peacebuilding process.

The democratization process in the DRC has been a distraction that has robbed the country of an effective peacebuilding process. The democratization process in the DRC has remained largely focused on provincial- and national-level changes, while neglecting the challenges at the grassroots level, which are likely to promote the democratic intent. The obsession of democratizing through the ballot diverted all the attention of MUNOC from the various local conditions and grievances, such that within a year after the elections, Eastern Congo was in a full-blown crisis. Scholars contend that the international community has been so focused on establishing democratic values in the DRC that it ignored various local factors that perpetuate violence (Eriksen, 2009; Zambakari, 2017). The transition of MUNOC to MUNOSCO in 2010 is evidence of the consistent policy failures. The latter remains trapped in the former operational framework despite the better facilities and increased number of personnel to "a maximum of 19,815 military personnel, 760 military observers, 391 police personnel and 1,050 members of formed police units" (Ngatu, Nojima, Boleme-Izankoy, Malonga-Kaj, Wumba, Kanbara, & Nakano, 2016) excluding the judiciary, civilian, and correction components.

Although MUNOSCO'S mandate is twofold—the protection of civilians and the stabilization and consolidation of peace—it remains a worrying phenomenon that MUNOSCO's operations are still alienated from local decisions.

Violence and the Social Cleavages of Power in South Sudan

The history of South Sudan is one of endemic violence which has been driven by multiple causes including territorial disputes, resource conflicts, ethnic tensions, religious difference, and interstate conflict.[7] The post-independence state of South Sudan has seen the emergence of ethnic tensions and differences as the central and major driver of conflict in the youngest African state. Ethnic tensions have always been part and parcel of the entire Sudanese crises, but they have often been overshadowed by the bigger conflict challenges which prioritized the independence of the South from the Arab North due to various disputes (i.e., territorial dispute, unequal distribution of resources such as oil, water and land, and extensive religious differences).

When the Republic of South Sudan obtained independence in January 2011, the suppressed political and social differences that are widely believed to be ethnically generated among the Sudan People's Liberation Movement (SPLM) began to emerge. Within three years following independence, a civil war broke out triggered by the political differences between President Salva Kiir and former Vice President Riek Machar. Vhumbunu (2016) confirms that the political relationship between these two has been strained and uneasy both within the party and in government. Vhumbunu (2016) further outlines how when he states:

> [T]he non-cooperative relations between the Office of the President and that of the Vice President, and contestations over skewed and irregular army recruitments in 2013, were also factors in the civil war, which was triggered by disagreements within the presidential guard over alleged orders to disarm Machar-aligned Nuer members as a result of an alleged coup. (p. 5)

The tension, which started as a political squabble between Kiir (of the Dinka ethnic group—the largest group in the country) and Machar (of the Nuer ethnic group—the second largest ethnic group) quickly escalated into violent ethnic clashes. The BBC (2014) reported that in as much as ethnic killings have been evident since the outbreak of the civil war, both Kiir and Machar command prominent supporters from each other's communities. Machar's supporters are believed to have instigated violence against Kiir's regime labeling it as corrupt and seize the oil-producing capital town of Bentiu. Therefore, the political leaders in South Sudan have resorted to the use of violence as a means of attaining their desired end.

Following the independence of the country, the government of South Sudan and the various key stakeholders (internal and external) which include the Intergovernmental Authority on Development (IGAD); the African Union (AU); the United Nations (UN); Civil Society Organizations (CSOs) became active in the country. Many of these countries were engaged in joint efforts to establish the institutions that would sustain South Sudan as an independent state, united together to seek ways to build the newly independent country of Africa. Da Costa and Karlsrud posited that the United Nations Mission in South Sudan (UNMISS) partly engaged a local peacebuilding approach in trying to address the challenges that might stir conflict in the future. The authors clarify that although the engagement of UNMISS was in the name of local peacebuilding, the engagement was only done with the local elites. The government of South Sudan and the stakeholders were virtually absent in the rural areas that exacerbated the wide divide between the center (top leaders-government) and the periphery (communities-rural area), which makes up the large percentage of the country.

The international community was quick to focus on building a state without addressing the crucial challenges of internal conflicts and political reconciliation (Tran, 2014). Both the government and international actors failed to offer fully established effective security sector reforms that could have been the bulwarks to withstand the outbreak of a civil war in 2013. It is important to note that such weakness is still evident and the division among IGAD[8] on the way forward regarding the peace agreements of South Sudan in 2015 and 2016 consecutively poses higher chances of failure in the peace process. The assumption by the international community that the new South Sudan's conflict tensions had ended with the separation of the South Sudan from (North) Republic of Sudan was the biggest mistake, which allowed the long-standing ethnic conflict that has infected the society. It is important to note that peace agreements in the case of South Sudan have consistently shown patterns of suspicions, tensions, and mistrust among the Dinka and Nuer ethnic groups. Thus, there is a deep need for mediation processes to help restore relationships and build tolerance to ensure sustainable solutions to the political challenges, which lies within the political differences and the needs of both Kiir and Machar through an incorporative strategy that brings all the issues into an agreement (Vhumbunu, 2016).

Why the Liberal Peace Approach Typically Fails

The interpretation of these cycles of violence and relapse of war following peace agreements, ceasefire, or post-conflict peacebuilding has been blamed on weak peace mechanisms (foreign approaches to peacebuilding which lack reconciliation, legitimacy, and inclusiveness) and weak institutions (which are guided by processes foreign to a particular conflict society/community in question). Since the late twentieth century, peacebuilding scholarship has started to question the ability of liberal peace in building sustainable peace in non-Western countries. In fact, the former UN Secretary-General Ban Ki-Moon's reflection on broader issues on peacebuilding in 2009 emphasized the theme of national ownership of peace with a clear understanding that peace processes that are guided by those who are not likely to live with it will likely fail (UN, 2009).

Donias (2015) buttresses the need for local ownership of peace when he avers "the inherent limits on the breadth, depth and duration of any external peace-building mission suggest that deep-rooted, sustainable change of the kind peacebuilding seeks to bring about requires the long-term support and commitment of a critical mass of domestic actors" (p. 2). However, the implementation of the broad-based national ownership peacebuilding remains troubled unless goals developed from partnership are prioritized instead of pursuing the interests of a single powerful organization (Murithi, 2008). For instance, the UN remains the most powerful and most resourceful institution in spearheading peace support operations in the world. Its engagement with African Union (AU) peace support operations should always carefully consider the temptation to impose ideas easily and be conscious of the consequences of frustrating the development of new and local ideas that may be locally owned. However, scholars observe that the UN and AU have been trapped in forging a syncretic system of specific peace ideas and strategies of addressing peace in the past decade, but their conduct has remained paternalistic in practice though both actors prefer to regard it as a partnership (Murithi, 2008; Vorrath, 2019).

Most liberal peace scholars have argued that these peacebuilding failures and setbacks in African countries "had more to do with improper sequencing or a lack of coordination or insufficient commitment by outsiders, not problems with the liberal idea itself" (Curtis, 2012, p. 11). In idealistic terms, one can stand to believe such an assessment. However, Sriram (2007) notes that such an assessment is driven by various under-examined assumptions of the African communities and has resulted in various unintended consequences. Murithi (2006) argues that it is a necessity to examine and consider alternative practices of peacebuilding on the continent that fall beyond the parameters of liberal peace. These alternative practices of peace may be identified within indigenous approaches to peace, informal economy, and social solidarity (within people-to-people initiatives, within community groups' engagement, within the representation of traditional structures (i.e., *Gacaca* courts of Rwanda or the *Xeer* legal system of Somalia, or within religious groups). Such alternatives may help in building up effective institutions that are necessary for a fully functional state.

Several features of liberal peace approaches weaken the process of building peace in Africa. These may be regarded as inhibiting factors to the successful building of peace in these complex conflicts. Various scholars studying African conflicts such as Curtis (2012), Keen (2012), Ducasse-Rogier (2004), Eriksen (2009), and Ramsbotham et al. (2011) have identified factors. For instance, the International Centre for Transitional Justice posits that the Congolese army is underfunded and ill-equipped, which has resulted in its inability to effectively provide security and instead commit criminal acts that include grave violations of human rights (ICTJ, 2016). This incompetence in security sector reform has become the source of conflict enhancement as the military has been found cooperating or competing with rebel groups in victimizing civilians and exploiting the natural resources of the country (ICTJ, 2016).

More so, international actors in peace have resorted to political mediation aided with peace agreements as the route to successful peace outcomes. The idea behind this strategy has been to forge political and economic liberalization as a way of branding sustainable peace but with little or no success among African countries (only Mozambique's [proxy war] is regarded as having had a successful intervention, however unstable (Kagire, 2016). Countries such as Angola and the DRC have endured failed peace agreements, and Sierra Leone's three peace agreements that were signed between 1996 and 1999 successively failed due to the multiplicity of warring parties. Rebels have pushed since then to get political legitimacy in the government structures, and the failure of such recognition war and violence is the threatened consequence (Kagire, 2016). Sawyer (2004) commending the Liberian Peace Talks (1996) clarifies that peace agreements "substantially, if not totally, controlled by armed groups whose leaders could hardly find in such arrangements sufficient incentive to blunt their greed and ambition" (p. 451), are not sustainable.

In instances where neighboring countries are involved in supporting rebel conflicts, complexity is most likely to be edified. The Global Policy Forum reports clarify that Ugandan and Rwandan militia groups have been supporting and influencing continuous conflict in the DRC (Macpherson, 2012; Snow, 2004). The invasion of the eastern Congo (North and South Kivu) by Rwandan troops furthered the crises in the already destabilized environment. Swart (2012) maintains that Rwanda's continued desire to keep its influence in the Kivus continuously undermined the political transition that had started in 2003. Though suggestions were made before by the UN Security Council in 2003 to sanction such countries, no effective stance has been taken to effect such actions.

Matagne (2011) in his assessment of the failures of liberal peace proponents in the DRC confirms how "top-down approaches were therefore implemented and they only allowed for short peace intervals in the eastern Congo because they did not take into account the complex dynamics at the local level" (p. 80). The extensive consequences of peace agreements' failure and the relapse of conflicts in Africa today require inclusive approaches that balance practical local knowledge and international efforts to complement the growth of local capacity by supporting the growth of local institutions across all level from the grassroots to the top levels of government. Hybrid peace approaches acknowledge the existence of both macro-level and micro-level tensions that affect the settlement of peace, and as a result, it allows for comprehensive approaches that investigate and scrutinize both local and international causes of peace process failure. Murithi (2008) acknowledges that the use and engagement of hybrid peace approaches in Africa may be helpful/instrumental in endorsing indigenous and endogenous peace architecture that addresses the core conflict problems that stand unique in each African conflict.

Are There Alternatives?

We have examined a few of the alternatives we consider very central in mitigating violent conflicts in Africa and promoting peaceful coexistence among the different ethnic nationalities. Among them includes:

Adopting the Principles of "Ubuntu"

African people have over the centuries developed a robust way of living that incorporates respect for leaders, traditional institutions, values, norms, and creeds. All these are deeply embedded in most cultures of Africans and has become a basis for daily social relations among the people. There is the need to look at different cultures to experience how they educate young ones about peace. African cultures are archives of a large body of knowledge on how to promote peace and maintain harmonious communities (Murithi, 2009). It is contradictory, however, that a large level of endless violence consistently ravages the continent of Africa. Nonetheless, it also shows that there is an urgent need to transmit the knowledge drawn from African cultures of peace, love, and respect passed down through the generations to the present generation and future generations of Africans as a pathway to sustainable peace.

Culture plays a crucial role in shaping the behavior of people and promoting peace among people. Therefore, it does not come as a surprise that local approaches for managing disputes around the world (particularly in Africa) become central. Thus, the need to pull together these experiences and use them in educating the young people in fostering culture as a symbol of peace arises. Without a doubt, cultural attitudes and values provide the foundation for the social norms by which people live (Murithi, 2009). Through cultural socialization, the young ones are taught to respect, forgive, share, protect, and preserve traditional values that have been bequeathed to them by their ancestors. This explains why conflicts are easily and often resolved within the family and community settings without necessarily going to the higher authorities for mediation. Further still, the culture of sharing with those who are less privileged (poor) is inculcated into the young ones. The concept of sharing is what is referred to as "Ubuntu."

Ubuntu is an African cultural trait, which speaks directly to the very essence of being human. It denotes generosity, hospitality, friendliness, caring and above all, compassion. For Ubuntu, the people share what they have. It suggests that our human nature (being) is caught up together, are connectedly bound up, in theirs. We belong in a bundle of life (Murithi, 2009). More so, the notion of Ubuntu is applied to justify the significance of building peace through the principle of reciprocity, inclusiveness, and a shared sense of destiny among different people. It provides a value system for giving and receiving forgiveness, as well as a rationale for sacrificing or relinquishing the desire to exact revenge for past wrongs. Ubuntu provides inspiration and gives guidelines for societies and their governments on the manner in which to formulate and legislate laws that will promote reconciliation rather than instigate violence or more conflicts. In simple terms, it can culturally revive our practical efforts to build peace and heal broken communities. Because of the interconnectedness between and among communities, in the event of conflicts, the disputants should know someone from the other community, and through these personal relations, disputes/confits are easily resolved.

If everyone accepts the principles of Ubuntu, then there are greater chances some people will have some feelings of either being wrong or accept responsibility for the wrong things they have done. In this case, a lawbreaker has been transformed and by extension his or her group has been transformed into a law-abiding individual and people. Similarly, a disputing person changes or transforms his or her group into a disputing group. This, therefore, suggests that if an individual is wronged, such a person could depend on the group to remedy the wronged; either way, the group has equally been wronged too. From this point, we can see the dynamics of group identification and the impact they play on conflict scenarios across the globe (Khoza, 1994; Murithi, 2009).

In societies where the Ubuntu principle is practiced, it has helped in resolving disputes, promoting reconciliation and peace aimed at healing past offences, and maintaining group/social cohesion and harmony at large. Often, consensus building was accepted as cultural support for the regulations and management of relationships between members of the community (Prinsloo, 1998). Sometimes, depending on the very nature of the conflict and/or disagreement, the process for resolving such conflict could start from the family level and then go to the village level, assuming it revolves around people of a particular ethnic group or sometimes between and among different ethnic nationalities located within a particular area.

Advancing "Propaganda of Oneness"

We proposed the use of propaganda to fuel togetherness and unity among diverse people. Just as warlords have employed the strategies of propaganda against their enemies in warfare, this approach should be adopted to promote unity in most conflict-ridden African countries. All media platforms—electronic, print, social media, and all forms of electronic devices should be hijacked to propagate the gospel of unity, oneness. Emphasis should be placed on the beauty of diversity among a people rather than disunity in a diverse people.

Through this, a nationalistic framework can be built by which all can be identified without any distinctions based on race, religion, tribe, or homeland creating a nation that encompasses the entire country. Any nation that is divided as a result of their inherent nature, and states where sectarianism has been deeply entrenched, will require aggressive propaganda to build a sense of togetherness, nationhood, and an all-inclusive identity that allows all different factions to assert their separate ones still (Elzubeir, 2017).

An interethnic, religious, and traditional body should be set up with the view to promote unity among diverse people. This body should be tasked with the responsibility of ensuring cooperation among diverse groups, encourage unity and friendship and further strengthen intermarriages between and among their people. Intercultural practices should equally be encouraged as a panacea to national development. This can be achieved by organizing cultural ceremonies that would bring these diverse nationalities together to share in the experiences of each group. Economic unity can also be promoted. This can be through trade, agricultural cooperation, and investments.

Engaging Youth and Women

Every nation on this planet earth prides itself more on its youths and the potential that they possess. A good chunk of young people across the continent of Africa have lost hope in their future, as opportunities to explore their potentials are limited. While the majority of these youths would desire quality education, convenient jobs to support their families, and assurance of financial security. Sadly, these opportunities are very few; hence, many of them have fallen prey to dangerous politicians to work for them as thugs to survive. Some have resorted to being used as foot soldiers of rebel leaders and religious fundamentalist. The sociological and/or economic analysis of the youth and their need, as well as strategies for survival, is significantly an unstudied field (Elzubeir, 2017). Thus, we aver that any all-inclusive plans for bringing stability in Africa must as a matter fact include intensive study of these inquiries.

We recommend that one important aspect of Africa's journey toward the sustainable building of peace and security would have to incorporate the organization of the youths into different sectors. Studies show that the increasing youthful population across the continent has been frustrated and agitated by lack of political space, unemployment, poverty, and inequalities leading them into non-conformity of action and behavior (Mukoma, 2018). Ozerdum (2015) argues that youth are often identified as drivers of conflict who are combative, rebellious, impatient, malleable, and sadly, risk takers. As earlier noted, these features are often taken advantage of by political elites, political parties, warlords, and extreme groups for their own good. According to Elzubeir (2017), "looking at the apparently unrestrained and irrational violence of the wars in Sierra Leone and Liberia, have hypothesized that Africa's youth are out of control; I refuse to believe this postulation for I believe that writers have not looked at the situation from the point of view of young people" (p. 4). This lack of intensive study of the plights of the young people is a huge gap that must be filled to be able to understand the challenges being confronted by these young people rather than categorized them as "uncontrolled." Therefore, we proposed that African youths should be structured into student unions, who are largely representative and quite influential civil organization for youth.

In tracing history, it is clear that student politics has too much influence in many African countries. Student Unions championed the October

Revolution that brought down the military regime of General Ibrahim Abboud in Khartoum in 1964. It is also on record that it was the youths who vigorously fought for the reformation of the Apartheid education system in South Africa. With the June 1976 student protests, marking one of the significant contributions that completely contributed toward young people participations toward ending the brutal system of Apartheid. Our second recommendation would be the organization of the young people into moderate religious and social organizations like church, mosque, and traditional African groups, whose influence over these youths have been overwhelming as it easily captures their energies and commitment (Elzubeir, 2017). Lastly and most importantly, we proposed that African youths should be deeply engaged in extracurricular activities such as sports and arts (music, dancing competition, etc.). Through this medium, the youths would not only be engaged among themselves but will create a platform for them to build bonds among youths of different ethnic nationalities. This will contribute in no small measure in promoting unity and, above all, peace.

In addition, UN Security Council Resolution 1325 (2000) advanced the need to engage in gender mainstreaming in peacebuilding with the intention to increase the involvement of women in peace processes. Almost two decades after the resolution, there is still very limited number of women involved in mainstream peacebuilding platforms across Africa. Worryingly, most of those that are already involved globally or locally in peace initiatives are "the educated elite, who in most cases have not even experienced the conflict thereof and are often detached from reality" (Zvaita & Mbara, 2019, p. 159).

We believe engaging women in peacebuilding is essential mainly because of two basic reasons. First, because women are the most victims of conflict, sexual exploitation, and abuse, it is essential to have them as key drivers of peacebuilding and conflict resolution (Agbalajobi, 2008). Women and children consist of the most victims of conflicts across the African continent. They form the largest number of refugees (women consist of 59% and children 51%) and internally displaced persons (Egbetayo & Nyambura, 2019). Thus, there is a need to rally more women into active peace participation addressing challenges affecting them.

Second, because African women are the fabric that holds families together and feel the need for peace in ongoing civil wars and conflicts more than men. For instance, the second Liberian civil war came to an end in 2003 after a mass protest by thousands of women who had organized themselves. More so, the Wajir women from the north-eastern province of Kenya are also an excellent example of how women involvement in conflict transformation and peacebuilding can result in sustainable outcomes. After realizing the continuous effects of conflicts which was resulting in series of murders, raping of women, robberies and disturbances in business and market places, the women organized themselves and initiated a peace mechanism that ended up attracting support and attention of the government which had declared a state of emergency in the province. Therefore, the need for engaging more women in African peacebuilding.

Concluding Remarks

This chapter has outlined the various factors affecting the sustainability of peace in Africa. The investigation of Somalia, the DRC, and South Sudan exposed the complexity that challenges the post-conflict reconstruction and peacebuilding. It critically engages the defective nature of liberal peace frameworks in African peace, by outlining how its inflexible nature often neglects the key values that may effect sustainable peace. As a result, emphasis is put on the need for local or contextual peace engagements coupled with hybrid peace strategies that mitigate the challenges to the building of sustainable peace in Africa. This allows for the emergence and recognition of some indigenous and endogenous peace practices in African communities that can be of benefit in guiding African scholars toward laying practices that preludes to long-term peace.

Notes

1. Clans are social units/ethnic groups. In Somalia there are four dominant clans which are the Hawiye, Darod, Isaaq, and Dir. Each has control over a specific geopolitical territory and Somalis demonstrate more loyalty to their clans than the state. See www. worldatlas.com/articles/etnic-groups-and-clans-in-somalia.html
2. MISSION DE L'ORGANISATION DES NATIONS UNIES POUR LA STABILISATION EN RD CONGO
3. Zaire's (now DRC) longtime dictator from 1965–1997.
4. AFDL was a coalition of Rwandan, Ugandan, Burundan, and some selected Congolese dissidents and disgruntled minority groups and nations that toppled President Mobutu SeseSeko.
5. Laurent Kabila was the president of DRC from 17 May 1997 who overthrew Mobutu SeseSeko through a coup.
6. Laurent Nkunda is a former General in the Armed Forces of the Democratic Republic of Congo and is the former warlord operating in the province of Nord-Kivu, sympathetic to Congolese Tutsis and the Tutsi-dominated government of neighboring Rwanda.
7. Interstate conflict between the Republic of Sudan and Republic of South Sudan.

8. Uganda and Sudan have acute political differences, Ethiopia and Kenya differ at times on the peace process to engage, and the addition of plus five USA, UK, Norway, China, the Arab League, and others opened room for more competing interests.

References

Abdulle, J. (2008). *Civil society in the absence of a State: Conceptual issues.* Berlin: Heinrich Boll Foundation.

Agbalajobi, D. T. (2008). The role of women in conflict resolution and peacebuilding. In R. Bowd, & A. B. Chikwanha (eds.), *Understanding Africa's contemporary conflicts: Origins, challenges and peacebuilding* (pp. 233–253). Addis Ababa: Africa Human Security Initiative.

Autesserre, S. (2011). Constructing peace: Collective understandings of peace, peacemaking, and peacebuilding. *Critique Internationale, 51*, 153–167.

Bräuchler, B., & Naucke, P. (2017). Peacebuilding and conceptualisations of the local. *Social Anthropology, 25*(4): 422–436.

Curtis, D. (2012). Contested politics of peacebuilding in Africa. In D. Curtis & G. Dzinesa (eds.), *Peacebuilding in Africa* (p. 116). Athens: Ohio University Press.

Dijkzeul, D. (2008). Towards a framework for the study of "No War, No Peace" societies. *Working Paper.* Switzerland: Swiss Peace. Retrieved from: https://www.files.ethz.ch/isn/55114/WP2_2008.pdf (accessed September 25, 2019).

Donias, T. (2015). Ownership: From policy to practice. In P. Jackson (ed), *Handbook of International Security and Development* (pp. 227–247). Cheltenham: Edward Elgar Publishing Limited.

Ducasse-Rogier, M. (2004). Resolving intractable conflicts in Africa: A case study of Sierra Leone. *Working Paper Series 31.* Hague: Netherlands Institute of International Relations. Retrieved from: https://www.clingendael.org/sites/default/files/pdfs/20040900_cru_working_paper_31.pdf (accessed March 9, 2018).

Egbetayo, V., & Nyambura, C. (2019, March 28). *Forced displacement in Africa has a female face.* Globalpartnership.org, Retrieved from: https://www.globalpartnership.org/blog/forced-displacement-africa-has-female-face (accessed September 25, 2019).

Elzubeir, M. (2017, December 4). My strategies for a stable Africa. *International Policy Digest.* Retrieved from: https://intpolicydigest.org/2017/12/04/my-strategies-for-a-stable-africa/ (accessed July 8, 2018).

Eriksen, S. S. (2009). The liberal peace is neither: Peacebuilding, state building and the reproduction of conflict in the Democratic Republic of Congo. *International Peacekeeping, 16*(5): 652–666. doi: 10.1080/13533310903303289

Hendrick, D. (2009). Complexity theory and conflict transformation: An exploration of potential and implications. *Working Paper 17.* University of Bradford: Department of Peace Studies. Retrieved from: http://citeseerx.ist.psu.edu/viewdoc/download?doi=10.1.1.613.9011&rep=rep1&type=pdf (accessed September 25, 2019).

Ibrahim, S. A. M. (2011). Does civil society in a stateless environment hinder or help in rees-tablishing the state? The case of Somalia. In Abdulkadi et al. (eds.), *Somalia: Exploring A Way Out*. Nairobi: National Civic Forum.

ICTJ. (2016). The Democratic Republic of Congo (DRC). Retrieved from: https://www.ictj.org/our-work/regions-and-countries/democratic-republic-congo-drc (accessed September 25, 2019).

Kagire, M. (2016, June 4). Congo President Kabila gives M23 rebels concessions. *The East African*. Retrieved from: http://www.theeastafrican.co.ke/news/Congo-President-Kabila-gives-M23-rebels-concessions--/-/2558/3232832/-/k9cltdz/-/index.html (accessed June 17, 2018).

Keen, D (2012). Peace as an incentive for war. In D. Curtis, & G. Dzinesa (eds.), *Peacebuilding in Africa*. Athens: Ohio University Press.

Khoza, R. (1994). Ubuntu: African humanism. *Occasional Paper*. Johannesburg: HSRC.

Koko, S. (2009). [Review of the book *The Resolution of African Conflicts: The Management of Conflict Resolution and Post-conflict Reconstruction*, by A. Nhema & P. T. Zeleza]. *ACCORD Conflict Trends 2009/1*. Retrieved from: https://journals.co.za/doc-server/fulltext/accordc/2009/1/accordc_2009_n1_a9.pdf?expires=1569417043&id=id&accname=58140&checksum=D2235B6AE697074F623F2789683156CC (accessed September 25, 2019).

Lake, D. (2015). Practical sovereignty and post conflict governance. In C. Crocker, F. O. Hampson, & P. Aall (eds.), *Managing conflict in a world adrift* (p. 118). Washington, DC: The United States Institute of Peace.

Lemay-Hébert, N. (2013). Critical debates on liberal peacebuilding. *Civil Wars*, 15(2): 242–252. doi: 10.1080/13698249.2013.817856

Linabary, J., Krishna, A., & Connaughton, S. (2016). The conflict family: Storytelling as an activity and a method for locally led, community-based peacebuilding. *Conflict Resolution Quarterly*, 34(4): 431–453. doi: 10.1002/crq.21189.

Macpherson, W. (2012, July 9). *Rwanda in Congo: Sixteen years of intervention*. Globalpolicy.org. Retrieved from: https://www.globalpolicy.org/security-council/index-of-countries-on-the-security-council-agenda/democratic-republic-of-congo/51744-rwanda-in-congo-sixteen-years-of-intervention-.html (accessed August 31, 2018).

Matagne, G. (2011). The trouble with the local in the Congo: the challenges of multilevel peacebuilding initiatives. *African Security Review*, 20(2): 80–85.

Menodji, M. H. A. (2013, February 4). *Problematic peacekeeping in the DRC: From MONUC to MONUSCO*. Global Policy Forum. Retrieved from: https://www.globalpolicy.org/security-council/index-of-countries-on-the-security-council-agenda/demo-cratic-republic-of-congo/52244-problematic-peacekeeping-in-the-drc-from-mo-nuc-to-monusco.html (accessed August 23, 2018).

Mukoma, N. (2018). *Blessed or cursed?—GGA*. [online] GGA. Retrieved from: https://gga.org/blessed-or-cursed/ (accessed August 30, 2018).

Murithi, T. (2006). Towards a symbiotic partnership: The UN peacebuilding commission and the evolving African Union/NEPAD post-conflict reconstruction framework. In Adekeye Adebajo & Helen Scanlon (eds.), *A dialogue of the deaf: Essays on Africa and the United Nations* (pp. 243–260). Johannesburg: Jacana.

Murithi, T. (2008). African indigenous and endogenous approaches to peace and conflict resolution. In D. J. Francis (ed.), *Peace and conflict in Africa* (pp. 16–30). New York: Zed Books.

Murithi, T. (2009). An African perspective on peace education: Ubuntu lessons in reconciliation. *International Review of Education, 55,* 221–233.

Newman, E. (2009). "Liberal" peacebuilding debates. In E. Newman, R. Paris, & O. Richmond (eds.), *New perspectives on peacebuilding.* Tokyo: United Nations University Press.

Ngatu, N., Nojima, S., Boleme-Izankoy, J., Malonga-Kaj, F., Wumba, D.-M., Kanbara, S., & Nakano, A. (2016). Disasters and related health issues in the Democratic Republic of Congo: Epidemiologic profile and perspectives for efficient health care delivery. *Current Politics and Economics of Africa, 9*(2): 227.

Oneal, J., & Russett, B. (1999). Assessing the liberal peace with alternative specifications: Trade still reduces conflict. *Journal of Peace Research, 36*(4): 423–442.

Osman, F. (2018). The role of civil society in Somalia's reconstruction: Achievements, challenges and opportunities. Retrieved from https://www.saferworld.org.uk/resources/news-and-analysis/post/775-the-role-of-civil-society-in-somaliaas-reconstruction-achievements-challenges-and-opportunities(accessed September 20, 2019).

Prinsloo, E. (1998). Ubuntu culture and participatory management. In P. H. Coetzee, & A. P. J. Roux (eds.), *The African philosophy reader* (pp. 41–51). London: Routledge.

Ramsbotham, O., Woodhouse, T., & Miall, H. (2011). *Contemporary conflict resolution: The prevention, management and transformation of deadly conflicts.* Cambridge: Polity Press.

Russet, B., & Oneal, J. (2001). *Triangulating peace: Democracy, interdependence, and international organizations.* New York: W.W. Norton.

Sawyer, A. (2004). Violent conflicts and governance challenges in West Africa: The case of the Mano River basin area. *Journal of Modern African Studies, 42*(3): 437–463.

Snow, K. (2004). *Rwanda's secret war: US-backed destabilization of Central Africa.* Globalpolicy.org. Retrieved from: https://www.globalpolicy.org/component/content/article/181/33592.html (accessed August 31, 2018).

Sriram, C. L. (2007). Justice as peace? Liberal peacebuilding and strategies of transitional justice. *Global Society, 21*(4): 579–591. doi: 10.1080/13600820701562843.

Somalia Corruption Report. (2019). Retrieved from: https://www.ganintegrity.com/portal/country-profiles/somalia/ (accessed September 20, 2019).

Swart, M. (2012). The legacy of the International Criminal Tribunal for the former Yugoslavia edited by Bert Swart, Alexander Zahar, Goran Slutter—Book Review. *Melbourne Journal of International Law, 13*(1): 358.

Tran, M. (2014, January 22). South Sudan failed by misjudgment of international community, says UN chief. *The Guardian*. Retrieved from: https://www.theguardian.com/global-development/2014/jan/22/south-sudan-failed-international-community (accessed August 23, 2018).

Tschirgi, N. (2015). Rebuilding war-torn societies: A critical review of international approaches. In C. Crocker, F. O. Hampson, & P. Aall (eds.), *Managing conflict in a world adrift*. Washington, DC: United States Institute of Peace.

UN Security Council. (2000). *Security Council resolution 1325 (2000) [on women and peace and security]*, 31 October 2000, S/RES/1325, Retrieved from: https://www.refworld.org/docid/3b00f4672e.html (accessed September 25, 2019).

UN Secretary-General. (2009, June 11). Report of the Secretary-General on peacebuilding in the immediate aftermath of conflict. *UNGSC, Sixty-third session*. Retrieved from: https://www.un.org/ruleoflaw/files/pbf_090611_sg.pdf (accessed September 25, 2019).

Vhumbunu, C. H. (2016). Conflict resurgence and the agreement on the resolution of the conflict in the Republic of South Sudan: A hurried and imposed peace pact? *ACCORD, Conflict Trends, 3*, 3–12.

Vorrath, J. (2019). Imbalances in the African peace and security architecture the current approach to capacity-building needs to be challenged. Retrieved from: https://www.swp-berlin.org/fileadmin/contents/products/comments/2012C29_vrr.pdf (accessed September 20, 2019).

Yamashita, H. (2014). Peacebuilding and "hybrid" peace. *The National Institute for Defense Studies New, Briefing Memo*, 1–4. Retrieved from: http://www.nids.mod.go.jp/english/publication/briefing/pdf/2014/briefing_e185.pdf (accessed September 25, 2019).

Zambakari, C. (2017). Challenges of liberal peace and statebuilding in divided societies—*ACCORD*. Retrieved from: https://www.accord.org.za/conflict-trends/challenges-liberal-peace-statebuilding-divided-societies/ (accessed September 20, 2019).

Zaum, D. (2012). Beyond the "liberal peace." *Global Governance, 18*(1): 121–132.

Zvaita, G. T., & Mbara, G. C. (2019). Engaging the values of local participation in African peace-building processes. *Journal of African Union Studies, 8*(2): 155–178. doi: 10.31920/2050-4306/2019/8n2a9.

Part III: Preventative, Restorative, and Systemic Engagement

5 Disrupting Cycles of Revenge and Boosting Community Resilience: A Forgiveness and Reconciliation Program at Boys and Girls Clubs

VINCENT R. WALDRON, CINDY BECKER, DAYNA KLOEBER, DOUGLAS
KELLEY, JONATHAN PETTIGREW, ROB RAZZANTE, KATRINA HANNA,
VONN MAGNIN, AND TONIA SMITH

> When you seek revenge, you end up hurting the other person more than they
> hurt you ... And then retaliation starts.
> —Hamari, Age 11, Boys & Girls Clubs member

> I've never seen anything like this at Boys & Girls Club. You are teaching kids
> important things they might not otherwise learn in their lives.
> —Rochelle, club manager

This chapter tells a story, a rich and complicated tale of researchers and students, community youth leaders and kids themselves, learning together about the role that forgiveness can play in fostering peaceful relationships. The narrative takes us from the halls of the local university to the community centers where children, many of them disadvantaged by poverty, learn skills that help them live more harmonious relationships and productive lives. The plot is driven by a central question. Can our decades of academic research on forgiveness be made useful to preteens, real-life kids who are discovering through sometimes-painful experience that relationships can be disappointing, conflict-filled, and even hurtful? Our approach to answering this question is an example of what we consider to be engaged scholarship—the kind that puts our theoretical understandings of communication and forgiveness in conversation with the experience-driven understandings of children and adults who serve as peacemakers in natural settings where conflict regularly emerges. In our view, peacebuilding is a process whereby harmful conduct is acknowledged by those who commit it, merciful responses are chosen over vengeful ones, and the parties agree to pursue relationships that are just, mutually respectful, and safe (Waldron, Kelley, & Kloeber, 2018).

As our story unfolds, the central characters grapple with a host of conflicts and surprising plot twists. Forgiveness theorists (Vince and Doug) puzzle with Dayna, creator of the forgiveness tree ceremony, over how to best translate their findings on the practices of adults to the youth served by Boys & Girls Clubs (B&GC). Our curriculum design team (Dayna, Cindy, Doug, and Rob) respond by designing a collection of games, stories, skits, and learning activities. Intervention researcher Jonathan confronts the challenge of measuring the effects of our forgiveness education pilot project. B&GC staff leaders (Vonn, Tonia, and a host of club managers and staff) face a conundrum. How could this university project compete with the highly choreographed, frenetic, and fun after-school-atmosphere of the typical club? Our on-site facilitators/instructors (Cindy and Dayna, along with a talented supporting team of students) are repeatedly called on to go "off-script," reinventing the curriculum in response to unexpected circumstances and the surprising relational insights of the kids. Our on-site observers and data analysts (including Rob and Kat) are challenged by the head-spinning complexity of conducting qualitative research in the buzzing hive of activity that is a Boys & Girls Club.

We begin with the backstory, a brief account of our academic research on forgiveness and its migration from university to community sites, such as schools, youth centers, and faith communities. The narrative progresses to describe our developing relationship with local branches of Boys & Girls Clubs, a national network of unique and highly praised youth-serving organizations. Next, the story of our forgiveness education curriculum is shared, including the adjustments we made as we gained more experience with three different clubs and their kids. Then the narrative builds to a climax as team members reflect on their hard-won understandings of how forgiveness concepts can be made useful to kids in community contexts.

The Backstory: A Primer on Forgiveness Scholarship

Forgiveness is one of several possible responses to hurtful or wrongful acts—a constructive and generous alternative to grudge-holding, avoidance, emotional detachment, or retaliation. In simple terms, forgiveness involves responding with kindness to those who have been unkind. But forgiveness is also a strong and self-respecting response to transgressions, one grounded in core moral commitments we make to ourselves, our relationships, and our communities. It is also a communication process, one that creates opportunities for (1) harmful conduct to be identified and held to account; (2) strong emotions to be expressed and validated; (3) apologies and amends to be offered and accepted; and (4) relationships to be renegotiated with the intent of creating a safe, just, and satisfying future for all parties. As Hamari observed in the opening quotation, forgiveness can disrupt cycles of revenge. And as Rochelle suggests, kids need forgiveness in their relationships. Adults too, we might add.

Why forgiveness communication matters. Although forgiveness is frequently explored as a psychological, political, or spiritual concept, we view it as a *communication process*, one that helps people (re)define the moral commitments that make their relationships and communities just, caring, and good, in the moral sense of that word (Waldron & Kelley, 2017). Philosophers and theologians have considered the willingness to forgive a mark of good character since ancient times (Griswold, 2007). Yet some scholars are skeptical, arguing that the value of forgiveness has been overhyped by a burgeoning self-help industry touting it as a relationship cure-all (Nussbaum, 2016). Nonetheless, numerous contemporary studies document its role in building more peaceful personal and community relationships in the United States and elsewhere (e.g., Worthington & Cowden, 2017). In community settings marked by conflict, forgiveness is often a crucial component of restorative justice, peace-building, and reconciliation processes.

In a series of survey and interview-based studies, Vince and Doug demonstrated that forgiveness is enacted in personal relationships through various kinds of discourse, some of which have more positive relational consequences than others (Kelley & Waldron, 2005; Waldron & Kelley, 2005; Waldron, 2017). For example, explicit forms of forgiveness granting ("I forgive you") tended to be more effectual than those which minimize a serious offense ("No worries. It's not a big deal.") or offer conditional forgiveness ("I will forgive you, but only if you do X."). In *seeking* forgiveness, offenders who explicitly acknowledged harm, and those that sincerely offered amends, were viewed more positively than those who fail to do so. In her thesis research, Dayna examined conditional forgiveness more closely, finding that it was often used in response to serious offenses (repeated infidelity or irresponsible drug use) and intended to provide the harmed partner with increased safety and an assurance that the violation would not reoccur (Kloeber & Waldron, 2017). In a large sample of romantic pairs, the verbalizing of explicit conditions appeared to arrest declines in relational satisfaction and create opportunities for relationship repair.

This academic research convinced us that forgiveness, and perhaps more importantly, the communication of forgiveness, could create more satisfying and peaceful relationships for couples, families, and communities. But the questions remained—how might we share this work beyond our traditional audience of fellow researchers and college students?

Tracing the Arc of Our Story: From University to Community

So, we challenged ourselves to apply forgiveness ideas and practices in community settings where forgiveness can be complicated by multi-layered relationships, painful cycles of revenge, and cultural norms that foster revenge or bullying. To make the sprawling forgiveness literature more accessible, Doug and Vince created the *Communication Tasks of Forgiveness* (CTF) model (see Figure 5.1), a set of seven interlocking tasks that tend be completed in successful forgiveness episodes (Waldron & Kelley, 2008; Waldron, Kelley, & Harvey, 2008).

The CTF helped us organize and teach communication practices that facilitate the accomplishment of each task. For example, "manage emotion" requires offended parties to find words for the emotions they feel (e.g., hurt, disappointment, fear) and offenders to legitimize those feelings ("I can see why you would feel disappointment"). Forgiveness-seeking typically requires, among other things, a full and sincere apology—one that clearly identifies the wrongful act, takes full responsibility, and pledges to do better.

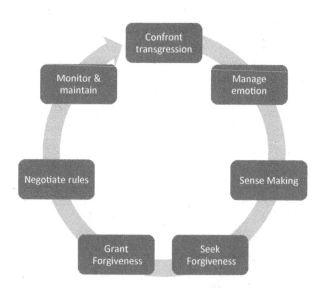

Figure 5.1. The communication tasks of forgiveness.

The CTF provides a communicative framework for forgiveness education in classroom settings, but if we were to take our show on the road, and out into the broader world, we needed more. First, we needed a way of inviting *whole communities*, not just individuals or couples, to explore forgiveness as a peaceful alternative to grudge-holding, alienation, and retaliation. Second, having worked mostly with adults, we needed to think about how to work with children. In short, we needed to devise a setting for our forgiveness story, a place where kids, and the communities they belong to, could help bring the story to life.

Revising the script: The forgiveness tree ceremony. Recognizing these needs, Dayna invented the forgiveness tree ceremony, which added a participative and artistic element to our community-based forgiveness education curriculum, which we have come to call the Forgiveness Tree Project (FTP). Dayna (Kloeber, 2014) worked with a group of undergraduate students to produce a brief video explaining the assumptions and steps of the ceremony: https://www.youtube.com/watch?v=G6s2cGfincY. Although it takes a variety of forms, the FTP typically involves brief instruction on what forgiveness is (and is not), forgiveness communication practices, group discussion, and the forgiveness tree ceremony itself—which invites audience members to construct a symbolic forgiveness tree for the community (for details, see Waldron, Kelley, & Kloeber, 2018).

The tree metaphor helps members discuss personal and community values that could motivate them to be forgiving (roots), how a strong sense of self supports healthy relationships (trunk), the strong bonds that give the community its meaning and shared sense of support (branches), and messages that help members grant and seek forgiveness when damaged individuals and relationships must be healed (leaves). The tree lends itself to discussion of forgiveness as a source of renewal and growth in communities that (like trees) are inevitably stressed, and sometimes scarred, by passing storms. The tree presented in Figure 5.2 was constructed by inmates in a county jail and displayed in the recreation room, a visual symbol of the community's commitment to be more forgiving in jail, and on the outside. Members pin their personal forgiveness messages/leaves (see Figure 5.3) to the tree and it is sometimes displayed in a public setting.

The tree offers a sheltered space in the community, where conflict can be aired, and forgiveness negotiated. As indicated in Table 5.1, the FTP has been implemented in a variety of settings: youth centers, faith communities, a jail, art galleries, colleges, and grade schools. As the FTP became more widely known in the local community, we received requests to work with a new and unfamiliar audience—kids.

Figure 5.2. The forgiveness tree.

A Younger Audience: "He's just mad cuz someone burned down his house"

Youth have too often been a neglected audience for communication research, including ours. Yet, the communication practices featured in the CTF model are first learned (or not) during childhood, as peer relationships become salient. Intervening at the appropriate developmental stage is important (Pettigrew & Hecht, 2015). For example, around the beginning of adolescence, youth begin to exhibit delinquencies—such as violence and other antisocial behavior, academic failure, risky sexual activity, and substance use (Guo, Hawkins, Hill, & Abbot, 2001). If we were to teach forgiveness as an alternative to antisocial responses such as revenge, we should heed the call of researchers who identified early adolescence as a key period for intervention (Pettigrew & Gal, 2019).

Indeed, our early efforts to involve FTP convinced us that forgiveness concepts resonated deeply with tweens and teens. Dayna pilot-tested the FTP at an elementary school in her neighborhood, inviting a group of junior high leaders to form a core group of forgiveness advocates who met for five lunchtime meetings. This core group then facilitated peer learning and helped

Figure 5.3. Personal forgiveness messages.

adults conduct the forgiveness tree ceremony in the school cafeteria. Dayna gained some powerful insights from that memorable group of junior high kids. As the following excerpt suggests, the hurtful incidents they described could be quite different from those described by adults, and peer pressure was often instrumental, for better or worse.

> During one of our lunchtime meetings, while talking about expressing emotion, one of the boys got upset and left the room ... One of the boys said, "He's just mad cuz someone burned down his house." I exclaimed, "What? What the? Well, that's horrible." A few more kids jumped in and explained ...; it was his house on a video game ... Some of the kids began to minimize their classmate's emotion that day. Then a group of others pushed back and said that had been exactly

Table 5.1. Inventory of forgiveness tree ceremonies (Kelley, Waldron, & Kloeber, in press).

Month/ Year	Community	Audience	Attendees	Community Speaker(s)	Breakout Sessions	Lecture	Discussion Circle(s)
September 2013	Sorority	Sorority members	100			✓	
March 2014	Northlight Art Gallery	Artists, curator, inmates' families, students	50	✓			✓
March 2014	Neighborhood Ministries Inner City Center	Staff, leaders	75			✓	
August 2014	Camp Solera	Freshman Residence Hall	300			✓	✓
October 2014	Glendale Community College/Civility Week	Students, faculty	90				✓
November 2014	Adult Detention Center	Inmates, detention officers, graduate students	45	✓	✓		✓
April 2015	ASU's Consent Week	Abuse survivors	60	✓		✓	✓
April 2015	ASU's Family Communication Consortium Forgiveness Education Week	Undergraduate and graduate students	35			✓	✓
May 2015	Forgiveness Tree Donors Thank You Event	Donors, community FTP champions, students	60	✓		✓	
May 2015	Oakwood Elementary School	Middle school students, teachers, staff	220	✓	✓	✓	✓
August 2015	Arizona Boys & Girls Club	Staff training	40				✓

Table 5.1. Continued

Month/ Year	Community	Audience	Attendees	Format			
October 2015	Arizona Boys & Girls Club	Tweens and teens (12–18 years)	120			✓	✓
December 2015	Franciscan Renewal Center	Adult Staff (counselors, clergy, cooks, custodians)	50		✓	✓	✓
Fall 2016, Spring 2017	Arizona Boys & Girls Club Three Locations: A, B & C	Tweens (10–12 years), first and second graders	90			✓	✓
August 2017	Arizona State University Freshman Orientation Class	College Freshman	15			✓	
Ongoing	Neighborhood Ministries Inner City Center	Children to adult, including staff	300	✓		✓	
Winter 2017	United Church of Christ & Unitarian Universalist Congregation	Adult congregation members	(40	✓		✓	✓

what we were talking about -- emotion. We aren't supposed to minimize others' emotion. –Dayna (from field notes)

When our campus hosted over one hundred teen leaders from Boys & Girls Clubs, we devised a variation on the FTP ceremony, one that rotated them in groups of twenty-five through a series of forgiveness "learning stations," ending with an opportunity for each child to inscribe a leaf and attach it to a massive forgiveness tree, hung on the wall of a campus ballroom. Having listened in as the kids discussed their most valued relationships and the estrangement they felt from former friends, siblings, and parents, Vince recorded these words:

> These kids are really hurting. They were pretty frank about the harm they had suffered and sometimes caused, in relationships with peers at school, with moms and dads and siblings. Some were angry and sullen, some expressed regret at their own bad behavior, but most just wanted to heal broken bonds, somehow. The messages they wrote on the leaves were empathetic ("Everyone makes mistakes. Even me"), realistic ("Forgiveness is hard!"), and often generous ("I forgive

you for using. I know you will be a better mom now."). The kids seem to know intuitively that forgiveness is important, and they want to learn more. –Vince (synthesized from field notes)

Thus, began our multiyear partnership with Boys & Girls Clubs.

Expanding the Story Line: Partnership with Boys & Girls Clubs

Forgiveness is something kids need in their relationships—Rochelle, Club Manager

One of Vince's graduate students happened to be working as an intern for Boys & Girls Clubs of the East Valley, one of three B&GC organizations in central Arizona. She arranged a meeting with her supervisors, including Tonia, who became a key supporter—an opportunity to share the history and goals of FTP and its relevance to B&GC. As it turns out, one of the three pillars of the B&GC mission features character development. FTP appeared to fit well with a new character-building approach that would soon be pilot-tested at multiple clubs.

Vince then accepted an invitation to share the FTP at a regional staff training session. He and one of his students outlined the approach and its fit with the B&GC mission. They invited staff to construct their own forgiveness tree. Some were a bit skeptical about incorporating a forgiveness component into the already hectic after-school schedule of homework, organized sports, and play. But most were enthusiastic. Many B&GC staff were previously youth members, a unique feature of this organization, and one that gives staff instant credibility with the kids. That day, several staff shared their personal struggles with youth who sought self-respect through aggression rather than the constructive approaches advocated by B&GC.

BG&C is a national youth services organization, serving roughly 433,000 children ages 6 to 18 years of age. Although youth members come from many backgrounds, a significant percentage might be considered "at risk" due to poverty, parental separation, or other factors. Nationally, roughly 56% of B&GC youth qualify for the federal school lunch program. National statistics indicate that boys comprise roughly 55% of the member population. We chose to pilot test the FTP at three clubs, chosen because the demographics of their youth populations and cultural milieus were quite varied and distinct. See Table 5.2 for a description of pilot Clubs A, B, and C.

The gender profiles of Clubs A, B, and C were like national trends, but the three clubs were different on other measures. Club A, located in an older suburb of the Phoenix-metropolitan area, was described as the "country club" of Boys & Girls Clubs by one staffer, and yet 56% of the children live

Table 5.2. Profiles of the Clubs A, B, and C.

	Variable	Club A	Club B	Club C
	Date of origination:	1986	1989	1987
	Youth members (total):	508	1,001	636
	Attending per day:	172	195	264
	% below poverty level:	56	20	60
	% in single parent homes:	37	43	54
Gender:				
	% Male:	53	57	53
	% Female:	47	43	47
Ethnicity/Race:				
	African American:	10	21	08
	Caucasion/White:	49	16	08
	Latino/a:	17	31	80
	Native American	nr*	11	nr
	Other/multi-racial:	24	21	04

* not reported separately at this clubs

below the federal poverty line (Club C had the highest rate, at 60%). Club B was the largest, with about 1,000 members, and the most diverse in racial/ ethnic make-up, including 11% Native American children. In contrast, 80% of children at Club C identified as Latina/o. At Club A, only 17% identified that way and 47% were Caucasian.

Youth attend their local clubs after school, typically until 5 or 6 p.m., when parents or other adults retrieve them. Many children receive an evening meal before returning to their homes. Adult staffers direct the kids in activities designed to prepare them for success in three areas: school/workforce preparation, healthy lifestyles, and character development.

Finding Our Theme. "Learning to give and accept apologies would be useful for our kids"

Vonn and Tonia, BG&C leaders and co-authors, recognized the need for forgiveness education. Tonia saw it as integral to the character development part of the mission. In her view, forgiveness skills could be instrumental in helping kids develop satisfying and morally sound relationships. Vonn directed our attention to an annual survey of youth satisfaction with Boys & Girls Clubs programs. In 2016, the results indicated that nearly half of those surveyed

(47%) were seeking additional assistance in managing conflict with peers. In his view, kids (and club staff) would benefit if kids could learn skills to help them resolve conflicts peacefully. Which skills? "Even just learning to give and accept apologies would be useful for a lot of kids," he suggested.

The need extended beyond individual kids to the climate of the club and the duties of staff. One club manager explained that certain children consumed an inordinate amount of staff time because they required adult assistance in handling even the smallest disputes. What should youth learn from our program? "Kids should learn to talk out their feelings before running to the staff," she suggested. Other staff shared their own views. One thought that youth at his club would benefit from learning that revenge had consequences for others.

> One kid yells at another one, then that kid yells back. Then their friends and siblings get involved and this one conflict leads to bad feelings for the whole group ... Most kids want to get along. But at home some learned to fight for respect rather than talk about what is bothering them. –Molly (B&GC staff)

With these lessons in mind, we worked to construct a forgiveness education curriculum that was responsive to the B&GC context. See Table 5.3 for an outline of the curriculum. On the recommendation of Vonn and Tonia, we targeted our instruction to members of Torch Club, a group of tweens (mostly 11–13 years old), identified as "rising leaders." Torch Club kids often assume leadership roles in their teen years and it was expected that they would model forgiving behavior for peers and younger children. These kids, numbering —twelve to fifteen at each club, would spend five or six after-school sessions with us (60–90 minutes) and then lead a larger group of —twenty to thirty younger children (8–10 years old) in a forgiveness tree ceremony. The ceremony was intended to reinforce the curriculum through public performance and commitment, position Torch Club kids as forgiveness advocates, and introduce younger kids to forgiveness concepts and practices.

We also designed a set of quantitative and qualitative measures to assesses the feasibility of the program. Each session was observed by a member of our research team, who took detailed notes (as did the instructors, immediately after the sessions). We also interviewed club leaders, staff, and the kids themselves. For the remainder of this chapter, we draw on that data, and our personal experiences, to reflect on what we learned.

What We Learned: Plot Twists and Turns

We thought we knew how the story would unfold, even if some tweaks were required by our younger audience and the club setting. Alas, the narrative was

Table 5.3. Curriculum outline.

I. Module 1: Discovering Forgiveness

 A. What is forgiveness?

 B. What forgiveness is not (e.g., weak, compliant, excusing bad behavior)

 C. Putting transgressions into words

 D. Forgiveness Tree Connection—A metaphor for forgiveness/ forgiving community

II. Module 2: Why Should I Forgive?

 A. Reasons to forgive (e.g., clearing the air, religious/cultural, healing self/ relationships)

 B. Establishing safe boundaries (adult help may be needed; avoiding toxic relationships)

 C. Consequences of unforgiveness/revenge (e.g., cycles of revenge, emotional burdens)

 D. Forgiveness Tree Connection—Branches (good relationships and their qualities)

III. Module 3: How Do I Forgive?

 A. *Hand of Forgiveness*: Mnemonic device for steps in communicating forgiveness

 B. Forgiveness Tree Connection—Roots (values, commitments)

IV. Module 4: Crafting Apologies

 A. Putting hurt and harm into words

 B. Elements of sincere apology

 C. Forgiveness Tree Connection—Leaves (messages foster renewal, change)

 D. Prep children to help with Forgiveness Tree ceremony

V. Module 5: Forgiveness Tree Ceremony

 A. Welcome the younger (8–10-year-olds)

 B. Basic discussion of hurt and forgiveness

 C. Show tree trunk and explain metaphor

 D. Rotate through FTP "Stations" (Torch Clubs kids lead art projects and discuss)

  a Roots Station: Why would you forgive a friend (or a friend forgive you)?

  b Branches Station: Which people do you care about? How are you connected?

  c Leaves Station: Write what you could say to a friend you hurt (who hurt you)

 E. Construction of tree: At each station help kids add roots/branches/leaves

 F. Gather around tree; discuss what it means to be a forgiving person/place/ community

enlivened by numerous unexpected events and circumstances, and the story line had to be changed, sometimes radically.

Teaching Forgiveness in Context: "After school, my club is controlled chaos"

As college instructors who are used to controlling our instructional spaces, we can assume a calm learning environment and a (mostly) attentive audience. In contrast, our first day in the club environment made one thing clear: If we were to teach these kids about forgiveness, we would need to work hard to keep their attention. Each of the three clubs offers a rich after-school environment tailored to kids of various ages, with computer labs, homework spaces, basketball courts, and free play areas. Caring adults keep gentle order and intervene when needed, and the kids move around the building in tightly choreographed shifts. But the hum of joyful conversation and the buzz of constant activity are facts of life in a Boys & Girls Club. Excited to be free from school, kids of all ages zip around joyfully, shouting greetings, and burning pent-up energy. Club managers tried to create quiet instructional spaces for us, but the results varied, and our instructional team labored to keep kids engaged. As this observation suggests, the hubbub of club life often invaded our instructional space.

> Megan and Dayna start the session by giving each other high fives as a way to reconnect [with the kids]. Megan starts a conversation with one boy who was in California last weekend. Dayna has a conversation with another peer. There is a counselor behind me with the door open, distracting students, with her walkie talkie. That counselor is yelling at her children. —Rob (observer, from field notes)

Cindy led the instructional team at Club A, our first pilot site. It was at her suggestion that we started providing pizza at every meeting as an incentive for kids to be there on time and stay focused in an environment characterized by competing activity, the din of after-school chatter, and occasional disruption.

> We had not considered the environment in the creation of the curriculum. That was a serious oversight. Numerous environmental factors were at play, including the P.A. system, the younger children coming in and out of our designated space, the noise from the gym, our kiddos having to leave to go to their basketball games and/or awaiting parents, as well as our providing pizza.

After observing several of our earliest sessions, Doug wrote in his field observation notes:

An important lesson has been going with the flow of the students' energy. A good example of this was Cindy's response to one student who was high energy and pressing to "toilet paper" something during the exercise where kids wrote on pieces of toilet paper. Cindy let the student toilet paper her, funneling the energy in a positive way that connected the students and leaders.

Indeed, we were reminded frequently that our curriculum was a tiny tributary in a gushing stream of valuable activities and frenetic energy that transpire every day at these clubs. Dayna facilitated the FTP at Club B and quickly learned to go with the flow.

> We had to show up with planned agendas and abundant activities, but it was imperative that we prioritize listening and engaging with kids ... In some cases, this meant scrapping an activity right in the middle. For example, when B&GC "National Pie Day" conflicted with one of our activities, we ended early and joined the kids in the gym, watching the kids smash pies in their brave leaders' faces. I recall the three of us realizing – sharing this community with the kids and leaders was way more important than teaching our forgiveness curriculum.

Understanding Kid Culture: "Forgiveness won't work in school because of bullies"

Our experience working with B&GC kids prompted us to revise our theorizing about forgiveness, as we realized that models based on adults inadequately address the culture of childhood communities. One cultural reality is the relative powerlessness that kids often experience in systems run by adults. The kids were often skeptical of apologies because they were often *forced* to apologize by teachers and parents. Martin, a realistic 12-year-old from Club B, described a conflict with another child, whom he derisively labeled "Trollnose" as the dispute unfolded in a classroom. Forced to apologize by his teacher, Martin shouted "Sorry Trollnose!" As a facilitator wrote in her field notes, "All of the kids moaned as they recalled their own experiences of being forced to apologize." With the help of the other Torch Club kids, Martin came to realize that a more generous apology was called for, and that providing one might be useful in creating some distance from a toxic peer. "I don't want anything to do with Trollnose, cuz he's got negative energy everywhere."

Some kids questioned if forgiveness was realistic in certain situations. For example, a young boy at Club C asserted, "Forgiveness won't work at school because of bullies." The topic of bullies was a recurrent theme across all sites. This realization compelled us to consider adjustments to our curriculum to account for the concern. Perhaps the most natural place to do so is in our discussion of relational safety in the context of boundaries and the role that adults (including B&GC staff) can play in discouraging bullying, while also assisting children to resolve disputes constructively. In this regard, we let the children know that they can choose to forgive a bully; however, forgiveness would not excuse the bully, imply reconciliation with a bully, or release adults from the responsibility of creating an environment where kids can see that safety prevails and rules are equally applied.

The kids at Club B were drawn from a neighborhood which had experienced ethnic conflict as its traditionally Native American population was partly displaced by a wave of immigrants from Mexico and Central America. Against this cultural backdrop of conflict, some of the children had been exposed to poverty and gang violence. Although their religious traditions valued forgiveness, families also prepared their offspring to defend their rights and honor. Field notes from Club B revealed that instructors were challenged to incorporate these cultural and family influences into the discussion.

> Topics such as suicide, retaliation, and physical violence more generally, are tough topics to discuss in relation to forgiveness. When a child's father tells him he will 'kick his ass' if he finds out that the child walked away from a fight– that's a tough spot as a facilitator.

Kids were surprisingly forthcoming in our sessions once they came to trust our facilitators, some sharing details about the hurtful encounters with peers and sometimes discussing their own transgressions against peers and siblings. We were struck by the heavy emotional burdens some of these young children were carrying, sometimes due to the strife they had witnessed among family members and peers. At a young age, many of these kids are embedded in a web of emotionally loaded relationships, some of which they kept tightly held, as if the peer group had signed a pact of secrecy and support. Our discussions of forgiveness allowed some kids to find new words to express the relational distress they were experiencing. At Club B,

> a few middle-school girls began to whisper and comfort one of their peers when another girl noted that not forgiving someone could cause the person to die by suicide. Based on the girls comforting their peer and by the peer becoming quiet and sullen, it seemed highly likely that this young girl knew someone who had recently died by suicide. —Dayna (from field notes)

Perhaps more than in our work with adults, we felt an extreme sense of responsibility for these kids, and we worked with B&GC staff to make sure they were looked after. Late in the project, having analyzed observational and interview data, we came to realize that our tree metaphor would be enhanced by more discussion of the "trunk." Signifying the individual's health and sense of personal power, the trunk is a springboard for discussions about a child's sources of strength and safety during emotionally demanding times. In this way, the child's personal well-being is placed in the center of the forgiveness tree, grounded by her values (roots) and the source of healthy and strong connections to others (branches).

Drafting (and Redrafting) the Curriculum: "We had to adjust quickly . . ."

The senior members of our team are parents, but our kids are older now. As we adapted the FTP for the Torch Club kids, it quickly became obvious that we had misread our audience. One problem: our material was too basic. These tweens knew a lot more about relationships and forgiveness than we had imagined.

> I distinctly remember that we underestimated the extent to which the kids might understand or know about forgiveness. We weren't prepared for them to be as knowledgeable as they were. We had to adjust quickly so that we were not talking down to them. . . . Our team would meet for dinner to discuss what had transpired during the previous session. Over the course of two to three hours, we brainstormed, made changes, and adapted the curriculum moving forward and going back. Change was constant. —Cindy (reported in her facilitator debriefing interview)

And yet, we noticed that some children, unlike most adults we work with, had a difficult time perceiving forgiveness as relevant to them. As Doug described in his research notes, it was easier to see how other kids needed it.

> The Forgiveness Roll-Up assignment encourages students to write names of students with whom they need to forgive or receive forgiveness. Three students couldn't think of anyone that they needed to forgive or who needed to forgive them (all three students were male). The [facilitators] tried to help by going through different scenarios where forgiveness might be warranted, but the students still didn't think forgiveness applied to them. At one point I talked with the students and asked if they could think of *friends* who needed to forgive or who needed forgiveness, and two of the students immediately brightened and began writing.

Another misplaced assumption involved the expression of emotion, a competency embedded in the second task in the CTF model. It turned out that some of these 10–12-year-old kids had yet to develop an emotional vocabulary. Quickly recognizing this, Cindy added a "feelings chart" to the curriculum, which proved quite helpful as kids struggled to express how they felt during conflicts with peers and family members.

> The "Feelings" chart has been used in every session when applicable, e.g. when we want the children to discuss their feelings. During the Hand of Forgiveness lesson ... we asked the children if any of them wanted a "Feelings" chart. Most of the children asked for a chart to help them to describe and name their feelings. While Courtney was completing the worksheet, she asked me to help her understand the feeling, "uncertain" in wanting to describe her emotions.

The B&GC staff helped us recognize ways to improve the curriculum. One staffer noticed that we emphasized "hands-on" activities over computer games and technology. In her experience, kids this age loved computer games and she suggested that integrating more games and technology into the FTP would keep them engaged.

What Works with Kids: The Bright Side of Our Story

We learned more about "what worked" with the kids from our interviews with the B&GC staff who observed our sessions, and from an analysis of the observational data provided by our own observers and facilitators. We began with the understanding that kids could learn forgiveness from stories (see Enright & Fitzgibbons, 2015), and several of our lessons invited kids to write their own stories, role-play parts in a relational drama, or critique the hammy, funny "performances" of our facilitators. One of these activities was the *Why I Like to Stay Mad* skit, in which two facilitators role-played in melodramatic fashion, an unproductive argument between three imaginary junior high characters. This skit, intended to convey the importance of boundaries and the dysfunction of holding grudges, was a big hit with kids at Clubs A and C. The staff member who led the Torch Club at Club C had this to say:

> It taught the students to be more intentional with their actions ... they gained more empathy and where other people are coming from. I really liked the idea of understanding other people's boundaries. I really liked that.

Kat played a key role on our data analysis team and her synthesis of what worked rings true. First, she noted, the FTP was most successful with the kids when it seemed different from "school." Indeed, "facilitators found that worksheets, specifically, should be used sparingly." So, what worked better?

> Giving kids a say in the curriculum was beneficial as well. Following a teasing issue between three kids, the facilitators at Club C created the Forgiveness Tree Project Rules to develop a safe environment for the participants. The kids

collaborated to make a poster that would display forgiveness rules to follow.—
Kat (synthesizing interview data)

Another strength of the curriculum was its utilization of relatable visual metaphors. Of course, the Forgiveness Tree is our guiding metaphor, and it seemed to help the kids organize and understand complicated concepts. Kids at Club B were sharing stories about when forgiveness was required, when one shared, "I think trees are a good symbol for forgiveness. Trees represent: growth, peace, [and it] has a lot of levels. Friendships work up into different levels, and when we forgive we become closer to people. Roots are crazy . . . your friendship can be crazy . . . lots of ups and downs."

Another successful metaphor was the "Hand of Forgiveness." Devised by Doug as a device for simplifying the CTF model, the hand associates each of the five fingers with important forgiveness lessons. For example, smallest finger is associated with the "pinky swear," a pledge to stick by the agreements that emerge from a forgiveness discussion.

> The kids were engaged and had fun with this activity. Shockingly . . . even Matt, who is usually disengaged, was engaged for the entire session. Caleb, who has not been a part of any previous sessions, was also very engaged. This was surprising to me . . . Andrea, who is normally quiet, was also engaged. This is the first session where I felt that all of the kids were truly engaged. When it was time for some of the kids to leave for basketball, they didn't leave, they stayed with us. That had not happened before . . . this was by far the more productive session we have had with the kids!" —Cindy (from field notes)

Learning activities that involved performance and active engagement were largely successful. For example, kids enjoyed concocting "lame apologies," such as "I am sorry your feelings were hurt, but that's too bad." Perhaps they had heard many of these. In our closing interview with the children, Max, a quiet boy from Club C, described the "crafting a good apology" lesson as his favorite part of the curriculum. He liked how the "roots" (of the forgiveness tree) made him remember to be strong and shared that he had recently apologized to a friend. The Torch Club supervisor at Club C thought the concluding forgiveness tree ceremony was the high point of the FTP sessions, because the kids were actively engaged as teachers and leaders of younger kids. Although it was clear to us that some of the younger kids were unable to process the idea of forgiveness, an observer of the ceremony at Club C wrote:

> Their [Torch Club kids] ability to articulate forgiveness concepts to the second-graders was impressive. They provided solid examples and presented numerous ways to communicate forgiveness. The forgiveness tree ceremony is

our opportunity to observe the Torch Club members teach the concepts they have learned ... from my observations, our approach is feasible ... it appears that the Torch Club members are retaining the information (observer field notes).

Research as Subplot: Adjusting Our Methods and Measures

In addition to adapting our curriculum, we adjusted familiar research methods to collect meaningful data on our pilot-test efforts. Vince scoured the literature, mostly in vain, for surveys of forgiveness that were appropriate for children. In the end, he pilot-tested an adult measure with a small group of children and adjusted the items that caused confusion. With Jonathan's help, he located outcome assessments that could be expected to change from pretest to posttest, if the FTP was having its intended effects. We decided on measures of empathy, constructive conflict management, attitudes toward violence, mood, and self-forgiveness. In the end, the quantitative data were a bit compromised by the noisy testing environment, a large variation in the comprehension levels of the kids, and the difficulty of locating some children for the posttest. Because the samples were small, and the curriculum was adjusted as we gained experience at the three sites, it proved impossible to assess the statistical effects of the program with any certainty. However, the self-report measures performed quite well, showing high levels of internal consistency. This increased our confidence in their usefulness in the next iteration of this project.

We learned much more from the vast amount of qualitative data we collected through the efforts of observers (posted in every session) and interviews with club managers, B&GC staff (present at every session), the Torch Club children (in focus groups), and our own team of instructor/facilitators. Thanks to an analysis conducted by Dayna, Cindy, Rob, and Kat, the data allowed us to assess the feasibility of the FTP in this setting and it generated numerous suggestions for improving the content and delivery of the curriculum. But research in the club environment offered unique challenges and responsibilities.

> While I had worked with children in the past, this was the first time I collected ethnographic fieldnotes when engaging children. As an observer, I would sit in the back of the room with my computer. Kids would rush into the room ready for their lesson and they paid little attention to me. There seemed to be little to no suspicion for why I was there taking notes. This served as a reminder for how vulnerable youth are and how ethical representations of youth need to be maintained integral. Rather than making assumptions of what kids were doing, I had to remind myself to only describe their behavior. —Rob (observer at Club B)

In some sessions, and especially with the forgiveness tree ceremony, our observers were overwhelmed by the variety and pace of activities, as kids rushed about, adults shouted directions, and the noise level escalated. It was impossible to record everything, but it helped that we collected observations from multiple perspectives: observers, facilitators, B&GC staff, and the kids themselves. As we contemplate the demanding role played by our facilitators and observers, all of whom were graduate students, it is clear to us now that we asked too much. As Dayna noted:

> Facilitating the learning sessions was exhausting and getting fieldnotes from facilitators was challenging (and I include myself here), especially from the doctoral students in the group who were doing this activity outside of their full-time (often 60+ hours/week) coursework and teaching loads. I think that this project will only be sustainable if we have either a) students enrolled in classes, or b) student workers, providing the ongoing labor.

Surprise Endings: "... it is incredibly easy to have genuine dialogue with children"

Despite working closely with our B&GC partners and having made significant adjustments along the way, our project still resulted in some surprises. One of those involved the kinds of kids that were most affected by forgiveness education. The original plan called for our audience to be comprised solely of Torch Club kids, the rising leaders. But unbeknownst to us, club managers assigned to us several kids who were experiencing interpersonal difficulties at the club, partly because they were unable to manage conflict. One of those was Rafer, who, according to the club manager at Club C, was noticeably changed by his introduction to forgiveness. Subsequent improvements in his relational skills rippled across his social network. This was confirmed at a debrief session held with the kids at Club C a few weeks after the FTP was completed. During that discussion, Kailee reported that she and Rafer had resolved peacefully some unresolved conflict during the lesson on crafting a good apology. As facilitator notes affirmed, she and Rafer got along "rather well" during subsequent sessions. From this surprising outcome, we concluded that our focus on children who have been identified as natural leaders should be expanded to include children who may be struggling to find their social footing at the club or elsewhere.

Another surprise ending was the amount of affection and attachment we felt toward these children over the course of just six training sessions. The forgiveness research conducted by Doug and Vince concerns deeply personal topics, but rarely do we develop close bonds with the people we study. We marveled at the connections that our talented facilitators, all of whom were graduate students, forged with these children. These connections were borne from their own sincere desire to help children grapple with the sometimes-painful complexities of human relationships. And they grew from the openheartedness of the B&GC kids and staff, many of whom were genuinely curious about our work and willing to go along with even our most puzzling schemes. More than the research we conduct "at a distance"—with our carefully worded surveys, structured interviews, and carefully controlled experiments—the hours we spent with these kids were meaningful, personal, and transformative. In reflecting on the project Cindy wrote:

> For me, the greatest take away was in the reality that it is incredibly easy to have *genuine dialogue* with children . . . profoundly deep conversations. I am still taken back all these months later by the realness in those moments. I can remember thinking what an honor it was to be a part of those conversations and the level of ethical responsibility I owed to the children for their honest self-disclosures.

The Story Continues

Having completed a promising pilot test and gathered considerable evidence on the feasibility of our project, we are seeking funding to expand forgiveness education more broadly. In our wildest dreams, forgiveness education is incorporated in Boys & Girls Clubs across the country. This community-based project required a considerable investment of administrative, instructional, and research energy as we collected evidence of its feasibility. But evidence-based programs are increasingly important for policy makers and private funders, for good reasons. Evidence-based interventions are generally well tested, have supporting materials (e.g., student workbooks), and offer training (Pettigrew & Gal, 2019). In addition to these pragmatic concerns, many organizations are highly invested in their clientele and want to serve them in the best possible ways. Organization leaders are reluctant to waste time and money on programs that have less chance of working, so they may turn to evidence-based curricula.

Qualitative data have proven useful in these efforts. Our analysis was conducted within the tradition of qualitative evaluation research generally, and more specifically, what Greene (1998) labeled an *interpretivist* approach. Here the key questions are not so much about summative program effects. Rather, qualitative assessment is useful in understanding the meaning participants derive from the experiences designed by trainers and how those understandings might facilitate or inhibit desired changes. Given an intervention that has proven useful elsewhere, qualitative data help researchers understand how/why it should be adapted to a particular population or unique context (Tucker Brown, 2011). It might reveal, for instance, that certain concepts (e.g., forgiveness) or metaphors (the forgiveness tree) have potent meanings because they are interpreted through a child's experiences with culture, religion, poverty, schools, and family conflict. It may also identify which program features can be replicated and transferred to other settings. In collecting and interpreting this data, we were cognizant of quality standards used to evaluate qualitative research of this type (e.g., Tracy, 2010), including richness of data, resonance, rigor, and transparency of methods.

This chapter is written at a time of great political and cultural divisiveness in our home nation (the United States) and elsewhere. Anger, grudge-holding, and retaliation often displace dialogue and compromise as favored responses to political differences. Although we hope children will reject rather than absorb these unforgiving attitudes, the intergenerational transmission of vengeance has been of concern in conflict-scarred regions, such as Northern Ireland. Our work builds on studies suggesting forgiveness education can reduce the hostility of children in such places (Enright & Fitzgibbons, 2015). It also responds to calls for studying the development of character in formative contexts, such as after-school programs (Clement & Bollinger, 2016). We are working in a tradition of intervention research that has been successful in improving the lives of families (e.g., Dishion, Nelson, & Kavanaugh, 2003; Guo et al., 2001; Smit et al., 2008), schools (e.g., Carney, Bronwyn, Louw, Okwundu, 2011; Gabrhelik, Duncan, Miovsky,Furr-Holden,Stasna, & Jurystova, 2012), and communities (e.g., Feinberg, Jones, Greenberg, Osgood, & Bontempo, 2010; Spoth et al., 2011).

Of course, we set out to answer a fairly simple question. Can our decades of academic research on forgiveness be made useful to preteens, real-life kids who are discovering through sometimes-painful experience that relationships can be disappointing, conflict-filled, and even hurtful? Although the story is far from complete, our current answer to that question is "yes." Thanks in part to the caring environment provided by Boys & Girls Clubs, kids can learn to be more forgiving, even in the face of disappointment and hurt. In fact, we found that many children are hungry for skills that will help them forge more peaceful and mutually respectful relationships. And that is a story worth helping to tell.

References

Carney, T., Bronwyn, J. M., Louw, J., & Okwundu, C. I. (2011). Brief school-based interventions and behavioural outcomes for substance-using adolescents. *Cochrane Database of Systematic Reviews, 1*, 1–63. doi: 10.1002/14651858.CD008969.pub3.

Clement, S., & Bollinger, R. (2016). Perspectives on character virtue development. *Research in Human Development, 13*, 174–181.

Dishion. T. J., Nelson, S. E., Kavanagh, K. (2003). The family check-up with high-risk youth adolescents: Preventing early-onset substance use by parent monitoring. *Behavior Therapy, 34*, 553–571. doi: 10.1016/S0005-7894(03)80035-7.

Enright, R. D., & Fitzgibbons, R. P. (2015). *Forgiveness therapy: An empirical guide for resolving anger and restoring hope.* Washington, DC: American Psychological Association.

Feinberg, M. E., Jones, D., Greenberg, M. T., Osgood, D. W., & Bontempo, D. (2010). Effects of the communities that care model in Pennsylvania on change in adolescent risk and problem behaviors. *Prevention Science, 11*(2): 163–171. https://doi.org/10.1007/s11121-009-0161-x

Gabrhelik, R., Duncan, A., Miovsky, M., Furr-Holden, C. D. M., Stastna, L., & Jurystova, L. (2012). "Unplugged": A school-based randomized control trial to prevent and reduce adolescent substance use in the Czech Republic. *Drug and Alcohol Dependence, 124*, 79–87. doi: 10.1016/drugalcdep.2011.12.010.

Guo, J., Hawkins, D. H., Hill, K. G., & Abbott, R. D. (2001). Childhood and adolescent predictors of alcohol abuse and dependence in young adulthood. *Journal of Studies on Alcohol and Drugs, 62*(6): 754–762.

Greene, J. C. (1998). Qualitative program evaluation: Practice and promise. In N. K. Denzin & Y. S. Lincoln (eds.), *Collecting and interpreting qualitative materials* (pp. 372–399). Thousand Oaks, CA: Sage.

Griswold, C. L. (2007). *Forgiveness: A philosophical exploration.* Cambridge, UK: Cambridge University Press.

Kelley, D. L., Waldron, V. R., & Kloeber, D. N. (2018). *A communicative approach to conflict, forgiveness, and reconciliation. Reimagining our relationships.* New York, NY: Routledge.

Kelley, D., & Waldron, V. (2005). An investigation of forgiveness-seeking communication and relational outcomes. *Communication Quarterly, 53*, 339–358.

Kloeber, D. K. (2014, January 16). *The Forgiveness Tree Project* [video file]. https://www.youtube.com/watch?v=G6s2cGfincY

Kloeber, D. K., & Waldron, V. R. (2017). Expressing and suppressing conditional forgiveness in serious romantic relationships. In J. Samp (ed.), *Communicating interpersonal conflict in close relationships: Contexts, challenges, and opportunities* (pp. 250–266). New York, NY: Routledge.

Nussbaum, M. C. (2016). *Anger and forgiveness: Resentment, generosity, justice.* New York, NY: Oxford University Press.

Pettigrew, J., & Gal, D. E. (2019). Implementing school-based programs. In J. D. Pozzulo & C. Bennell (eds.), *Working with trauma-exposed children and adolescents: Evidence-based and age-appropriate practices* (pp. 278–294). New York, NY: Taylor & Francis.

Pettigrew, J., & Hecht, M. L. (2015). Developing school-based prevention curricula. In K. Bosworth (ed.), *Prevention science in school Settings: Complex relationships and processes* (pp. 151–174). New York, NY: Springer.

Smit, E., Verdurmen, J. E. E., Monshouwer, K., & Smit, F. (2008). Family interventions and their effect on adolescent alcohol use in general populations; a meta-analysis of randomized control trials. *Drug and Alcohol Dependence, 97*, 195–206. doi: 10.1016/j.drugalcdep.2008.03.032.

Spoth, R., Redmond, C., Clair, S., Shin, C., Greenberg, M., & Feinberg, M. (2011). Preventing substance misuse through community–university partnerships: Randomized controlled trial outcomes 4½ years past baseline. *American Journal of Preventive Medicine, 40*(4): 440–447.https://doi.org/10.1016/j.amepre.2010.12.012

Tracy, S. J. (2010). Qualitative quality: Eight "big-tent" criteria for excellent qualitative research. *Qualitative Inquiry, 16*, 837–851.

Tucker Brown, A. (2011). *Using qualitative methods to evaluate public health programs.* National Center for Chronic Disease Prevention and Health Promotion. Available at: http://www.cdc.gov/dhdsp/pubs/docs/cb_november_8_2011.pdf

Waldron, V. (2017). *The middle years of marriage: Challenge, change, and growth.* New York: Peter Lang.

Waldron, V., & Kelley, D. (2005). Forgiveness as a response to relational transgression. *Journal of Social and Personal Relationships, 22*, 723–742.

Waldron, V., & Kelley, D. (2008). *Communicating forgiveness.* Newbury Park, CA: Sage.

Waldron, V. R., & Kelley, D. K. (2017). Negotiated morality theory: How family communication shapes our values. In D. O. Braithwaite, E. A. Suter, and K. Floyd (eds.), *Engaging theories in family communication: Multiple perspectives* (2nd ed., pp. 233–253). New York, NY: Routledge.

Waldron, V., Kelley, D., & Harvey, J. (2008). Forgiving communication and relational consequences. In M. Motley (ed.), *Studies in applied interpersonal communication* (pp. 165–184). Newbury Park: Sage.

Worthington, E. L., & Cowden, R. G. (2017). The psychology of forgiveness and its importance in South Africa. *South African Journal of Psychology, 47*, 292–304.

6 Cultivating a Space for Restorative Justice in Kansas: Exploring Opportunities for Restorative Justice through Dialogic Deliberation

GREGORY D. PAUL

Wrongdoing tends to spark several questions. Chief among them is the question of what should happen in response to wrongdoing. Although the conventional answer involves blaming and then punishing the person(s) deemed responsible for the wrongdoing, that answer tends to be deficient. For one, it ignores the many factors that contribute to people's tendency to engage in wrongdoing, whether those are individual, relational, organizational, or societal. For another, it relies on a response (punishment) that tends to be ineffective at teaching people new behaviors or helping them grow (Johnstone, 2001; Zehr, 2002). A better answer stems from an approach to justice that (1) accounts for the structural and systemic factors that influence people's behavior, (2) attempts to address those factors proactively and reactively, and (3) seeks restoration for both the wronged and the wrongdoer. This approach does not deny individual responsibility. Rather, it also recognizes the influence that relationships, systems, and structures play in shaping and changing human behavior.

In the context of responding to wrongdoing, this approach to justice is called restorative justice (RJ). Although there are numerous definitions of restorative justice, at its heart RJ emphasizes multidimensional restoration following harm to make things right individually, relationally, and societally (Daly, 2016; Gavrielides, 2008; Johnstone & Van Ness, 2007; Paul & Borton, 2017; Roberts, 2010; Rugge & Cormier, 2013). Generally speaking, RJ is an approach or orientation to resolving conflict, building peace, and restoring relationships that rests on values of learning; growth; healing; and support for individuals, relationships, and society at large (Borton & Paul,

2015; Braithwaite, 1999; Doolin, 2007; Okimoto, Wenzel, & Feather, 2009; Tsui, 2014; Zehr, 2009; Zehr & Mika, 2010). Scholars tend to distinguish restorative justice from *retributive* justice, which takes a tit-for-tat approach to justice, reciprocating negative behavior with negative consequences (Bergseth & Bouffard, 2007; Paul & Schenck-Hamlin, 2017; Tsui, 2014). Several processes fall under the umbrella of RJ, including victim-offender mediation (VOM), victim-offender conferencing (VOC), peace circles, and family group conferencing (McCold, 2000; Raye & Roberts, 2007). Each of these processes share common practices, such as dialogic communication and restoration (Paul & Riforgiate, 2015; Umbreit, 2001).

Although the use of restorative processes has expanded into a variety of contexts (Borton, 2016; Green, Johnstone, & Lambert, 2013; Johnson & Johnson, 2012; Morrison, 2006; Paul & Riforgiate, 2015; Shaw, 2007), RJ proponents identify numerous areas for further growth. For many practitioners, RJ is not limited to a process used in a particular context (e.g., VOM/VOC in the context of juvenile justice). Rather, it is a way of being, relating, and making meaning that focuses on restoring peace by restoring just relationships between people and justice positions in society (Vaandering, 2011; Zehr, 2002). Consequently, practitioners are focusing on how to develop social systems—not just the adoption of a particular process—that support growth in the use of restorative processes and practices in communities.

Such work is happening in a number of areas, including in several cities in Kansas, where there are a handful of restorative justice organizations. These organizations have been working in schools, with justice officials, and in their communities to expand their work and reach for a number of years. This chapter offers a summary of a series of conversations focused on developing such social systems that took place in four Kansas communities in 2016. These conversations aimed to bring stakeholders together to explore what was needed to develop support systems for youth in those communities when they engaged in wrongdoing. The conversations surfaced a number of steps stakeholders could take to develop positive support systems for youth and their families with the long-term goal of building stronger, more peaceful communities.

Transforming Conflict and Building Peace through Restorative Justice

Conflict transformation is distinct from simply settling an issue under negotiation or coming to agreement on a conflict issue. It involves approaching conflict issues, people, and relationships in ways that positively address the immediate situation, account for structural and systemic factors that contribute to the situation, and develop a framework that can contribute to the construction of a sustainable peace (Lederach, 2003). Transformation efforts address conflict on multiple levels with the goal of building positive, sustainable, and life-giving systems (Jameson, Bodtker, & Linker, 2010; Ledearch, 2003).

The emphasis on a multi-leveled, proactive, and responsive approach to addressing problematic situations corresponds with tenets of RJ (Zehr, 2009). Typically, when injustice occurs, such as when someone breaks a law or acts in a way perceived to be unjust toward another person or group, getting justice within a Western framework typically involves punishing the wrongdoer, whether through revenge (McCullough, 2008) or through the justice system (Braithwaite, 1989; Wachtel & McCold, 2001). This "eye for an eye" approach, as captured in the theory of justice world beliefs (Lerner, 1980; Paul & Schenck-Hamlin, 2017; Strelan, 2007), largely approaches accountability negatively (Newbury, 2008), focusing on ways to bring negativity to someone who brought negativity to others. Critics of this approach highlight its lack of effectiveness, its insufficient attention to the people harmed by the wrongdoing, and its backward-looking (as opposed to forward-looking) orientation (Paul & Borton, 2013; Umbreit, 2001; Wenzel, Okimoto, Feather, & Platow, 2008; Zehr, 2002).

A more effective approach to justice, some argue, can be found in restorative justice. RJ prioritizes values such as empowerment, learning, healing, growth, connectedness, and peace, as persons with a stake in the problematic situation dialogue with one another to experience (or at least set the groundwork for) restoration in situations of injustice (Borton & Paul, 2015; Braithwaite, 1999; Doolin, 2007; Okimoto et al., 2009; Tsui, 2014; Van Ness & Strong, 1997; Zehr & Mika, 2010). Such restoration can involve multiple types of reparation—symbolic, material, and emotional—as needed by victims (Paul & Swan, 2018). It also can include other outcomes that promote healing, growth, and potentially relational repair for victims and offenders (Paul & Dunlop, 2014). RJ proponents argue that restorative practices are more effective than conventional justice practices at helping all parties achieve closure, feel satisfied, and be able to move forward (Bergseth & Bouffard, 2007; Calhoun & Pelech, 2013; Gabbay, 2005; Lipsey, 1995; Vanfraechem, 2005). By working to restore justice in these specific instances, parties work to lay the foundation for sustained peace.

This approach to RJ, called here a *proceduralist* approach, tends to focus on the adoption of RJ procedures within existing systems. The proceduralist approach tends to define RJ rather narrowly, focusing on characteristics that make criminal justice procedures "restorative" rather than "conventional." From a proceduralist perspective, RJ offers an alternative process for responding to wrongful behavior in its focus on dialogue versus debate, storytelling versus argument, multidimensional restoration versus unidimensional compensation, accountability through reparation versus accountability through punishment, and victim inclusion versus victim exclusion.

Whereas the proceduralist approach aims to build a sustained peace within specific instances, the *structuralist* approach to RJ focuses on building integrated social systems that promote social justice and build a sustained peace. In other words, the vision of a structuralist tends to be bigger than a program or process; it instead is focused on the goal of building a social system through the use of *restorative practices* in which all elements of society work together to eliminate inequality, bias, and discrimination in all forms and in all contexts (e.g., social, economic, judicial, and more). Structuralists, then, see RJ as a *social movement* that aims to restore social justice for those who have experienced discrimination and bias not only in the justice system but also schools, communities, governments, workplaces, families, and other organizations. Thus, RJ is understood more broadly as a way of being, relating, acting, and communicating than as a specific process carried out in a specific setting.

Both approaches share a common foundation that draws on the symbol of "restorative justice" that is constituted by common values such as humanity, connection, learning, growth, and healing. Yet, the scope of their practices varies greatly. Within the proceduralist approach, there is greater focus on processes such as VOM and VOC as substitutes for or supplements to conventional criminal justice processes. In VOM/VOC, primary stakeholders (victim, offender, and facilitator) and interested secondary stakeholders (supporters of the participants and affected community members) come together to share their experiences of the wrongful situation, negotiate reparation, and decide together on what type of relationship they want to maintain going forward (Umbreit, 2001). Research suggests that such processes are effective at heightening victim satisfaction (Kurki, 2003), reducing offender recidivism (Latimer et al., 2005; de Beus & Rodriguez, 2007), lowering state costs (Gabbay, 2005), and facilitating closure (Armour & Umbreit, 2006).

A structuralist perspective, however, focuses not only on the implementation of specific processes but also on the creation of material, personal, relational, economic, and societal conditions that are consistent with restorative values. It sees the container or "black box" approach to RJ (Paul, 2016b) that focuses solely on the implementation of RJ processes within a given setting is overly narrow. This wider approach means that RJ work can include a wide variety of behaviors and efforts (together known as restorative practices) that are designed to promote restored social justice for all.

The question confronting practitioners working from either of the approaches is similar: *How can one create settings that are ripe or conducive for RJ?* From a proceduralist perspective, the answer to this question largely consists of arguments demonstrating restorative practices' relative effectiveness compared to conventional practices (Bergseth & Bouffard, 2007; Calhoun & Pelech, 2013; Gabbay, 2005; Lipsey, 1995; Vanfraechem, 2005) and research about factors that influence openness to RJ processes (e.g., Paul, 2015, 2016a; Paul & Swan, 2018; Paul & Schenck-Hamlin, 2017). The thinking is that decision-makers will gravitate toward procedures that are more efficient and effective at accomplishing desired outcomes. One concern with the proceduralist approach is that restorative processes implemented in conventional environments may have difficulty thriving because of incongruent aims (Paul & Borton, 2017). Moreover, there is at least some pressure on justice officials to demonstrate support for justice outcomes as conventionally described by the public at large. Structuralists address this concern by trying to replace existing systems with new systems that are conducive to the values and practices associated with RJ. The question for structuralists is less, "does it work more effectively," and more, "what do we need to change to make it work?"

It was this interest in evaluating the ripeness of communities for RJ that provided the impetus for a series of community conversations geared toward growing the work RJ in Kansas. This chapter provides a summary of the themes that emerged from those conversations, focusing on the practices and values that conversation participants felt should be embraced in order to create conditions that facilitated positive youth development. Although the conversations were largely centered on issues pertaining to youth, the ideas emerging from those conversations have important implications for transforming conflict and building peace in communities.

Conversation Framework and Contexts

The genesis for the idea of hosting community conversations came out of a connection with Cynthia Nietfeld, a practitioner involved in regional RJ efforts. As we learned of each other's backgrounds and interests in growing RJ locally, we landed on the idea of hosting deliberative conversations in communities around Kansas that focused on ways to implement restorative practices in those communities. Funded by Kansas State University's Center for Engagement and Community Development and the Kettering Foundation, we set out planning our next steps in four communities around

Kansas: Manhattan, Topeka, Wichita, and McPherson/Newton. These four communities were chosen based on their demographics; locations; and efforts made in the areas of juvenile justice, restorative justice, and youth support.

Guided by literature and support from the National Issues Forum and the Kettering Foundation, we followed similar processes for all four sites in terms of community entrance, conversation framing, and conversation hosting. First, Nietfeld would make contact and meet with community stakeholders to introduce the project, get a feel for their work, and invite them to a "framing meeting." This would typically take several weeks to meet with various stakeholders from law enforcement, the court system, schools, mental health organizations, and other community agencies. Second, we conducted a framing meeting in which we facilitated conversation among stakeholders to introduce one another, discuss goals related to juvenile justice, identify issues affecting the accomplishment of those goals in their communities, and identify other stakeholders participants felt should take part in the upcoming community conversation. This was as much a "feeling out" meeting as it was a framing meeting, as all of us were trying to make sense of one another and the work to be done. We tried to demonstrate our desire to support ongoing efforts rather than be outsiders parachuting in with a sense of us "knowing what's best." We were not always successful with all groups, as we experienced difficulty with a contingent of law enforcement officials in one area who were uncertain what to make of us. This was more the exception than the rule, however, as we found that most stakeholders appreciated being able to amplify their work in their communities.

Buoyed by the positive energy and momentum from the framing meeting, we would then work on developing an issue guide, recruiting facilitators and participants, and managing logistics. The issue guide, which all participants had at their community conversations, grew out of stakeholders' ideas and goals identified during the framing meeting. It framed the conversation within local and state contexts; identified three topic areas to be covered in conversations; and provided various "pro" and "con" lists, tensions, and questions for participants to consider. Concurrently, we worked on recruiting facilitators and conversation participants. Most facilitators were connected to a dialogue and deliberation group at Kansas State University and had prior experience. Participant recruitment occurred through organizations and existing relationship networks. Nietfeld and I tended to find our niche in these responsibility areas as we negotiated our various other responsibilities and commitments.

One hundred eighty-six people (thirty-six in Manhattan, fifty in McPherson/Newton, thirty-eight in Topeka, and sixty-two in Wichita) participated in the community discussions. Included among participants were police officers, school resource officers, teachers, professors, mental health professionals, parents, youth, and other interested community members. At the conversations, which took place in public places (a church, a library, a nature preserve, and a convening space on a university campus), circle tables were set up and food was provided for all attendees. Participants were welcomed by facilitators and thanked for their attendance. At the beginning of each of the four events, we described the purpose of the conversation as a first step in identifying practices to support youth, identified conversation guidelines, and answered procedural questions. Participants were given informed consent forms for conversations to be audio-recorded, to which they could provide or withhold their consent. At the conclusion of the conversations, each group reported out themes or important points in their conversation for all participants to hear. The meeting ended with a discussion of next steps for community members to take. Immediately following the discussion, we worked to generate a report reflecting participants' words, ideas, and suggestions. We then emailed that report to all participants within a week following each conversation.

Transcriptions of discussion recordings generated 778 single-spaced pages. Following the thematic analysis process laid out by Braun and Clarke (2006), transcripts were read multiple times to identify recurrent themes in the conversations. Analysis involved coding data into emergent categories and then comparing those categories with each other to explore relationships among them. The focus during the coding process was on identifying specific action steps (i.e., manifest content) and connections among those steps to enable a wider systems-level view of factors that would address youth wrongdoing and promote positive youth and family support.

Creating Communities of Support

Based on framing meeting discussions in each of the four locations, each community conversation took slightly different directions. In Manhattan, the focus was on "positive youth development," looking at supporting families and youth through formal education, community resources, and formal justice procedures. In McPherson/Newton, the focus was on "creating connections, supporting families, and building community." Participants explored ways that communities, schools, and the legal system could prevent and respond to times when youth got into trouble. In Wichita, the meeting was framed as a way for participants who were "ready for change" to learn about and discuss responses to youth behavior together, focusing on the community's role in school discipline policies, juvenile justice changes, and support for positive youth development. In Topeka, the focus was on "cultivating cultures where families can thrive," with particular attention to positive family, school, and community cultures.

The discussions surfaced several practices, policies, and potential problems connected with preventing and responding to youth wrongdoing and creating communities of peace and support. Conversation participants identified relational and systemic factors that could support youth development and be responsive to youth needs in their communities. Two general themes that emerged were (1) growth through learning and (2) proactive and reactive support for both youth and parents. These themes connected closely with restorative responses to wrongdoing.

Growth through Learning

One of the central themes in the four community conversations pertained to the importance of learning so that youth and caregivers could "invest in themselves" and grow. Participants indicated that growth was a constant need for both youth and adults alike, and that growth was most likely to occur if someone was alongside youth and their caregivers teaching them both formally and informally and helping them learn more about themselves and others.

Areas of growth. Key areas of growth related to personal development, relationship development, career development, and general "soft skills and communication." Participants felt that youth needed to learn more about several topics, including emotional intelligence, goal setting, mindfulness, bullying, poverty, cultural competency, and general social skills. A Wichita participant reflected positively on her school's program that helped students learn about personal goal setting and build relationships with specific teachers and with a consistent group of peers over their time in the program. This was similar to a program in Manhattan in which teachers met with a small group of children for 20 minutes, one day per week, to develop peer relationships among those children. A Manhattan participant indicated,

> Everybody has something … going on in their life at different times and stuff. And I think mixing those kids together where there's some- some kids that haven't been in trouble or maybe some- just different things and then realizing that you're all kind of in the same boat. It's just a little bit- it looks a little bit different for each kid and they start to … really accept one another and kind of look at them different.

A teacher in McPherson/Newton noted the positive changes happening in her classroom while teaching children social skills.

> One of the things that we do in the morning for our morning meeting is we learn how to talk to each other, we learn how to pay a compliment, how to accept a compliment. They don't know how to do that. You should have seen my kids the first day we did it. When we first implemented morning meeting, it would go around and I would say, 'Okay so now you turn to the person to your left and say good morning, how are you?' They wouldn't look at each other and they won't, you know. Then I would stop and say, 'Okay now the right thing to do, when you're in a conversation with somebody, is you have to look at ...' To watch the transformation in these kids in the amount of time that we've been doing it.

By understanding themselves and others and building close relationships with peers and teachers, youth can build a network of supporters who can help them work through difficult situations.

Participants also indicated that parents and caregivers also needed growth in social and relational skills and networks. This growth often came by developing healthy peer relationships and sharing information and experiences about parenting and community resources. Organizations such as Parents as Teachers and Early Head Start gave parents a peer-support network that could "build relationships with parents to help them learn effective ways to encourage their children" (Manhattan). A Topeka participant expressed hope for a program in which "the kids are getting help, [and] their parents are also getting help in that system. We'll see how that works out, but it sounds like a really good system." In Wichita, a participant described the formation of a "parental advisory committee" for parents whose children were in juvenile detention, in which parents would receive peer support coupled with family functional therapy. As stated by Topeka participants, "it's all about educating parents right from the beginning," recognizing that parents "are the first educator of [their] child."

Facilitators of growth. In addition to discussing *what* youth and parents should be learning, participants also discussed *who* should be teaching: teachers, mentors, and peers. A McPherson/Newton participant noted,

> If you get it at a young age, when you see that start to happen, and you get somebody in there that shows them unconditional love,... it gets them that choice to just want to better and strive better and create a lasting relationship with that person that sticks around and shows them unconditional love, I think that would be good—mentor, youth support, relationships.

Likewise, another McPherson/Newton participated noted,

I think it's easy for an adult to come and tell a kid. But I think sometimes it takes somebody of their age group. Somebody that is living the same age group with them. … Maybe by being that friend, something they see every day, they can help steer them and introduce them to more kids their age … positive kids.

For youth, having both peers and adults who were able to support and model positive ways of behaving and relating was crucial for connection. Likewise, for parents, being able to connect with other parents who could provide emotional, instrumental, and informational support was valuable, particularly given the difficulties faced with parenting.

Roadblocks to growth. Participants identified a number of difficulties facing parents that necessitated such support, including parents' experiences as children, poor mental health, lack of awareness of community resources, lack of understanding of current pressures youth face, and lack of time to attend parenting classes. A Manhattan participant gave voice to these issues, saying,

They are used to yelling at the kids or 'You get me in trouble because the school's calling me now.' It's all negative. It's all punitive ….They didn't know any other method of practice. And going to parenting school? 'I don't have time for that. I have to go to work. I have three jobs I have to take care of.' So they don't have time for parenting classes.

The aforementioned statement pointed to a second issue—insufficient access to resources. Participants noted that although "parents need resources and help, number one," "there's a lot of mental health services for children, but not a lot for parents … Parents can't get access to services." Participants also expressed frustration that services weren't available when parents needed them. A Topeka participant reflected this concern, saying, "Parents might want to go in the daytime. Can they come in the evening? Where are they? Are they a match with the time for the parent to actually use them? There are services, but can we really use them, because I've got to work these crazy hours." Transportation to services was also a problem, given that people often relied on public transportation, which was inefficient and problematic. Given the difficulty, it was vital for parents to have someone around them who could teach them not only about parenting practices but also about human development, positive communication, and conflict management skills.

In short, participants felt that it was essential to promote growth of youth and parents through learning inside and outside the classroom from teachers, peers, and mentors. By continuously learning about themselves and others around them, youth and their families would be better able to make sense of their experiences, provide support for those around them, and work through difficult situations.

Proactive and Reactive Support

Dovetailing with the importance of growth through learning was the theme of support for youth and families. This support, formalized as "circles of support," "positive youth supports," "support systems," and "multi-tiered systems of support," was necessary for people regardless of whether they were facing challenging and uncertain situations. Participants spoke to the importance of having proactive and reactive systems of support.

Building support systems. As noted earlier, participants across all four sites spoke about the need for both youth and families to be surrounded by supporters who could proactively provide emotional, informational, and instrumental support. In school settings, participants discussed the need for mentoring programs to have more extensive access within schools so that students could talk with a mentor when needed. A Wichita participant indicated that

> There's so many non-profit organizations in Wichita. We are not at a shortage of non-profit organizations or community organizations that are doing their own mentoring or tutoring programs that can help. It's just getting them attached to the school so they're not picking and choosing kids out of nowhere.

These programs should be open to everyone so as not to single out particular youth, as a Manhattan participant noted. Moreover, participants stressed the need for positive peer relationships that modeled appropriate ways of behaving, developed understanding connections, and fostered awareness and understanding of oneself. A Wichita participant also asserted that businesses should support employees taking time off of work to go into a school and serve as a mentor. For parents, participants positively reflected on the work of Parents as Teachers. Funded by public and private dollars, Parents as Teachers is a community agency that works with parents to provide training and information about other community programs to parents.

Proactive support for youth also came through activities. A number of participants noted that activities provided a sense of fulfillment, provided life skills, and reduced unsupervised times that were associated with wrongdoing. A mother in Wichita noted that her son's love for drama and participation in plays is "what keeps him on track." Another Wichita participant discussed the need to "engage [youth] after hours" and "connect kids to positive activities." A Manhattan participant likewise asserted that

> The number one cause of recidivism is not having positive youth activities. It's not what's going on in the home, it's not socioeconomic status, it's not gender, it's nothing. It's whether or not there is anything else for them to do other than commit a dumb mistake.

This sentiment was echoed in McPherson/Newton, where participants talked about "thinking about what do we do to busy that mind and those hands and keep them out of trouble."

Another source of support was from parents, particularly through engagement in schools and youths' lives. Again, participants across all four areas that parental involvement in education was key to youth success and learning. A McPherson/Newton teacher noted that "the best luck I have with students is when parents are involved. Getting parents involved with kids and with schools too." A Manhattan participant agreed, saying

> You have to involve the, engage the families too ... The more for an idea to have salience, it helps to come from multiple perspectives. And so for being taught while you're at school about these practices and then you go home, they can be reinforced by your parents. You have a bunch of different voices speaking into that and reinforcing that idea.

In Wichita, a participant noted,

> The reality is a lot of people don't have parents who they can go home to and get help with homework and they don't have parents who care to hear about their day or how they are preforming at school. And I am sure that you are aware of that already, like I am not trying to label that. But that is the part that I am concerned with in our community is even those who do have parents, the lack of parents who care who are showing up for those things.

For participants, parent involvement in school and in children's lives was crucial for success. This involved more than parent–teacher conferences. It involved providing the parents tools to know how to communicate with their youth and parent them positively and constructively.

Roadblocks to support. The main issue that arose when discussing support systems was traced back to funding and poverty. In terms of youth activities, participants frequently cited the lack of funding as a deterrent to youth participation. For example, a Manhattan participant noted, "There's a lot of different types of programming, but unfortunately that stuff isn't free." A Wichita participant echoed the concern, saying, "That's the problem with after school activities. They've got to catch the bus and I know there's a late bus as well, but try to deal with transportation when you don't have neighborhood schools anymore." Likewise, parents working multiple jobs to make ends meet face extraordinary hurdles in being present at home and in schools. A Wichita participant compared family wealth to a "social airbag" giving people access to additional resources. However, families in poverty are less likely to have such a support cushion, instead having to rely on community organizations that they may not be able to coordinate with due to needing to work multiple jobs. Consequently, funding was a key concern in terms of providing support structures to youth and parents alike.

Another concern was connected to the need for organizations to collaborate and coordinate rather than compete with each other. A Topeka participant indicated,

> I see a lot of different agencies doing a lot of the same work, and we're not talking to each other. I think that might get confusing, a lot of times. I would like to see something that's a little more streamlined, us all working together rather than building silos, so it's a little easier to get the services you need.

In Manhattan, participants noted that such collaboration would enable organizations who don't provide a particular service to find other organizations that do and then connect people with those organizations. In Wichita, a participant indicated that

> We have to figure out a way to merge efforts, which I think we're trying to do in our community. We're at a place [where] we're working together to look at a crossover youth practice model where the children's home, the department of corrections, and the school district, and mental health services, and addiction services, and all of the stakeholders at the table that provide public services to youth and families can be very early on.

However, funding and the fear of losing funding to other organizations were ever-present concerns that drove organizations to be more siloed and competitive.

The picture that emerged was one akin to an integrated team that wrapped around people in need. Rather than operating in silos, organizations should be working together to bring relevant organizational members to the table and support people who needed them. Those key constituents included members from nonprofit organizations, particularly mentoring organizations; schools; the justice system; and mental health agencies.

Learning, Support, and Collaboration in Responses to Wrongdoing

The principles of growth, learning, support, and collaboration were evident not only in ideas for how to help youth and parents grow, but also in ideas for how to address youth wrongdoing. A McPherson/Newton participant noted,

> You want them [i.e., youth] to take responsibility for their actions. You want them to have accountability to the person or persons they caused harm to. And lastly, you want them to have growth so that they aren't making the same mistakes and not continuing down the path they obviously are. I think the ultimate goal of any discipline is that you correct negative behavior.

These principles of responding to wrongdoing were rooted in perceived causes of wrongdoing and perceived flaws in conventional responses to wrongdoing.

Factors influencing wrongdoing. Mirroring concepts discussed earlier, participants felt that youth wrongdoing was a function of multiple factors. As a McPherson/Newton community member stated,

> You have to look at the whole child, and it's beyond just a judgment for what he did. I think you have to look at the whole person and the circumstances. I'm not saying they should get off for what they did, but did you at least need to look at, is it a family issue? Is there more going on?

In particular, people highlighted the interdependent factors of mental health, self-concept, and family pressures.

Mental health was seen as an important but under-addressed factor driving youth wrongdoing. A youth participating in one of the conversations relayed her own experience:

> I know I'm not supposed to but in high school I got into a suspension. I did it on purpose just so I could sit in a quiet room and do my homework. I had terrible OCD and ACD. I could not take tests or do anything in front of the kids. Even if just the resource was a number of kids, I had to be alone ... I had a Prairie View person come in. I went to the resource officer with me because she was the only person who knew I loved school. I'm a nerd. I love doing other people's homework for fun. She knew that it was just being quiet, not that I didn't want to do it. She helped me get the resource to be alone in the room and she helped me with a bunch of stuff.

A Manhattan participant provided another example, linking outbursts linked to autism with throwing a chair, which could lead to a battery charge. A Wichita participant noted,

> It's a huge problem about mental health, and that's more than just our community. I think there's not much known about effective mental health treatment for children or adults. Maybe what the community needs is to acknowledge that we need to spend more money learning about how to treat mental health issues.

Coupled with untreated and/or undiagnosed mental health were problems associated with family life, including lack of structure and problematic parenting practices. The lack of structure, according to a Manhattan community member, meant that youth did not respond well in schools when adults asked them to follow directions. Failing to follow directions in turn led to problematic behavior that disrupted the classroom, which led to other issues. Moreover, the lack of structure often reflected other problematic parenting practices or parents' inability to be present with their children due to working multiple jobs. A McPherson/Newton participant asserted that

> It's wrong of us to assume that these kids know better, because they may not have ever seen anything different. Maybe they're seeing lying, stealing, drug dealing in their home and then when they get in the system, we're like, 'Shame on you, you should have known better.' [They need] and advocate, somebody who is going to hold their hand, more or less, teach them, 'You know, what you did was wrong, and this is what it looks like when you do it the right way.'

Such advocacy was reflected in programs like the ones discussed in Topeka that focused more on prevention rather than postvention, educating parents about constructive parenting practices.

One outgrowth of these and other factors was the development of a poor self-concept or lack of constructive social skills. A Manhattan participant asserted that "it's like their basic needs totally are messed up. And so it's hard to learn or be, I mean, even proud of who you are. It just leads down a whole chain of thing." A Wichita man reflected on his own experience, indicating that self-image and neighborhood pressures, combined with a lack of present parents, led to his incarceration earlier in his life. A youth in McPherson/ Newton similarly noted that his experience in group homes taught him problematic ways of behaving.

Problematic responses to wrongdoing. Based on these beliefs about factors that led youth to getting into trouble, participants shared a number of ideas about ineffective and effective responses to wrongdoing. Participants largely panned conventional responses, particularly out-of-school suspension (OSS), mandatory reporting, and overcriminalization. Participants felt that OSS, which they criticized as being "stupid" and "ridiculous," merely exacerbated problems by giving a consequence that did not address the causes of problematic behavior. A teacher commented,

> I've been a teacher for 27 years, and I've never been a proponent of out of school suspension for anything. I agree we're short staffed and things like that. But I guess, right there, that's one that I feel like, when there is an issue with a child, a student usually, it could be an addiction, it could be a mental health issue, behavior disorder, or just an emotional situation. I guess that's been my frustration for 27 years is we don't address the problem, which is kind of a community family problem.

By not addressing the factors contributing to problematic behavior, schools were simply compounding the issue by causing youth to fall further behind in their school work. A number of participants connected school suspensions with the school-to-prison pipeline, in part because OSS leaves youth unsupervised, "which means if they're kicked out of school, that's when they get in trouble. . . . If a kid is suspended, all you do is given him a much wider window to get in trouble." Moreover, participants noted that OSS was sometimes seen as "rewarding [youth] for that behavior." As another McPherson/ Newton person noted, "I would like to have seen more options versus ISS [in school suspension] or out of school suspension, either one. OSS, out of school suspension, is the dumbest thing in the world because they just go home and sleep."

Just as participants felt that OSS was problematic, they also faulted overcriminalization of what they perceived to be typical youth behavior. A Manhattan participant noted,

> But it's one of those things where we have seen a criminalization of what was once typical teenage behavior. Like, as you know, a fight in school among high school students now comes with a battery charge, which did not use to be the case. So now it's going to intake at JIAC for what was once, you know, in school suspension. You need to figure it out. These are your peers. The world is crowded, and dirty, get your elbows in sort of behavior is now coming with a criminal record.

A teacher in Topeka echoed this sentiment, saying,

> To me, the biggest one, and then one that drives me nuts sometimes, is their [failure] to stop the criminalization of school misbehavior. This happens in our school. I'm trying to wean myself out as much as I can . . . A student doesn't want to give you their cell phone is not a reason to call the officer to the classroom. He's not the right person . . . There's many other things. It's stopping the criminalization of misbehavior.

This criminalization was driven in part by the fuzzy relationship between law enforcement and school officials. A Manhattan participant provided a hypothetical example to illustrate the issue:

> I can speak in very general terms. School administrators are responsible for administrating the school and maintaining order in the school. Police are not very good at that. That's not really what they're there for. Police are very good at dealing with enforcement issues at the school refers to them. Now, it's a double-edged sword. You have two kids, one stole something from the other kid and the other kid punches him in the face over because there was a confrontation. So is that a school matter that should be handled by the school or is that a matter that should be handled by the police as a theft and a battery? Well, congratulations, if you're a school administrator, you get to decide, and whatever you decide, you know [is it].

The decision to keep matters "in house" versus referring to law enforcement has significant implications for involved youth. If police take over, criminal charges could be pressed. As a McPherson/Newton participant stated, "If you lock them up and you give them the title of the crime when they're young, then it goes like people don't want to hire them because of the crime they did. Kind of ruins their chances of getting a good job ... It just ruins their life."

Interestingly, another source of problems for participants was mandatory reporting. As mandatory reporters, teachers and administrators are responsible for reporting to authorities certain issues that they become aware of, including those related to mental health and abuse. The problem that arises is that these same school officials are being asked to develop trusting relationships with youth, which could lead to disclosures by students of issues that officials are required to report. Consequently, youth are left doubting whom to trust, in part because they fear the consequences of sensitive disclosures. This was reflected by a McPherson/Newton parent, who indicated, "I had a daughter say the wrong thing to a mental health person and landed her in a mental health institution for a week. You have to be very careful, and you learn that early on." A different McPherson/Newton participant also pointed to the problem that mandatory reporting created.

> There's a couple of obstacles too. As they take a kid in, before they give them the suspension, and they ask them, they do a counseling session. Why did you do this, what's wrong at home? Two things happened with my daughter. One, she isn't a sharer. She's a very private person. Two, kids that are raised in poverty in the system learn not to tell. They know everybody they talk to is a mandatory reporter. Depending on what's going on, they won't say, because they won't want to have to go through that ... They don't have anyone in the school system they can trust because everybody is a mandatory reporter.

Thus, even when trying to dig into underlying causes of youth wrongdoing, policy-driven barriers make the discovery of those causes more difficult due to lack of trust. This affects both students and parents. In Wichita, where parents must swipe ID cards to enter schools, a participant shared her experience of parents asking other parents to go into a school to pick up their child. The problem? The ID check automatically revealed warrants for arrest, which school officials were mandated to report. Thus, parents were afraid to go into schools, even though school officials wanted parents to be more involved.

Restorative responses to wrongdoing. These issues provide the context for approaches to responding to youth wrongdoing that participants felt were more helpful. Such responses focused on learning, accountability, connection, and concern for the whole person, with the goal of keeping youth out of the justice system and addressing factors causing youth wrongdoing.

Perhaps most reflective of this approach was a school in Wichita which was actively implementing both multi-tiered systems of support and restorative justice to prevent and respond to youth wrongdoing. As a Wichita participant described it, this approach was:

> A demonstration project in restorative practices, which is the umbrella under which restorative justice fits. And to make a long story short, essentially when people do wrong in our society, what we often ask is what happened and then we ask who's responsible and then we ask how do we punish them? What we're working toward instead is asking, what happened, who was harmed, and how and what do we do to make things right? That's a very different approach. The question we often don't get to when we're dealing with juvenile justice is what do we need to do to make things right. Because the law says if this infraction happens and this is what's supposed to happen as a result of that, but that's not usually very helpful. It's generally we punish people, whether it's in school or in society.

The consequence of that approach, as stated by another participant, was a 10–12% reduction in school suspensions.

Restorative processes, whether in schools or in communities, shared a number of characteristics. First, they were responsive to youth needs, particularly in situations where trauma might be involved. A McPherson/Newton participant commented,

> They need to know that there are consequences to their actions, but they also need to know that they're not their action or their consequence. You cannot punish the trauma out of a kid. If they're having a meltdown because of something traumatic and they threw a chair, I'm not going to spend 15 minutes lecturing them about that chair.

By surfacing outside factors that might be contributing to wrongdoing, an individualized response that combines multiple resources can be created that will address those factors as well as the consequences of those factors. Second, restorative processes avoided removing students from support systems, instead working to surround students with a support structure and keep them connected to already existing sources support (e.g., sports teams). A McPherson/Newton participant commented,

> I think that would help bring more community members from all over the place, the restorative justice initiation. That would-that could bring in community members from all different areas and can really start developing more of a community around the kids that need that type of assistance, you know, and need to be kind of turned around.

Third, they kept the youth out of the conventional justice system and associated school-to-prison pipeline. If there are practices set up that divert youth from the conventional justice system, whether teen court, peer mediation, victim-offender mediation, or the like, youth are able to take responsibility for their behavior without the stigma and baggage associated with criminalization. Fourth, restorative processes emphasized learning and changing to a "growth mindset." As described by a Manhattan participant,

> So the kid's not bad, the behavior's bad. That is a subtle shift, but it's something that's really, in terms of how you view yourself, really important that you can change. And if you made a mistake, you have hope that you have an opportunity to improve.

A student echoed the importance of learning, stating:

> You know. They have to experience what it's like to get that and somebody take it from them. They have to experience this person had to work 6 hours to make this or breaking something. This person had to work. They have to work that many hours or whatever to account for that. Maybe I shouldn't. It's a lot of work to get to this. Kind of show them what it's like to get what they did. Say they broke into somebody's house and stole a TV or something. This is how long I had to work to get to this. Life hours to get to this. You just take it. You know. I guess kind of show them what they have to do to get something.

Fifth, restorative processes held youth accountable. A McPherson/Newton participant noted, "At some point, you have to make sure you're not enabling this kid. You've got to take action. When it happens, you've got to act, not let it slide." This accountability provides structure for youth and helps them to learn the individual, relational, and systemic consequences of their behavior.

A sixth characteristic should also be noted. The shift to restorative processes goes hand in hand with developing a positive, non-adversarial relationship with law enforcement. Participants in the four locations commented on the problematic relationship youth have with law enforcement. For example, one discussant noted, "One thing that comes to mind fairly readily, because it's been in the news a lot, is that law enforcement is not necessarily a friend." A participant in a different area felt that police "are out to get high school kids. Out to get them. Teachers will tell that, parents will tell you that, they are out to get kids no matter what it is." However, participants also indicated that a positive step that they were starting to see was a closer and more regular relationship between youth and police. Whether, as a Wichita participant noted, taking a mentoring role or working actively to build rapport, building closer relationships with youth could help deescalate situations and shift the focus in responding to wrongdoing from punishment to support.

Discussion

Lederach (2003) shows that conflict transformation offers "life giving opportunities for creating constructive change processes that reduce violence, increase justice in direct interaction and social structures, and respond to real-life problems in human relationships" (p. 14). For all of the pain and loss induced by wrongdoing and injustice now and in the past, individual, relational, and societal transformation also is possible. Whether we take advantage of those opportunities is driven largely by how we make sense of those injustices and our response to them, which in turn is a function of individual, relational, and systemic factors. From the conversations in four Kansas communities, it is clear that the path toward learning, growth, and peacemaking requires a collaborative effort among multiple stakeholder groups that provides adults and youth the resources and opportunities to process their past and learn constructive ways of acting with each other, with their peers, and with the community at large. Taking this path can produce systems in which restorative processes and practices can thrive.

The collection of practices outlined earlier reflect principles of peacemaking that align with the concept of restorative justice and its associated values such as moral learning, growth, supportiveness, and accountability (Paul & Dunlop, 2014; Wachtel & McCold, 2001). For such practices to thrive, they must be connected to a network of other practices with similar ideological foundations (Paul, 2016b; Paul & Swan, 2018). However, it is not enough simply to pick and choose which practices to offer. Practices feed off of each other and constitute an ecology suitable for the growth of restorative processes and practices in communities. Combining mentoring practices with mental health offerings with after-school activities with restorative processes can create conditions where youth, their caregivers, and the community can learn and move forward.

In many ways, this echoes Block's (2008) discussion of restorative communities that shift conversations

> from problems to possibility; from fear and fault to gifts, generosity, and abundance; from law and oversight to social capital and chosen accountability; from the dominance of corporation and systems to the centrality of associational life; and from leaders to citizens. (p. 47)

At the heart of these shifts, as with the concept of justice, is the idea of accountability (Block, 2008). Conventional systems tend to be bureaucratic in nature—impersonal, controlling, isolated, rule-driven. It is not at all surprising that conventional justice systems, political systems, and community systems reflect similar principles. Each system suffers from common faults: lack of engagement, divisiveness, poor judgment, low self-efficacy, lack of coordination, lack of shared learning, and distrust (Mathews, 2014). These faults are rooted in part in an absence of positive accountability to one another. Yet, what conversation participants were calling for was a turn away from conventional systems and a move toward restorative systems characterized by "citizens' willingness to own up to their contribution or agency in the current conditions, to be humble, to choose accountability, and to have faith in their own capacity to make authentic promises to create the alternative future" (Mathews, 2014, p. 48). Such systems are characterized by accountability-as-care, involving a turn toward each other, a recognition of interdependence, and an appreciation for ongoing dialogic conversation.

How, then, do we begin to create conditions for restorative communities to emerge? And how can engaged scholarship contribute to the creation of those conditions? Answers to these questions lie in the answers to several related questions.

Who should be at the table? The short answer is everyone, because community develops in the mundane conversations of everyday life. The longer answer is that, if focused on developing processes or systems, multiple stakeholder groups should be deeply involved in creating restorative systems: youth; caregivers; education officials; community organization representatives; law enforcement officials; justice system officials; elected officials; experts in sociology, human development, and communication; and more. Participants will bring with them expertise from both their lived experience and their professional experience. Moreover, the relationships held by these participants will enhance the quality and reach of the change effort.

This, of course, begs the question of how to go about recruiting, motivating, and encouraging people to gather around the table. This work seems to be done most effectively by those already living and working within the communities where the work is occurring. In our experience, as outsiders in most of these communities, recruitment was the hardest part. Nietfeld was active in going into communities, introducing herself to people in particular positions, describing the project, and getting a foot in the door. This created a snowball effect that tended to attract others. Of course, we had to be mindful of local politics, of which as outsiders we were sometimes problematically unaware. While outsiders can help to start a project, it seemed to us that insiders were the only ones who could carry it to completion.

This also begs the question of who should be at the table in terms of the composition of the engaged research team. Given the diversity of themes and subject areas, it seems especially important for this work to be done by a team of people with diverse skill sets, backgrounds, and outlooks. Nietfeld and I knew quite a bit about RJ, but we didn't know as much as we should have in other areas that came up. Having a team that is committed to the same end goal while using their diverse expertise and skill sets can help to ensure the ability to address systems level issues that arise. Moreover, ensuring that local community members are part of the team helps to ensure the ability to address local-level issues that arise. Of course, as discussed a little later in this chapter, such teams can experience meaningful tensions that force everyone to keep asking questions that are central to the effort, including who should be around the table and what should they do while at the table.

What kinds of processes should stakeholders follow? There are a variety of facilitated discussion models that can be suitable. Our use of the framework provided by the National Issues Forum was useful for prompting discussion about particular question dimensions, though it would likely have been more useful had we been discussing specific action steps and comparing costs and benefits of those steps. Because we were not yet at that point, we realized we needed to back up a bit to focus more on developing a common set of goals and perspectives rather than specific action steps. Regardless, providing stakeholders the opportunity to meet regularly with each other to identify goals and value commitments, explore background issues, identify action steps, and decide on how to proceed with action steps can be helpful. At each of these points, engaged scholars have an opportunity to provide useful background research and data to be considered during discussions.

How regularly should parties meet? Developing and maintaining systems of support is an ongoing process that needs regular conversation and planning. Meeting frequently to share concerns, imagine possibilities, and detail action steps is crucial. For community conversations, it is imperative that those conversations act as starting points rather than ending points. One-off conversations are less effective than ongoing conversations that have community buy-in. Creating momentum for ongoing rather than one-off conversations is also tied in with people recruited to participate in the process. Insiders who are invested in the work will continue that work long after outsiders have come and gone.

What outcomes are likely to occur? In some ways, the collaborative process described earlier *is* an important outcome, reflecting principles of collaboration and multivocality that will persist for as long as conversations continue. Such persistence is vital—the creation of ripe conditions is not a once and done performance. Outcomes are created and recreated through ongoing dialogue and deliberation among stakeholders. These outcomes are likely to vary by community, as communities have different needs, concerns, and characteristics. Moreover, these outcomes are likely both extrinsic and intrinsic, unfolding over time. Thus, having a narrow view of effectiveness in this work can be overly limiting and can potentially end up sacrificing long-term change for short-term evidence of change.

What tensions may occur? Tensions do not have to be negative or problematic—they can be productive and animating. To be clear, tensions are part of restorative justice (Gavrielides, 2008; Paul & Borton, 2017). Any process that involves creating transformative systems is likely to run into tensions regarding process, outcomes, and scale. Particularly with restorative justice, where there are differences between proceduralist and structuralist aims, approaches to accomplishing system transformation likely will differ. These tensions likely will influence issue framing, stakeholder involvement, discussion goals, timelines, types of arguments/evidence valued, and scope of change sought. Facilitators and change agents would do well to surface their underlying beliefs about restorative justice to work through these tensions on an ongoing basis. Indeed, these underlying beliefs and values influence the communication dynamics also at work in engaged scholarship (Connaughton et al., 2017).

Our experience was no exception. We discovered as we finished the first round of discussions that we approached RJ rather differently—I as a proceduralist outsider and researcher who was relatively new to Kansas and Nietfeld as a structuralist quasi-insider and community change agent who had contacts in a variety of communities. These tensions caused us to stop and start, to evaluate and reevaluate our aims, and to explore one another's expertise and passions. We often needed to recalibrate in terms of what we were asking facilitators to do during the meetings, what we were expecting by the end of the meetings, and what we should do following the meetings. It was difficult and at times frustrating, knowing that we had (mostly) similar long-term aims but preferring different approaches to accomplishing those aims.

The work also opened my eyes anew to the tensions of doing this work within a conventional university context. As an assistant professor on the tenure track at the time of this engagement, I found myself wrestling with questions like: how do I devote sufficient time to this work while fulfilling my other teaching, research, and service responsibilities (not to mention family responsibilities)? Will this work "count" toward research? How do I blend my research and community support goals? How do I explain to someone not in the academy that I have to care about conventional research products like articles and book chapters and that I can care about both research *and* community engagement—that they are not mutually exclusive? How do I explain to university decision-makers who may hold more conventional definitions of research that engaged and public research is just as (if not more) meaningful than traditional research that tends to be relatively insular and siloed? Does my conventional research matter as much as helping to create transformative systems that will support youth and families? As an academic, am I always consigned to being an outsider, even in my own community? In many ways, working to meet my academic obligations while helping build youth support systems was exhausting and energizing, frustrating and rewarding, confusing and clear, guilt-inducing and satisfying. Trying to do this with someone who approached the world differently than I did heightened these emotions. Yet, it was our differences that also helped this work progress.

Moreover, even as this work wound down, my grappling with these questions never did. The questions undergirded a period of deep frustration with the academy and its conventional silos, aims, and processes, leaving me wondering whether I wanted to continue my academic career when there was more I wanted to do. They then provided me a way through that frustration as I reconstructed my scholarly choices so that I could work to being an academic committed to building and supporting others in building communities of peace through dialogue, democracy, and engagement. These questions keep me centered and searching while I work toward the hope that we can transform the academy-community relationship through engaged scholarship.

Conclusion

While "community" occupies an important place in the literature on restorative justice, it remains a rather amorphous concept (Walgrave, 2002). On the one hand, community as "communities of care" (Bolivar, 2012; Schiff, 2007) support participants in restorative justice processes such as victim-offender conferences. On the other hand, and as illustrated in these conversations, community as collaborators include those people and groups that are working to create large-scale systems that are conducive to the growth of restorative practices. This shift in our thinking about community moves us away from "black box" thinking on restorative justice (Paul, 2016b) and toward a systems-level understanding of restorative justice in which restorative principles are integrated into a larger system sustained by diverse groups of interdependent, collaborating stakeholders. Such collaboration ideally involves ongoing dialogic and deliberative conversations that identify desired goals and outcomes, potential hurdles, community resources, communication plans, and courses of actions within specific timeframes.

This systems perspective of restorative justice extends an argument about the utility of a bona fide groups perspective on victim-offender conferencing

(Paul, 2016b). Such a perspective highlights principles of identity, membership, interdependence, and (importantly) context. Widening our lens, we see the vital role of context in the continuation of restorative justice. It simply is not enough to perform restorative justice in a vacuum and hope that it persists. For restorative processes and practices to be around for the long haul, practitioners and researchers must work to cultivate a *system* that is ripe for persistence. This means that restorative justice work must involve designing support systems characterized by restorative principles of connection, learning, and growth and adapted to fit specific cultural contexts. Although the process for developing such systems is long and difficult, the potential rewards it offers in the forms of lives, relationships, and communities are rich and well worth the effort.

References

Armour, M. P., & Umbreit, M. S. (2006). Victim forgiveness in restorative justice dialogue. *Victim and Offenders, 1,* 123–140. doi: 10.1080/15564880600626080.

Bergseth, K. J., & Bouffard, J. A. (2007). The long-term impact of restorative justice programming for juvenile offenders. *Journal of Criminal Justice, 35,* 433–451. doi: 10.1016/j.jcrimjus.2007.05.006.

Block, P. (2008). *Community: The structure of belonging,* 2nd ed. San Francisco: Berrett-Koehler.

Bolivar, D. (2012). Community of care from a victim-perspective: A qualitative study. *Contemporary Justice Review, 15,* 17–37. doi: 10.1080/10282580.2011.589671.

Borton, I. M. (2016). Transforming marital conflict through restorative justice. In P. M. Kellett & T. G. Matyok (eds.), *Transforming conflict through communication in personal, family, and workplace relationships* (pp.131–140). New York: Lexington Books.

Borton, I. M., & Paul, G. D. (2015). Problematizing the healing metaphor of restorative justice. *Contemporary Justice Review, 18.* doi: 10.1080/10282580.2015.1057704.

Braithwaite, J. (1989). *Crime, shame, and reintegration.* New York, NY: Cambridge University Press.

Braithwaite, J. (1999). Restorative justice: Assessing optimistic and pessimistic accounts. *Crime and Justice, 25,* 1–127. http://www.jstor.org/stable/1147608. doi: 10.1086/449287

Braun, V., & Clarke, V. (2006). Using thematic analysis in psychology. *Qualitative Research in Psychology, 3,* 77–101.

Calhoun, A., & Pelech, W. (2013). The impact of restorative and conventional responses to harm on victims: A comparative study. *British Journal of Community Justice, 11,* 63–84. doi: 10.1080/10282580.2010.498238.

Connaughton, S. L., Linabary, J. R., Krishna, A., Kuang, K., Anaele, A., Vibber, K. S., & Jones, C. (2017). Explicating the relationally attentive approach to conducting engaged communication scholarship. *Journal of Applied Communication Research*, *45*, 517–536. doi: 10.1080/00909882.2017.1382707.

Daly, K. (2016). What is restorative justice? Fresh answers to a vexed question. *Victims & Offenders*, *11*, 9–29. doi: 10.1080/15564886.2015.1107797.

de Beus, K., & Rodriguez, N. (2007). Restorative justice practice: An examination of program completion and recidivism. *Journal of Criminal Justice*, *35*, 337–347. doi: 10.1016/j.jcrimjus.2007.03.009.

Doolin, C. (2007). But what does it mean? Seeking definitional clarity in restorative justice. *The Journal of Criminal Law*, *71*, 427–440. doi: 10.1350/jcla.2007.71.5.427.

Gabbay, Z. D. (2005). Justifying restorative justice: A theoretical justification for the use of restorative justice practices. *Journal of Dispute Resolution*, *2*, 349–397.

Gavrielides, T. (2008). Restorative justice—the perplexing concept: Conceptual fault-lines and power battles within the restorative justice movement. *Criminology & Criminal Justice*, *8*, 165–183. doi: 10.1177/1748895808088993.

Green, S., Johnstone, G., & Lambert, C. (2013). What harm, whose justice?: Excavating the restorative movement. *Contemporary Justice Review*, *16*, 445–460. doi: 10.1080 /10282580.2013.857071.

Jameson, J. K., Bodtker, A. M., & Linker, T. (2010). Facilitating conflict transformation: Mediator strategies for eliciting emotional communication in a workplace conflict. *Negotiation Journal*, *26*, 25–48. doi: 10.1111/j.1571-9979.2009.00252.x.

Johnson, D. W., & Johnson, R. T. (2012). Restorative justice in the classroom: Necessary roles of cooperative context, constructive conflict, and civic values. *Negotiation and Conflict Management Research*, *5*, 4–28. doi: 10.1111/j.1750-4716.2011.00088.x.

Johnstone, G. (2001). *Restorative justice: Ideas, values, debates*. Portland, OR: Willan.

Johnstone, G., & Van Ness, D. W. (2007). The meaning of restorative justice. In G. Johnstone & D. W. Van Ness (eds.), *Handbook of restorative justice*. (pp. 5–23). Portland, OR: Willan.

Kurki, L. (2003). Evaluating restorative justice practices. In A. von Hirsch, J. Roberts, A. Bottoms, K. Roach, & M. Schiff (eds.), *Restorative justice and criminal justice: Competing or reconcilable paradigms?* (pp. 293–314). Portland, OR: Hart.

Latimer, J., Dowden, C., & Muise, D. (2005). The effectiveness of restorative justice practices: A meta-analysis. *The Prison Journal*, *85*, 127–144. doi: 10.1177/0032885505276969.

Lederach, J. P. (2003). *The little book of conflict transformation*. Intercourse, PA: Good Books.

Lerner, M. (1980). *The belief in a just world: A fundamental delusion*. New York: Plenum.

Lipsey, M. (1995). What do we learn from 400 research studies on effectiveness of treatment with juvenile delinquents? In J. McGuire (ed.), *What works: Reducing reoffending- Guidelines from research and practice* (pp. 63–78). New York: Wiley.

Mathews, D. (2014). *The ecology of democracy: Finding ways to have a stronger hand in shaping our future*. Dayton, OH: Kettering Foundation Press.

McCold, P. (2000). Toward a holistic vision of restorative juvenile justice: A reply to the maximalist model. *Contemporary Justice Review*, 3, 35–414.

McCullough, M. E. (2008). *Beyond revenge: The evolution of the forgiveness instinct*. San Francisco: Jossey-Bass.

Morrison, B. (2006). School bullying and restorative justice: Toward a theoretical understanding of the role of respect, pride, and shame. *Journal of Social Issues*, 62, 371–392. doi: 10.1111/j.1540-4560.2006.00455.x.

Newbury, A. (2008). Youth crime: Whose responsibility? *Journal of Law and Society*, 35, 131–149. doi: 10.1111/j.1467-6478.2008.00418.x.

Okimoto, T. G., Wenzel, M., & Feather, N. T. (2009). Beyond retribution: Conceptualizing restorative justice and exploring its determinants. *Social Justice Research*, 22, 156–180. doi: 10.1007/s11211-009-0092-5.

Paul, G. D. (2015). Predicting participation in a victim-offender conference. *Negotiation and Conflict Management Research*, 8, 100–118. doi: 10.1111/ncmr.12049.

Paul, G. D. (2016a). But does it work? The influence of perceived goal attainment effectiveness on willingness to use legalistic and restorative responses to offensive behavior. *Communication Studies*, 67, 239–258. doi: 10.1080/10510974.2015.1121157.

Paul, G. D. (2016b). A bona fide group perspective of restorative justice: Implications for researchers and practitioners. In P. M. Kellett & T. G. Matyok (eds.), *Transforming conflict through communication in personal, family, and workplace relationships* (pp. 125–130). New York: Lexington Books.

Paul, G. D., & Borton, I. M. (2013). Exploring communities of facilitators: Orientations toward restorative justice. *Conflict Resolution Quarterly*, 31, 189–218. doi: 10.1002/crq.21073.

Paul, G. D., & Borton, I. M. (2017). Toward a communication perspective of restorative justice: Implications for research, facilitation, and assessment. *Negotiation and Conflict Management Research*, 10, 199–219. doi: 10.1111/ncmr.12097.

Paul, G. D., & Dunlop, J. (2014). The other voice in the room: Restorative justice facilitators' constructions of justice. *Conflict Resolution Quarterly*, 31, 257–283. doi: 10.1002/crq.21091.

Paul, G. D., & Riforgiate, S. E. (2015). "Putting on a happy face," "getting back to work," and "letting it go": Traditional and restorative justice understandings of emotions at work. *Electronic Journal of Communication*, 25, 3–4.

Paul, G. D., & Schenck-Hamlin, W. (2017). Beliefs about victim-offender conferences: Factors influencing victim-offender engagement. *Conflict Resolution Quarterly*. doi: 10.1002/crq.21190.

Paul, G. D., & Swan, E. C. (2018). Receptivity to restorative justice: A survey of goal importance, process effectiveness, and support for victim-offender conferencing. *Conflict Resolution Quarterly*. Advanced online publication. doi: 10.1002/crq.21238.

Raye, B. E., & Roberts, A. W. (2007). Restorative processes. In G. Johnstone & D. W. Van Ness (eds.), *Handbook of restorative justice* (pp. 211–227). Portland, OR: Willan.

Roberts, M. L. (2010). Evaluating evaluation: An investigation into the purpose and practice of evaluation in restorative justice based programs (Unpublished master's thesis). Canada: Simon Fraser University.

Rugge, T., & Cormier, R. (2013). Restorative justice in cases of serious crime: An evaluation. In E. Elliot & R. M. Gordon (eds.), *New directions in restorative justice: Issues, practice, evaluation* (pp. 266–277). Portland, OR: Willan.

Schiff, M. (2007). Satisfying the needs and interests of stakeholders. In G. Johnstone & D. W. Van Ness (eds.), *Handbook of restorative justice* (pp. 228–246). Portland, OR: Willan.

Shaw, G. (2007). Restorative practices in Australian schools: Changing relationships, changing culture. *Conflict Resolution Quarterly, 25*, 127–135. doi: 10.1002/crq.198.

Strelan, P. (2007). The prosocial, adaptive qualities of just world beliefs: Implications for the relationship between justice and forgiveness. *Personality and Individual Differences, 43*, 881–890. doi: 10.1016/j.paid.2007.02.015.

Tsui, J. C. (2014). Breaking free of the prison paradigm: Integrating restorative justice techniques into Chicago's juvenile justice system. *Journal of Criminal Law & Criminology, 104*, 635–666.

Umbreit, M. S. (2001). *The handbook of victim-offender mediation: An essential guide to practice and research.* New York: Jossey-Bass.

Vaandering, D. (2011). A faithful compass: Rethinking the term restorative justice to find clarity. *Contemporary Justice Review, 14*, 307–328. doi: 10.1080/10282580.2011.5 89668.

Vanfraechem, I. (2005). Evaluating conferencing for serious juvenile offenders. In E. Elliot & R. M. Gordon (eds.), *New directions in restorative justice: Issues, practice, evaluation* (pp. 278–295). Portland, OR: Willan.

Wachtel, T., & McCold, P. (2001). Restorative justice in everyday life. In H. Strang & J. Braithwaite (eds.), *Restorative justice and civil society* (pp. 114–129). New York: Cambridge University Press.

Walgrave, L. (2002). From community to dominion: In search of social values for restorative justice. In E. G. M. Weitekamp and H-J Kerner (eds.), *Restorative justice: Theoretical foundations* (pp. 71–89). Portland, OR: Willan.

Wenzel, M., Okimoto, T. G., Feather, N. T., & Platow, M. J. (2008). Retributive and restorative justice. *Law and Human Behavior, 32*, 375–389. doi: 10.1007/ s10979-007-9116-6.

Zehr, H. (2002). *The little book of restorative justice.* Intercourse, PA: Good Books.

Zehr, H. (2009). The intersection of restorative justice with trauma healing, conflict transformation and peacebuilding. *Journal of Peace and Justice Studies, 18*, 20–30. doi: 10.5840/peacejustice2009181/23.

Zehr H., & Mika, M. (2010). Fundamental concepts of restorative justice. In C. Hoyle (ed.), *Restorative justice: Critical concepts in criminology* (pp. 57–64). New York: Routledge.

7 Fraught Times: Engaging Systemic Issues of Hate Online

JOHN DREW AND DEVIN THORNBURG

The transformative integration of social media into our daily lives has introduced a plethora of profound implications for global peace strategies writ large, and some of which are still emergent and, yet, increasingly disruptive. While there have been many positive and revolutionary outcomes associated with the horizontalizing of information distribution that the internet (and social media networks in particular) has triggered (Gilder, 1994; Rheingold, 2003; Jenkins, 2006; Benkler, 2006; Castells, 2011; Safranek, 2012), we posit that there are some relatively new socio-technological developments associated with today's social media landscape that now pose multiple threats to our species' struggle for greater world peace. These dangers which include international terrorism, heinous hate crimes and election meddling, among others, demonstrate the emergence of a new horizon in global information warfare, and thus, require an updated framework for what engaged scholarship around peace and conflict should include. What's more, some of the most powerful and influential technology companies in the world (Google, Facebook, and Twitter) are driving some of these historic changes but are doing so without actually maintaining full control—or even awareness—about how their technology is being adopted and exploited, the consequences of which have been profoundly destabilizing and show little sign of abating. We argue that it is useful to understand the contemporary social media landscape as a "superorganism" (Kelly, 2010), and one whose increasing socio-technological complexity may in fact be diminishing contemporary prospects for sustained peace. But rather than succumb to the remarkable power of this so-called "superorganism," we find it imperative to consider how online conflict fundamentally requires scholars engaging in strategies for peace to expand how they engage with conflict more broadly speaking. Indeed, we tend to think of scholarly engagement in general as being involved on the ground with a place in the physical world—but engaged scholarship, we argue here, now urgently necessitates deep involvement in online conflict realities as well.

To this end, we have identified two highly distinct but troublingly related instances where the contemporary social media landscape has been carefully exploited to perpetuate divisiveness, violence, and deep conflict; yet, despite great public attention around these two particular case studies, their sustaining socio-technological survival mechanisms remain largely intact. These examples include the rise and alleged fall of ISIS and the digital election strategy of Donald Trump. When these two phenomena are analyzed in the context of the world's deepening refugee crisis and the concomitant rise in nationalism and xenophobia worldwide (Harvey, 1996), we believe they pose an even greater threat, and especially since the underlying mechanisms that brought both Trump and ISIS great power continue to operate freely, and yet, opaquely to many people.

Intended Audience

Before we can explore why today's social media landscape necessitates fresh approaches to what engaged peace-related scholarship might look like, however, it is useful to define what we mean by peace and who we consider as our audience for this type of research and practice. To be sure, there are myriad voices and strategies both within academia and outside of it that are currently engaged in the very difficult task of promoting peace in places mired in human violence and we are not in a position to account for such diversity and complexity within our species' broader efforts to reduce said violence. Instead, our address here is tailored for academics and both government and non-government organizations alike that have become increasingly concerned about and (counter) active around the multitude of ways in which hateful and violent messaging are spread specifically in online environments. Indeed, our hope is that by critically analyzing the texture and composition of some of the newest and more destructive socio-technological developments within mainstream social media environments, we are able to share some strategic recommendations for more systematic peace-driven interventions in online spaces in the future. We also remain aware that the very notion of peace is a relative one but for the purposes of our analysis we consider peace as an ideal where both individuals and communities are able to survive without mental or physical stress imposed by other human beings and we refer to it in a similar context to the way in which the League of Nations was conceived following the aftermath of World War I (see Armstrong, 1982). While difficult to achieve or sustain, its existence as an ideal may still serve as benchmark in which to compare new trends over time, such as the emergence of ISIS and its deft use of social media to broaden its reach and violent ideology.

ISIS and Social Media

While Jihad-related terrorism dates back to the 1980s (Bar, 2004), many scholars point to the origins of ISIS in Iraq in 2003 as a result of the U.S. invasion and occupation, when its then-leader Abu Musab Zarqawi pledged an allegiance to Al-Qaeda, the group responsible for the attacks on the World Trade Center and the U.S. Pentagon two years before. A U.S. airstrike killed Zarqawi in 2005, and the group subsequently became the Islamic State of Iraq (ISI), led by Abu Omar al-Baghdadi. As the Iraqi war continued, al-Baghdadi was killed and replaced by Abu Bakr al-Baghdadi.

Mainstream media depictions of the Iraq war through the decade were largely focused on searching for "weapons of mass destruction" and the effort to topple Saddam Hussein, less on the activity of ISI, or Daesh, its Arabic acronym. This focal point changed dramatically with the beginning of the U.S. withdrawal from Iraq and the simultaneous commencement of the Syrian civil war in 2011, with ISI growing in its influence and size in both countries (hence, the name change to ISIS: Islamic State of Iraq and Syria). As jihadis from Europe, Chechnya, North Africa, Jordan, and Saudi Arabia, to name a few territories, made the journey to join the announced "caliphate," the group aggressively began to exploit social media to project power to the West. The publishing of beheadings of Syrian soldiers, international journalists, and humanitarian workers became commonplace across social media platforms such as Twitter, Facebook, and YouTube and brought a surge of international attention to the organization. Indeed, on November 13, 2014, Baghdadi used social media to release a 17-minute audio tape calling on ISIS sympathizers to "erupt volcanoes of jihad everywhere" (Kirkpatrick, 2014) and sympathizers heeded his call: as of 2015, and by a significant margin, ISIS has been responsible for the highest number of terror attacks worldwide (National Consortium for the Study of Terrorism and Responses to Terrorism, 2017). And while ISIS's geographic territorial hold has since been eliminated, ISIS's violent messaging and psychological hold very much lives on precisely because of social media's unique capacity to persist and be easily searchable across networks over time (Boyd & Ellison, 2007). Indeed, we ask, in a social media landscape literally flush with millions of fake accounts (Confessore & Dance, 2018) and where violent, hateful, and strategic messaging among terrorists and bots alike is constantly being posted and reposted, and highly, if not entirely anonymously, to what degree are governments in a position to respond?

Social media messages from ISIS are typically filled with themes and visual imagery of glory, adventure, and purpose and often tell a consistent and highly visual story that self-sacrifice is honorable and justify violent means and this is significant given that Kruglanski et al. (2014) have proposed that the theology or philosophy of many terrorists may not be as compelling among potential recruits as the psychology of it. In addition to the human need for cognitive closure explained by Kruglanski (1989), Kruglanski et al. (2014) argue that the need to feel personally significant is very much at play when one begins to consider pathways toward violent extremism. Noting that closure may be a heightened need around the globe in the current moment—given various contemporary and global waves of immigration, economic recession, and political instability—Kruglanski et al. (2014) argue that a fundamentalist ideology provides clarity of choice and contingencies between actions and consequences. Put simply, a sense of control and a potential way forward is often offered and we would like to suggest that this sense of clarity may in fact be heightened by the nuances of social media environments.

For one, social media has become global, social, ubiquitous, and cheap (Shirkey, 2008), which means that the messaging and propaganda tool organizations like ISIS have proven so adept at exploiting are highly accessible and can have tremendous reach. Second, when one couples the psychological vulnerability and social marginalization of young men and women that have been forced to abandon their homelands as a consequence of war and extreme violence, among other factors, and yet somehow manage to migrate to countries with very different cultural traditions, customs and social norms, and where they are increasingly made to feel unwelcome by anti-immigrant media, laws, policing patterns, and general public vitriol associated with shifting demographics and national resource burdens, it should come as no surprise that a smartphone connected to social media may subsequently serve to offer some psychological respite, if not socio-political refuge. Indeed, what makes social media platforms like Twitter, Facebook, and YouTube so financially successful lies in their profound capacity to keep their users connected to their families, friends, followers, and the social and political trends the user most closely identifies with. This means that when a particularly marginalized youth is trying to socially and economically navigate life in a fundamentally new country and respective social, political, and religious landscapes, social media has the power to serve as some sort of virtual lifeline, whereby the user is able to partially connect with other like-minded people experiencing similar fears, anxieties, aspirations, doubts, hardships, and personal challenges, and even if those people are relative strangers and/or remain in the homeland or in an entirely different nation.

The significance offered through the extremism of ISIS, and particularly vis-à-vis their social media exploits, allows for a sense of greater purpose and meaning to be peddled, which has long been established as a psychological need (Lifton, 1999) and is further heightened by a sense of loss that extremism on social media can emphasize. Individuals often experience uncertainty over questions of existence and morality. They are not certain about their purpose in life and their obligations to humanity. They are not sure which behaviors are appropriate. These questions are, arguably, insoluble and thus amplify uncertainty (Hogg, Adelman, & Blagg, 2010).

Kruglanski et al. (2014) suggest that the desire for personal significance can sometimes follow an accelerated path to violence and combat, resulting in the hopeful dominance over others and often the channeling of a need for sex and aggression into meaningful and sacred motivation. And such motivation now seems nearly infinitely abundant thanks to the social media that ISIS sympathizers and recruiters produce, all of which reinforce the perception of ISIS as ruthless, powerful, and in search of the divine, and namely "because their power derives from their ability to inspire dread out of proportion to the threats they actually pose" (Koerner, 2016). Furthermore, as Koerner (2016) argues, by embracing the internet's crowdsourcing tools and capacity, ISIS recruiters do not try to control who dispenses their message, which only further serves to bolster popular perception of their powerhold since this messaging is now pervasive across platforms and is being amplified by thousands of both private and public social media accounts.

ISIS sympathizers actively invite and encourage potential new sympathizers to create largely anonymous social media accounts and across a wide variety of platforms (Koerner, 2016) in the service of spreading their violent messages and religious extremism.

This crowdsourcing of propaganda responsibilities has never been witnessed before, and to this day, Twitter, Facebook and Google have yet to unanimously figure out how to put a clear and firm stop to it, despite being called upon to testify about the situation by both the U.S. (Hern, 2018) and U.K. governments. And while Facebook claims that their Artificial Intelligence (AI) technology is now able to detect (before any human user has flagged it) 99% of Islamic State and Al-Qaeda-related content that the company ultimately removes, Facebook executives still caution that the system remains imperfect namely because it is not designed to work across all languages and stylistic differences among all terrorist groups (Kahn, 2017). Moreover, even as some sources such as Peter Neumann, who runs the International Center for the Study of Violent Extremism and Political Radicalisation at Kings College, London, indicate that there has been a relative decline in terrorist content on major social media platforms in recent years, many argue, including Neumann, that much work remains to be done.

For example, the Counter Extremism Project (CEP), which is a non-governmental organization that monitors terrorist groups and their supporters recently released a study (CEP, 2018) that monitored ISIS video uploads to YouTube from March 8–June 8, 2018, and determined that 91% of ISIS videos uploaded to YouTube during this time were uploaded more than once. Furthermore, while 76% of ISIS videos remained on YouTube for less than 2 hours, there were 278 unique user accounts involved, 163,391 unique views were tabulated and 60% of the accounts that were identified as having uploaded a ISIS video were still allowed to remain a part of the YouTube community, even after their videos had been removed. Perhaps even more troubling, however, is that the phenomena of digital persistence, both in the form of users and specific social media content, is not beholden to a singular platform. Indeed, if a user, or a piece of content, is removed from one platform, many digital scholars argue that there is a host of other, and in some cases still emergent, digital platforms that offer additional avenues for posting and cross-posting, and some of these platforms, such as the messaging service Telegram, are encrypted and make it nearly impossible to intercept what is being posted in the first place.

In sum, what ISIS has shown the world in a very short period of time amounts to three key takeaways: (1) Terrorist organizations can build brand power and ultimately recruit more soldiers by maintaining a persistent and highly visual digital media presence and one that feeds off of increased marginalization among select populations such as immigrants and war refugees; (2) Crowdsourcing of propaganda can further amplify perceptions of power and allows terrorist organizations to rely less on central command structures which effectively makes them more difficult to monitor; (3) While large social media companies like Facebook, Twitter, and YouTube have gotten better at removing dangerous content, their regulation tactics are far from perfect and should serve as a stark reminder how much public information spaces have been disrupted by nefarious actors that now have robust digital strategies to promote and disseminate violence and hate online.

The Election of Donald Trump

While there have been many efforts to understand the political ascendency and subsequent election of Donald Trump to the U.S. presidency, including by social scientists and humanists, Pettigrew (2017) makes a strong case for five major social psychological phenomena that can help characterize Trump's most vocal if not divisive, and in some cases, violent support base. These phenomena include an affinity for authoritarianism, a preference toward social dominance orientation, a tendency for racial prejudice, a lack of contact with diverse groups, and a shared sense of "relative deprivation" in comparison to other groups deemed less deserving. Perhaps not surprisingly, mainstream media accounts of Trump's election success have rarely accounted for all of these characteristics simultaneously. We would like to suggest that there is yet one additional phenomenon that deserves to be added to this list: the social-technological phenomena of dark posts on social media and the Trump election team's deft use and deployment of customizable, social media-based advertising tools in the run-up to his historic election.

In at least one significant way, the Trump election team's rampant dissemination of dark posts on Facebook using Facebook's Custom Audience advertising tools and the psychological data illegally harvested by Cambridge Analytica's now defunct voter profiling enterprise shares a profound similarity with ISIS's approach to galvanizing sympathy for their particular organization. Rather than attempt to appeal to their potential fan base with objective facts and reality and through door-to-door campaigning, the Trump election team eventually spent upwards of $75 million a month on digital advertising (and mostly on Facebook) to saturate social media with graphic images, videos, gifs, and other multimedia content laden with lies, half-truths, cruel depictions, and divisive text designed to psychologically appeal to potential supporters or, on the flip side, to turn potential Hillary Clinton supporters sour and dissuade them from voting—and it worked (Kreiss, 2016). For example, according to the U.S. Census Bureau, the number of African-American voters who participated in the election declined sharply in 2016, the largest decline in turnout among African-Americans since collection of this data began in 1988. While some of this decline may be attributed to historically high turnout among African-Americans for former President Obama's election and reelection campaigns, it has since been widely reported that Trump used "provocative content to stoke social media buzz, and he was better able to drive likes, comments, and shares than Clinton . . . effectively winning him more media for less money" (Martinez, 2018).

Notably, dark posts are invisible to everyone, but the recipient and Facebook promotes them as "unpublished" posts that "allow you to test different creative variations with specific audiences without overloading people on your Page with non-relevant or repetitive messages" (Facebook's Custom Audience tool, 2018). This high-tech functionality, coupled with millions of posts that were carefully, and in many cases, crafted by Trump's election team and independent allies (Martinez, 2018; Frier, 2018; Kreiss, 2016), dramatically impacted Hillary Clinton's ability to turn out potential swing voters, and in the end, a variety of graphic, often cruel and highly targeted social media content very much helped hand Trump his election victory (Kreiss, 2016; Green et al., 2016). Perhaps more importantly, however, this particular case study also showcases the new and still emergent ways in which a previously fringe and loosely organized political faction with a penchant for hateful messaging can, with proper funding, now inundate the internet with strategic media content and turn previously quiet sympathizers into activists (Thompson, 2017), and in some cases, such as what was so tragically witnessed in Charlottesville, Virginia, in August 2017, violent crusaders (Shapira, 2017). This stark reality should give scholars and government agencies pause and especially when one considers the broader international context in which online hate now operates within.

A Global Refugee Crisis and the Concomitant Rise in Xenophobia Worldwide

The UN defines a refugee as "someone who has been forced to flee his or her country because of persecution, war, or violence" and as of May 2018, an estimated 25.4 million refugees around the globe fall into this category. What's more, the number of displaced people in the world has never been higher. Indeed, according to a June 2018 UNHCR report (Edwards, 2018), by the end of 2017, there were 68.5 million forcibly displaced people in the world, among them 25.4 million refugees. Alarmingly, 2017 was also the sixth consecutive year that the number of forcibly displaced people in the world surpassed peak World War II levels, and most indications suggest this number will continue to rise in the near future.

As of January 2018, about one-fifth of the world's displaced, over 13 million people, were born in Syria, more than one million of whom now find themselves displaced in Europe. In 2016, the United States resettled nearly 85,000 refugees within its borders, the most since 1999. The largest numbers of these refugees came from the Democratic Republic of Congo, Syria, Myanmar, and Iraq and a record number of them identify as Muslim. As in the United States, there has been much discussion in Europe regarding which refugees should be permitted to legally resettle, with great attention focused on national origin and religious affiliation.

Escalation of nationalistic and xenophobic responses to voluntary and forced immigration in a wide range of countries have been reflected and reinforced by countless Western media outlets in recent years, and the surge of refugees worldwide has made many domestic populations now wary of immigration writ large. Indeed, in eight of ten European nations surveyed in spring of 2016 (Connor, 2016), half or more adults in those countries said incoming refugees increases the likelihood of terrorism, and half or more respondents in five of those same countries feel that the newcomers will disproportionately take jobs and social benefits away from locals. Moreover, in none of these countries did a majority see increasing diversity as a positive development. And perhaps not surprisingly, during the 2016 U.S. presidential campaign, the divide between Democrats and Republicans on immigration issues was particularly stark. In another Pew Research Survey conducted in early August (Doherty, 2016), 79% of those who "strongly support" President-elect Donald Trump favored the building of a wall between the United States and Mexico, while only one in ten voters who supported Democratic candidate Hillary Clinton favored it.

It may also come as no surprise that the rise in use of social media around the globe has significantly affected perception, policies, and practices with regard to immigrants in particular, and sadly, has led to a steep rise in hate speech worldwide. For example, among Canadians, it was reported that from November 2015 and November 2016 hashtags such as #banmuslims, #siegheil, #whitegenocide and #whitepower were widely adopted (Marketplace, 2017) and there was a corresponding 600% increase in Canadian hate speech on platforms such as Facebook and Twitter (Naffi, 2017). In Germany, and about the same time, the federal police agency conducted sixty searches in private homes in fourteen different provinces and subsequently opened forty investigations in response to those searches, the majority of which involved the posting and sharing of anti-Semitic, xenophobic, and other extremist messages (Toor, 2016). Notably, by this same time period, Germany had accepted more than one million asylum seekers, largely from Syria and Iraq. In the United States, according to California State University's Center for the Study of Hate and Extremism, hate crime in the country's ten largest cities rose 12% in 2017, which marks the highest level of hate crime in the United States in over a decade. This increase was also the fourth consecutive annual rise of hate crime in the United States in a row.

Analysis and Conclusions

More than two years into the Trump presidency, it has become abundantly evident that the contemporary moment is one of marked division and great global uncertainty. But beyond the political divisions and new uncertainties stemming from today's White House and its various domestic and international policies, we would like to make the case that the relatively new socio-technological realities associated with today's social media landscape amount to an equally fraught moment and whose dynamic characteristics now requires more intensive investigation on behalf of scholars and activists worldwide. Indeed, through both the rise of ISIS and Donald Trump, we have witnessed two relative political newcomers discover entirely new forms of communicative power that have since reshaped humanity's course forever. In the case of ISIS, terrorist and extremist networks worldwide have been given genuinely innovative and new lesson plans for how to disseminate terror with fundamentally greater efficacy. And in the case of Donald Trump, future election teams in countries all over the globe will now most certainly look to his own team's highly divisive, yet ultimately successful, digital election strategy and draw playbook tips from it. Moreover, given the global refugee crisis and the heightening capacity among both individuals and terrorist and political organizations to exploit social media in the service of fear mongering and hate messaging against those who are on the move and so frequently blamed for shifting demographic trends and national resource burdens, it behooves peace activists and scholars to sincerely identify just what we are collectively now up against.

To this end, we believe it is fruitful to now turn to an argument that Kevin Kelly (2010) makes in his book, *What Does Technology Want*. According to Kelly, we are now living in the age of the "technium" whereby it is easy to identify numerous technologies that have evolved to include political, economic, and sociocultural power of their own and which may no longer be entirely controlled or contained by the technology's inventors or administrators, not to mention government regulators. Kelly refers to such technologies as "superorganisms" and we would like to suggest that social media platforms like Facebook, Twitter, and YouTube deserve such categorization and respective intellectual analysis precisely because their creators and administrators are unable to prevent all of their users from using their platforms in the ways they were originally conceived of functioning. Indeed, when Mark Zuckerberg first invented Facebook in his college dorm room, it was impossible for him to imagine that one day his burgeoning software would be responsible for the private and personal data of more than two billion people on the planet. Nor could he imagine how one day both terrorist organizations and U.S. presidential candidates alike would use his platform toward their own, often nefarious, political ends and with considerable consequences, including violence. What Zuckerberg and other tech executives at YouTube and Twitter have built and unleashed upon the world no doubt deserve our collective awe, but we think it is equally important to now clearly articulate the fact that these executives no longer maintain full control over their creations, and more specifically, now find themselves profoundly implicated in a new era of political destabilization, and particularly with respect to the behavior patterns of the most sinister and destructive users of their platforms.

Second, we would like to argue that if we genuinely want to try and understand just how much control, and therefore power, have been relinquished to social media technologies like Facebook, YouTube, and Twitter, it is now imperative that journalists, government regulators, scholars, and activists alike actively engage and robustly experiment with some of the same social media tools and digital strategies that have helped ISIS and Donald Trump become international sensations. To more fully understand just how Donald Trump, or Russia's Internet Research Agency for that matter (Chen, 2018), were able to game Facebook's *Custom Audience* and *Audience Insight* tool to help deliver Trump the 2016 U.S. presidency, one must in fact begin to buy (and on a regular basis since the tools are always evolving) Facebook (and increasingly Instagram) advertising space, and tediously experiment with the myriad ways in which the company's *Custom Audience* and *Audience Insight* tools allow its clients to target highly precise user demographics and constituencies, and in a variety of ways that the majority of Facebook and Instagram users remain largely unaware of.

To this end, and by way of conclusion, we would like to briefly draw upon Michelle Fine's (2016) work related to what she and her colleagues refer to as "critical bifocality." Fine, a social psychologist whose work spans over thirty years, describes critical bifocality as a "research and design practice" that takes seriously the following four commitments:

1.) Expertise is widely distributed but a particular wisdom about injustice is cultivated in the bodies and communities of those most intimately wounded by unjust conditions.
2.) Research on oppression must be linked to research on accumulation of privilege.
3.) Research on history, structures, and lives is powerfully produced by contact zones of divergent standpoints.
4.) Research is most valid and "of use" when designed by/alongside and in the interest of social justice movements and then circulated through lawsuits, academic papers, community performances, social media, and products of meaningful engagement with community life and movement actions (pg. 358).

Indeed, in the era of neoliberal global capitalism and where Silicon Valley continues to reap unprecedented financial gains without responsive or effective government oversight, Fine calls for research designs that "interrogate how history, structures, and lives shape, reveal, and refract the conditions we study" (p. 347). This is partially to say that if we want to cultivate better peace strategies in the era of social media, the first order of business is to clearly articulate which histories, structures, and residual inequities define the technology's financing, business priorities, and structural evolution. Mark Zuckerberg is a white, male, billionaire who went to Harvard, after all, and to this day, has yet to be held even remotely accountable for Facebook's highly problematic role in the 2016 U.S. presidential election, for example, nor for Facebook's reoccurring capacity to be exploited by foreign actors and violent extremists. The same can be said for the owners of Google and YouTube and yet we now have quantitative evidence that social media can act "as a propagation mechanism between online hate speech and real-life incidents" (Muller & Schwarz, 2018).

To this end, Fine points to the "radical margins" of society and "contact zones of divergent standpoints" as the places where engaged scholarship "of use" must truly materialize since "wisdom about injustice is cultivated in the bodies and communities of those most intimately wounded by unjust conditions" (p. 358). So what might this approach to engaged scholarship look like in today's social media landscape? Well, for one, the people undertaking such research must in fact identify and then build meaningful relationships with those that are being most left behind by the relentless advancement of neoliberal global capitalism, such as refugees and the 68.5 million people that have been displaced from their homes worldwide. While many of these people may be struggling to simply survive, the presence and, in many cases, vital use of smartphones among refugees and displaced peoples has been well documented (Maitland & Xu, 2015; Gillespie et al., 2018; Göransson, 2018). What is less scrutinized, however, are the ways in which this "radical margin" of global society experience social media and particularly social media that casts them in negative light. To what degree are these members encountering hate speech that specifically targets them, for example, and what are the specific technical instances within social media platforms most responsible for propagation of said hate speech? Such research remains a giant undertaking and yet we now know that ISIS and other violent extremist groups have learned to exploit social media and specifically target those who feel most marginalized by their social and economic circumstances, including the harsh realities of displacement and/or forced migration.

Finally, a second and equally colossal undertaking in addition to working alongside refugees, to name one "radical margin," to identify how social media may be impacting them, should consist of the mass production of social media content that broadcasts the experiences of these members with compassion, empathy, and positivity. This is to say that for every instance of hate speech encountered in the social media landscape, there should be at least a tenfold counter response, and one that is developed in direct collaboration with those most victimized by hate speech. This counter-response should celebrate and psychologically boost global society's most abandoned by the unforgiving inequities associated with neoliberal globalization, war, racism, climate change, and economic poverty. For example, Kruglanski et al. (2014) assert that one possible counter-strategy toward coping with violent extremism is in fact to broadcast the experience of those individuals who at one point may have flirted with extremist thought but who later decided not to become terrorists and are subsequently leading productive and meaningful lives. They argue that this allows for a counter-narrative to be more widely established and harnesses the same forces that lead to the attraction to extremism in the first place. Thus, if simplicity of the message and cognitive closure are what leads some individuals to extremist thought, the counter-narrative must be equally simple and assured, and we ultimately add, significantly more pervasive in social media environments that remain largely unregulated and dominantly guided by shareholder value as opposed to what might make the world less violent, for example.

To close, the pathways forward are inherently complex. It is unlikely, for example, that social media platforms will disappear given how globally popular and lucrative they have become. It also remains unlikely that their administrators will ever be able to remove all instances of hate speech from them, nor are they likely to turn away windfall advertising revenue in the form of dark posts purchased by future politicians. That is unless governments decide to better regulate them and intervene in how they technically and financially operate. Indeed, putting pressure on governments to hold social media companies more accountable for how unruly their platforms have become is certainly one strategy activists and scholars should pursue moving forward. Exhibiting critical bifocality in the digital realm is another.

References

Armstrong, D. (1982) The origins of the League of Nations. In *The rise of the international organisation: A short history. The making of the 20th century*. London: Palgrave.

Bar, S. (2004, June). *The religious sources of Islamic terrorism*. Retrieved from: https://www.hoover.org/research/religious-sources-islamic-terrorism

Benkler, Y. (2006). *The wealth of networks: How social production transforms markets and freedom*. New Haven: Yale University Press.

Boyd, D. M., & Ellison, N. B. (2007). Social network sites: Definition, history, and scholarship. *Journal of computer-mediated Communication, 13*(1): 210–230.

Castells, M. (2011). *The rise of the network society* (vol. 12). Hoboken, NJ: John Wiley & Sons.

Chen, A. (2018, February). *What Mueller's indictment reveals about Russia's internet research agency.* Retrieved from: https://www.newyorker.com/news/news-desk/what-muellers-indictment-reveals-about-russias-internet-research-agency

Confessore, N., & Dance, G. (2018, July). *Battling fake accounts, Twitter to slash millions of followers.* Retrieved from: https://www.nytimes.com/2018/07/11/technology/twitter-fake-followers.html

Connor, P. (2016, December). *International migration: Key findings from the U.S., Europe and the world.* Washington, DC. Pew Research Center. Retrieved from: http://www.pewresearch.org/fact-tank/2016/12/15/international-migration-key-findings-from-the-u-s-europe-and-the-world/

Counter Extremism Project. (2018, July). *The e-Glyph Web Crawler: ISIS content on YouTube.* Retrieved from: https://www.counterextremism.com/sites/default/files/eGLYPH_web_crawler_white_paper_July_2018.pdf

Doherty, C. (2016, August). *5 facts about Trump supporters' views of immigration.* Washington,DC. Pew Research Center. Retrieved from: http://www.pewresearch.org/fact-tank/2016/08/25/5-facts-about-trump-supporters-views-of-immigration/

Fine, M. (2016). Just methods in revolting times. *Qualitative research in psychology, 13*(4): 347–365.

Frier, S. (2018). *Trump's campaign said it was better at Facebook. Facebook agrees.* Retrieved from: https://www.bloomberg.com/news/articles/2018-04-03/trump-s-campaign-said-it-was-better-at-facebook-facebook-agrees

Edwards, A. (2018). *Forced displacement at record 68.5 million.* Geneva: UN Refugee Agency.

Gilder, G. (1994). *Life after television: The coming transformation of media and American life.* New York, NY: W.W. Norton.

Gillespie, M., Osseiran, S., & Cheesman, M. (2018). Syrian refugees and the digital passage to Europe: Smartphone infrastructures and affordances. *Social Media+ Society, 4*(1), 2056305118764440.

Göransson, M. (2018). *Apping and resilience: Policy brief how smartphones help Syrian refugees in Lebanon negotiate the precarity of displacement.* Clingendael: Clingendael Institute.

Green, J., & Issenberg, S. (2016, October). Inside the Trump bunker, with days to go. Retrieved from: https://www.bloomberg.com/news/articles/2016-10-27/inside-the-trump-bunker-with-12-days-to-go

Harvey, D., & Braun, B. (1996). *Justice, nature and the geography of difference* (vol. 468). Oxford, UK: Blackwell.

Hern, A. (2018, January). *Facebook, Google and Twitter to testify in Congress over extremist content.* Retrieved from: https://www.theguardian.com/technology/2018/

jan/10/facebook-google-twitter-testify-congress-extremist-content-russian-election-interference-information

Hogg, M. A., Adelman, J. R., & Blagg, R. D. (2010). Religion in the face of uncertainty: An account of religiousness. *Personality and Social Psychology Review, 14*(1): 72–83.

Jenkins, H. (2006). *Convergence culture: Where old and new media collide.* New York, NY: New York University Press.

Kahn, J (2017, December). *U.K. lawmakers slam Facebook, Google, Twitter on hate speech.* Retrieved from: https://www.bloomberg.com/news/articles/2017-12-19/u-k-lawmakers-slam-facebook-google-twitter-on-hate-speech

Kelly, K. (2010). *What technology wants.* London, UK: Penguin.

Kirkpatrick, D., & Gladstone, R. (2014, November). *ISIS chief emerges, urging "Volcanoes of Jihad".* Retrieved from:https://www.nytimes.com/2014/11/14/world/middleeast/abu-bakr-baghdadi-islamic-state-leader-calls-for-new-fight-against-west.html

Koerner, B. (2016, April). *Why ISIS is winning the social media war* Retrieved from: https://www.wired.com/2016/03/isis-winning-social-media-war-heres-beat/

Kreiss, D. (2016). *Prototype politics: Technology-intensive campaigning and the data of democracy.* Oxford, UK: Oxford University Press.

Kruglanski, A. W. (1989). *Lay epistemics and human knowledge: Cognitive and motivational bases.* New York: Plenum Press.

Kruglanski, A. W., Gelfand, M. J., Bélanger, J. J., Sheveland, A., Hetiarachchi, M., & Gunaratna, R. (2014). The psychology of radicalization and deradicalization: How significance quest impacts violent extremism. *Political Psychology, 35,* 69–93.

Lifton, R. J. (1999). *The protean self: Human resilience in an age of fragmentation.* Chicago, IL: University of Chicago Press.

Maitland, C., & Xu, Y. (2015, March 31). A social informatics analysis of refugee mobile phone use: A case study of Za'atari Syrian refugee camp. TPRC 43: The 43rd research conference on communication, information and internet policy paper. Available at SSRN: https://ssrn.com/abstract=2588300

Marketplace, CBC. (2017, January). Racist language use. Retrieved from: https://www.cbc.ca/marketplace/blog/about-our-analysis-of-intolerant-language

Martinez, A. (2018, February 23). *How Trump conquered Facebook— Without Russian Ads.* Retrieved from: https://www.wired.com/story/how-trump-conquered-facebookwithout-russian-ads/

Müller, K. & Schwarz, C. (2018). "Fanning the Flames of Hate: Social Media and Hate Crime," CAGE Online Working Paper Series 373, Competitive Advantage in the Global Economy (CAGE).

Naffi, N. (2017, November). *Online hate speech in Canada is up 600 percent. What can be done?* Retrieved from: https://www.macleans.ca/politics/online-hate-speech-in-canada-is-up-600-percent-what-can-be-done/

National Consortium for the Study of Terrorism and Responses to Terrorism. (2017). *Annex of Statistical Information Country Reports on Terrorism 2016.* A Department of Homeland Security Science and Technology Center of Excellence, Maryland.

Pettigrew, T. F. (2017). Social psychological perspectives on Trump supporters. *Journal of Social and Political Psychology*, 5(1): 107–116.

Rheingold, H. (2003). Smart Mobs: The Next Social Revolution. New York, NY: Basic Books.

Safranek, R. (2012). The emerging role of social media in political and regime change. *ProQuest Discovery Guides. March*, 1–14.

Shapira, I. (2017). *Finding the white supremacists who beat a black man in Charlottesville.* Retrieved from: https://www.washingtonpost.com/local/finding-the-white-supremacists-who-beat-a-black-man-in-charlottesville/2017/08/31/9f36e762-8cfb-11e7-84c0-02cc069f2c37_story.html?noredirect=on&utm_term=.28ae6480ef0f

Thompson, A. C. (2017). Racist, violent, unpunished: A White Hate Group's campaign of menace. Retrieved from: https://www.propublica.org/article/white-hate-group-campaign-of-menace-rise-above-movement

Toor, A. (2016, July). *German police raid homes over Facebook hate speech.* Retrieved from: https://www.theverge.com/2016/7/13/12170590/facebook-hate-speech-germany-police-raid

Part IV: Volunteer and Citizen Scholars: Reflections and Lessons Learned

8 Practicing Mediation as an Engaged Scholar: A Personal Memoir

GWEN A. HULLMAN

During my first day of a forty-hour mediation training, the director of the local mediation center addressed our training class. Before our first role-play he cautioned, "Whatever you do, don't make the conflict any worse than it already is." His comment gave me pause. Until that moment, I had never considered that outcome as a possible result of my efforts to help. He essentially warned that mediators' decisions could harm participants and worsen their divide. His explanation was convincing, and a bit disconcerting. I had never come across this possible scenario in the conflict resolution books I had read and taught with. Despite several years of teaching communication, I realized in that training moment that there was much more I needed to learn about the reality of conflict and mediation. I sensed an important gap between my academic training and perspective about conflict resolution, and the practitioner perspective about conflict resolution. Was I encountering a possible disconnect between theory/scholarship and practice/real application (Van de Ven & Johnson, 2006), and how would I learn to bridge the two as I engaged with people and their conflicts in the world around me?

My personal journey into being an engaged communication scholar—applying what I knew in community settings—had begun with this reality check. I was an assistant professor of communication studies at the University of Nevada in Reno. I enrolled in a training program jointly sponsored by the Extended Studies Division of the University of Nevada and the Reno Mediation Center, a nonprofit mediation center that served the local small claims court and surrounding community. This program provided opportunities to assess my communication knowledge and skills, recognize how communication training prepared me for mediation, and to contribute to the role of mediation in my community. Ultimately, my experience as an engaged scholar transformed the classroom experience I sought to offer to my students, and my relationship to the community in which I lived. This chapter tells my story of how engaging, and helping others with what I know, changed important aspects of my own scholarly life and identity.

Assessing My Communication Skills in Mediation

Mediation is a communicative process in which a neutral third party assists participants in a negotiation (Putnam, 2013). Many beginning mediation programs consist of forty-hour, hands-on training. As much as it was a process of learning new techniques, mediation training was also—for me—a process of unlearning things (Gold, 1985). The vocabulary used in the mediation training was at first confusing to me. Training language has developed over time from mediators across various backgrounds, such as law, education, business, and counseling. I recognized many of the concepts presented in the training, but called them by different labels based on my exposure to communication studies research. Some labels were not interchangeable in equal ways (word for word), which required me to deconstruct and reconstruct abstract ideas. Framing, for example, was a concept I had often discussed in my interpersonal communication courses. Framing meant choosing the way in which an idea, question, or request would be presented to another person (Entman, 1993). In this sense, one can frame a sentence negatively or frame one positively. Framing the mediation, however, referred to applying a larger framework to an entire conversation or situation. A new frame would encourage participants to focus on the issue in a different way (Gray, 2006). For example, the parents of a bride are upset with a photographer's wedding pictures because some important family members are not included in any of the photographs. The photographer, in turn, is upset that the customer does not value her work. She notes that several guests were uncooperative when asked to pose for photos. A useful frame for the conversation may be, "How could we preserve memories of an event after the event is concluded?" Intuitively, the idea of providing a new frame made sense to me, but for a while, every time I heard the word "framing," I had to think about which "framing" I was supposed to be doing. The interdisciplinary nature of mediation practice provided a broader lens through which I could view the concepts. Although I initially felt confused, I eventually gained much knowledge by integrating the new perspectives.

I was, however, uneasy about my initial reaction to the training program. The mediators at the center made an investment in me as a volunteer, and they had expectations of what I would contribute to the local court mediation program and the community mediation center. They agreed to serve as advisory board members to develop our new Master of Arts degree, which focused on conflict management. They already had assisted me. I wanted to maintain that relationship by reciprocating. I also recognized that I served as an additional connection for them to the local university. I had concerns about what might happen if the training did not work out well. I did not want to disappoint myself and others, and I also felt some pressure from the important relational exchange I had set up with my trainers. But I persisted, and we enjoyed mutually beneficial results.

I sat with human resource specialists, judges, managers, and retired professionals. I recall feeling frustrated that the training was not coming as easily as I had expected. I had a Ph.D. in communication studies and I did not see that my education was helping me in the present moment. Further diminishing the confidence I initially had was a comment from another participant in the training. A judge at my table announced that he could not understand how any of us in the class without a legal background could possibly become mediators. His lack of confidence in the rest of us did not help me manage my own self-doubt in these early stages of learning.

I was in a state of conscious incompetence (Howell, 1982). Attempting to be positive, I tried to think of the training as a great opportunity to learn. I liked being a helpful person and I thought that helpfulness would translate into mediation skills, but I learned that the translation would not be seamless. I served a harmonizing function during my childhood and young adult life, and I tended to get along with just about everyone. I reflected on my early attempts to reconcile conflict in my childhood. I had a relative who would give my younger sister noticeably less expensive, somewhat generic gifts compared to ones she would give me. Our birthdays were one day apart so it was easy for us to compare gifts. We shared a cake and a party as far back as I could remember. My sister eventually noticed that the gifts I received were "better" than the gifts she received. At one point, she voiced her dismay to our relatives. As far as I know, neither of my parents helped her address the situation. I decided to manipulate/manage the situation because I was uncomfortable. I started making positive comments to my sister about the gifts she received. My intent was to give her the impression that her gifts were more desirable than my gifts. I sometimes asked her to trade gifts with me. On many occasions, she agreed. One year I received an embroidered, multi-colored, commercially branded sweater. My younger sister received an inexpensive bottle of perfume from a local drug store. She was not old enough to appreciate perfume, and her young age was the angle I took to persuade her to trade gifts. As I reflected on this situation from my past during mediation training, I realized that I really did not "fix" anything with my interventions, and

I possibly allowed the pattern to continue because of my actions—merely managing the conflict. Perhaps I even made the situation worse, as the mediation trainer forewarned?

During my first years as a mediator, I continued to analyze my own communication skills through a mediation-training lens. I concluded that I took too much responsibility for other peoples' conflicts and for solving them. My own relationships, I had self-diagnosed, were conflict avoidant. Lieberman, Foux-Levy, and Segal (2005) contended that critical self-assessment is part of a mediation-training program. Their assessment fit my experience. I was able to identify my strengths and weaknesses because of the continuous training and feedback. I began to develop confidence in my newfound skill set. It is a goal for training programs to build confidence in their participants (Lincoln, 2001), although confidence came later for me after practice had begun to create competence. I continued to pursue the mediation path even though it was difficult because I believed that the process of mediation was good for my community, and good for me as a communication scholar and teacher. I saw that mediation offered a way to empower people to create their own ideas of justice and seeing how people did this in real conflicts could only deepen my skills as someone who taught related courses.

My Mediation Training in Action and in My Own Life

I adopted a communication-based process of conflict resolution referred to as facilitative mediation (Alexander, 2008). In this type of mediation, the mediator acts as a third-party neutral without contributing specific resolutions to the discussion. This style of mediation empowers participants to identify the issues, brainstorm possible solutions, and evaluate possible solutions. Advocating for this process helped me to give control of the conflict to the participants and retain control only of the process. I saw facilitative mediation as a way to empower people in the community to co-create their own versions of justice and to resolve their own issues in ways that is best for them (see Garcia, 2000).

My expertise as a communication scholar provided a valuable foundation upon which to learn the practice of mediation. The Reno Mediation Center offered a connection for me and many other community members to practice the skills we had learned. Maxwell (1997) argued that allowing trained mediators to practice their skills in the community facilitates community empowerment. I liberated myself from "helping" people solve their conflicts. Instead, I focused on empowering them to resolve conflicts for themselves. Not all mediations resulted in agreements, but many resulted in at least some movement in the positions of the people involved, or their understanding of others' perspectives.

During my initial years of mediating, I watched countless small claims cases go before judges. At the time, disputants had the option of using a court mediator or going before the judge. I would arrive early to the small claims courtroom, deliver a presentation about the free mediation option, and then ask people to volunteer to use the mediation service. On days when no one volunteered, I stayed in the courtroom and listened to the cases. I studied the cases to examine the underlying issues, which tended to "leak out" during the hearings. I hypothesized whether the participants would have been better off solving their problems through mediation. The judges were bound to decide cases based on the legal issues before them and could not possibly get to most of the important underlying issues in the courtroom (see Roehl & Cook, 1985). As I heard the cases, I often found myself wishing those involved had volunteered for mediation.

One such case involved a woman who was suing her ex-mother-in law for half the cost of a television. They jointly purchased the television. The judge asked each of them to present evidence related to the purchase. Evidence included receipts, warranty paperwork, recollection of agreed-upon terms, and related joint living expenses. However, the women also revealed other information irrelevant to the specific dispute over the television. This information did, however, point to the heart of their underlying relational conflict. The woman had a young son, who was the ex-mother-in-law's grandson. They all had lived together at one time. The ex-mother-in-law had not communicated with her grandson in quite some time, and clearly missed him. She was quite upset and disappointed that he was not there that day in the courtroom. I was troubled the women were in court over a $300 television because their problem seemed much deeper than the television. I watched this case almost ten years ago. I still remember the faces and emotions of the people involved. I still wonder whatever happened to them after they left the courtroom that day. Cases such as this one motivated me to return to the courtroom month after month to invite participants to volunteer for free mediation.

Eventually, the judges decided that mediation would be mandatory for almost all small claims cases. Disputants were much more prepared for their cases after trying mediation, even when mediation did not end in agreement/ resolution. Sometimes, judges temporarily lifted restraining orders so that mediation could be used. Parties in small claims court were not always happy about seeing a mediator before seeing a judge. They also were not always shy about sharing those views with me. On one hand, I was excited about man-datory mediation because I knew I would be guaranteed mediations when

I went to the courthouse. In addition, half of the cases on the docket were now mediated, providing a less adversarial way for people to resolve conflict. Mandatory mediation also alleviated the burden on judges and long waits for court dates. As a scholar of mediation, I was torn about the mandate for it. One reason why facilitative mediation works is because people agree to mediate voluntarily. In the case of mandatory mediation, disputants did not volunteer to be there at all. The involuntary nature of mandatory mediation, it could be argued, violates facilitative mediation philosophy (see Boettger, 2004; Vettori, 2015 for arguments). From my own standpoint, I disagreed with the mandatory nature of the mediation program, but continued to support it because I could see that the process was working for many who tried it in good faith. The mandatory mediation process was not the ideal way to practice facilitative mediation, but it was still beneficial.

Mediation, I was finding, was beneficial to the disputants' relationships and many times provided a way for them to move forward. I began to think of mediation as building a community, one relationship at a time. One question I always ask at the beginning of a mediation is, "Have you discussed this with one another before today?" Anecdotally, there was a 50/50 chance this was the first face-to-face conversation the disputants had about the issue. Because mediation requires people to talk directly to one another, I believe mediation has the power to re-connect people. In some cases, there never was a conversation about the dispute. Through mediation, parties can start that conversation. Many times, the conversation empowers them to make decisions together and decide what happens next. Alternatively, through the legal process, a judge talks with each party separately in a courtroom. Rarely do disputants talk directly to one another in court. The judge then decides the solution, which is certainly necessary sometimes, but not empowering for the community members. The court process also fails to facilitate opening lines of communication between the disputants again and, therefore, is not always helpful if reconciliation is a goal of conflict resolution.

I once co-mediated a case at the Reno Community Mediation Center for two neighbors who had not spoken to each other in years. After their conflict began, they avoided each other. They looked out of their windows before going outside to make sure they would not meet. The conflict spilled over into their children's relationships and their neighbors' relationships. The aftermath of the conflict seemed worse for the neighborhood than the original dispute. However, at the conclusion of a two-hour mediation, they left the mediation center together. They were talking about their kids and catching up on everything they had missed. Resolution certainly was part of that mediation conversation, but so was relationship repair (Trego, Canary, Alberts, & Mooney, 2010).

I worked with a co-mediator during that mediation who was gifted at asking the right questions. Asking questions really is an art form (Barthel & Fortson-Harwell, 2016). Close-ended questions were not useful to me in mediation except to establish a time line or to clear up a confusing detail. Open-ended questions, however, worked well to gain information about participants' interests and to challenge them to look at problems differently. Open-ended questions seemed less threatening for participants as well, especially if the questions arose from genuine curiosity. I leaned heavily on my background in teaching interpersonal communication to understand the function and structure of questions in mediation conversations. A question that elicits thoughts about the ideal neighborhood would have been a potential start to the aforementioned conflict conversation after the opening statements. For example, "You've both talked about how this situation has impacted the way you behave toward one another and in your neighborhood; what does an ideal neighborhood look like to both of you?" A good question can encourage participation and progressive movement through the mediation conversation. A good question utilizes information participants have contributed, focuses responses on something positive, and encourages a future-focused conversation (Barthel & Fortson-Harwell, 2016). Using an ideal neighborhood as a frame could be a way that people start talking about what they will do instead of what they have already done. Future talk is empowering because both participants can contribute to the new vision without necessarily having to hash out responsibility for the past, unless that's important to them. Many mediation-training programs suggest talking about what people can agree to do in the future. Instead of staying focused on the current situation (which is where the participants are stuck), a question can begin the process of formulating a shared goal or an outcome (Barthel & Fortson-Harwell, 2016). I have found in my own practice that open-ended questions challenge my own assumptions as well as the participants' assumptions and work well to get the conversation started.

The mediation center training taught me how to suspend judgment and rely more on conditionalism (Burgoon & Langer, 1995). At first, I started practicing this skill by hypothesizing all the possible motives and missing pieces of a conflict narrative that differed from my original conclusion (e.g., perhaps this was the reason she yelled, maybe he was having a bad day). This strategy works when there is time to ponder and reflect. It is not feasible to ponder and reflect, though, when mediating a conflict. I tried to hold back on superimposing any details on any narrative. I accepted that I might never know certain details. I began focusing on mindfulness (Burgoon & Langer, 1995) and applying it to the mediation processes that I facilitated. I proposed a segmented silence technique for mediations that includes periods of thoughtful reflection for both mediators and participants (Hullman, 2016). I doubt I would have developed this technique had I not been practicing mediation. This technique and my mediation training helped me practice withholding unnecessary judgment.

Although I became adept at withholding judgment through mindfulness, becoming a community mediator had some unintended consequences for me. I started to have trouble making personal decisions and negotiating on my own behalf. I became indecisive and over-analyzed peoples' behavior and communication. Had I become too neutral and analytical—a trained incapacity resulting from being a mediator? I changed my voter registration to independent, I disliked voting in faculty senate as I often focused on seeing the merits of both sides of arguments, and I agonized over what school my daughter would attend. I thought more about past conversations and spent more time in my head thinking about possible outcomes. I certainly had trained my mind to refrain from making premature internal attributions about others' behaviors. As a result, people accused me of being naïve. I became a more patient person but also hesitant to take action. Furthermore, when it was time for me to negotiate on my own behalf, I was not always happy with my performance. I knew cognitively how to negotiate, but had trouble activating the scripts (Greene & Graves, 2007). It was a challenge to withhold judgment sometimes and not other times. I struggled to adapt my new skills across situations in my own life (Duran, 1983).

My relationship with my community changed in other ways as well. Reno, in 2009, based on my personal experience, was a small town. As a mediator, I needed to maintain a reputation as a neutral party. As this requirement became more central to the role I played, I found I wanted to become less integrated into any one particular group of people. Mediation was confidential as well. However, people from mediations I had facilitated would approach me in public settings to give me updates and tell me about their personal situations. I never revealed how I knew them to the people I was with. These conversations were uncomfortable, and by avoiding them, I could see that, over time, I was becoming more isolated. Eventually, I learned how to manage those conversations through selective disclosure and topic shifts.

I concluded that, overall, I had changed positively because of mediation practice. I was curious whether anyone else noticed. As I worked on this memoir, I asked my spouse if I had changed since I started mediating. He said he had noticed several differences in the way I interacted with others. For example, he noticed that I tended not to take things personally, as I had done in the past. He said I was much more willing to offer circumstantial motivations to explain negative behaviors. He also stated that in the height of my involvement, I seemed less willing to use my own intuition to form an opinion, and instead remained uncertain. His perceptions of how I changed supported my own conclusions. Mediation training has the potential to influence positive communication skill development (Lincoln, 2001; Malizia & Jameson, 2018). Overall, I believe mediation training and practice further developed my communication skills.

Giving Back to the Mediation Community

After a few years mediating for the court system and community center, I began training new mediators. The training consisted of co-mediating disputes and then debriefing with one another after the mediations concluded. I appreciated the director's confidence in me to take on this role. It was satisfying to support the mediation community center and court program by co-mediating with new mediators. I also learned from new mediators who demonstrated techniques that I could adopt later on as well.

I had an opportunity to contribute to the continuing education of my fellow mediators in my community by sharing scholarship. After mediating for about five years, I planned and facilitated a two-hour listening workshop for local mediators. The workshop was based on a listening course that I created at the University of Nevada and adapted for mediation practice. Mediators are tasked with being good listeners, but many receive little formal training in listening. My experience during the workshop was that my community of mediators appreciated the information and recognized its relevance in their practice. Teaching the workshop was meaningful for me. I saw the event as a contribution to the community of mediators who had welcomed me and trained me.

Seven years later, I found myself back in the same training room at the Extended Studies Building at the University of Nevada, Reno. This was the same beginning mediation-training program I had attended. This time, I was on a panel of mediators sharing the mistakes I made as a mediator and what I learned from those mistakes. I also spoke of the personal satisfaction that I received on my journey from communication scholar to community mediation practitioner. My mediation experiences changed the way I taught mediation and conflict resolution, and many of my other classes as well.

Engaged Teaching

My experiences as a mediator enhanced my role as a teacher of conflict resolution. I began teaching the conflict resolution course in the Communication
Studies Department and added an alternative dispute resolution course at
the graduate and undergraduate levels. The coursework was beneficial to the
students who learned conflict resolution skills and practiced them in their
personal and professional lives. Greater awareness and utilization of the mediation programs in the local Reno area was a direct result of their experience
in my classes.

Experiential learning became a central component of my teaching. I continued to provide theoretical foundations and research opportunities to students. In addition, I wanted the students to "feel" the material as actors. They
gained an appreciation of how difficult conflict resolution and mediation can be
in practice. This experience was unsettling for students who had mastered the
academic knowledge of conflict and mediation, but had trouble demonstrating basic mediation skills in practice where things moved quickly. These students could produce a well-written essay about the implications of displaying
basic mediation skills, such as the ability to remain neutral or ask an unbiased
question (Putnam, 2013), but often fell far short of enacting those behaviors in a role-played mediation. The observable gap between my students'
knowledge and skill was akin to Ashcraft's (2002) concerns about practical
ambivalence in graduate programs. I found evidence of practical ambivalence
in my pedagogy, and sought to re-balance what I focused on for the students.
I needed to include more emphasis on the practice of conflict and mediation
communication. I was also surprised that other students seemed like natural
mediators despite their struggles in mastering the academic assessments of
mediation theory and research. For them, including graded assessments of
skill performance built self-confidence and reinforced the academic material.
Furthermore, in the spirit of Barge and Shockley-Zalabak's (2008) arguments
regarding engaged scholarship, I needed to focus more on how students can
learn to harness the creative power of effective conflict resolution and focus
less on dissecting conflicts for the sake of demonstrating analytical and critical
prowess.

I included mediation professionals in syllabus planning and in the classroom experience to help my students understand how to translate what we
do in the classroom into what we do in practice. Barge and Shockley-Zalabak
(2008) argued that cooperation with nonacademic practitioners is a way to
provide opportunities for the co-creation of knowledge, thus enhancing the
students' experiences in the classroom. Through the interactions among

students and professionals, the students learned the social/community relevance of theories and research findings (Barge & Shockley-Zalabak, 2008). In turn, our local practitioners gained valuable insight into the latest findings on new mediation techniques or labels that were new to them. As the students worked through role-plays and other simulation exercises, they were able to create scripts for how to approach conflict situations (Schank & Abelson, 1977). Their scripts were the result of feedback not only from me but also from each other and local mediators in the community.

The relationship between the mediation center and the university flourished and we built valuable bridges between us. The mediation center became interested in student interns to support their work in the community. We were able to provide scholarships for students to complete the forty-hour beginning mediation training. The local mediators assisted in developing a proposal for a campus mediation program. A local mediator also began teaching as adjunct faculty in our department. The lines between scholarship, teaching, and practice were blurring in positive ways. All of us learned from one another in ways that Boyer (1996) argued were possible. The result was enhanced scholarship, learning, and creativity. The culmination of my experience as a mediator was transformative in nature for me personally. It made me a better scholar, a better teacher, and a better communicator.

I currently serve as a Department Chair and Associate Professor of Communication Studies at Ashland University in Ohio. Although I am no longer involved in mediating small claims disputes, mediation principles and practice follow me into department meetings, conversations, and the classroom. It has become a little voice that tells me to search for interests, rather than positions, in my personal relationships and my work relationships. I choose to find common ground in department meetings and classroom discussions, and listen intently with the goal of understanding. Mediation practice has been valuable to me, and I have witnessed how it benefits others as well. To that end, I am currently working on a joint conflict resolution minor with the Director of the Center for Nonviolence, the Criminal Justice Department, and Student Services. Through this program, students will have opportunities to experience meaningful conflict resolution and mediation practice, and my hope is that mediation will be transformative for them as well.

References

Alexander, N. (2008). The mediation metamodel: Understanding practice. *Conflict Resolution Quarterly, 26,* 97–123. doi:10.1002/crq.225.

Ashcraft, K. L. (2002). Practical ambivalence and troubles in translation. *Management Communication Quarterly, 16,* 113–117.

Barge, J. K., & Shockley-Zalabak, P. (2008). Engaged scholarship and the creation of useful organizational knowledge. *Journal of Applied Communication Research, 36,* 251–265. doi:10.1080/00909880802172277.

Barthel, T., & Fortson-Harwell, M. (2016). Practice note: Asking better questions. *Conflict Resolution Quarterly, 34,* 43–56. doi:10.1002/crq.21170.

Boettger, U. (2004). Efficiency versus party empowerment: Against a good-faith requirement in mandatory mediation. *Review of Litigation, 23,* 1–46.

Boyer, E. L. (1996). The scholarship of engagement. *Journal of Public Service and Outreach, 1,* 11–20.

Burgoon, J. K., & Langer, E. J. (1995). Language, fallacies, and mindlessness-mindfulness in social interaction. *Communication Yearbook, 18,* 107–126. doi:10.1080/238089 85.1995.11678909.

Duran, R. L. (1983). Communicative adaptability: A measure of social communicative competence. *Communication Quarterly, 31,* 320–326.

Entman, R. M. (1993). Framing: Toward clarification of a fractured paradigm. *Journal of Communication, 43*(4), 51–58. doi:10.1111/j.1460-2466.1993.tb01304.x.

Garcia, A. C. (2000). Negotiating negotiation: The collaborative production of resolution in small claims mediation hearings. *Discourse & Society, 11,* 315–343. doi:10.1177 %2F0957926500011003003.

Greene, J. O., & Graves, A. R. (2007). Cognitive models of message production. In D. R. Roskos-Ewoldsen & J. L. Monahan (eds.), *Communication and social cognition: Theories and methods* (pp. 28–36). Mahwah, NJ: Erlbaum.

Gold, L. (1985). Reflections on the transition from therapist to mediator. *Mediation Quarterly, 9,* 15–26. doi:10.1002/crq.39019850904.

Gray, B. (2006). Mediation as framing and framing within mediation. In M. S. Hermann (ed.), *The Blackwell handbook of mediation: Bridging theory, research, and practice* (pp. 193–216). Malden, MA: Blackwell.

Howell, W. S. (1982). *The empathic communicator.* Belmont, CA: Wadsworth.

Hullman, G. A. (2016). Segmented silence in mediation: Mitigating the effects of cognitive overload. In P. M. Kellett, & T. G. Matyok (eds.), *Transforming conflict through communication, in personal, family, and working relationships* (pp. 189–200). Lanham, MA: Lexington.

Lieberman, E., Foux-Levy, Y., & Segal, P. (2005). Beyond basic training: A model for developing mediator competence. *Conflict Resolution Quarterly, 23,* 237–257. doi:10.1002/crq.135.

Lincoln, M. G. (2001). Conflict resolution education: A solution for peace. *Communications & the Law, 23,* 29–40.

Malizia, D. A., & Jameson, J. K. (2018). Hidden in plain view: The impact of mediation on the mediator and implications for conflict resolution education. *Conflict Resolution Quarterly, 35,* 301–318. doi:10.1002/crq.21212.

Maxwell, J. P. (1997). Conflict management and mediation training: A vehicle for community empowerment? *Mediation Quarterly, 15*, 83–96. doi:10.1002/crq.3900150203.

Putnam, L. L. (2013). Definitions and approaches to conflict and communication. In J. G. Oetzel & S. Ting-Toomey (eds.), *The SAGE handbook of conflict communication* (2nd ed., pp. 1–39). Thousand Oaks, CA: Sage.

Roehl, J. A., & Cook, R. F. (1985). Issues in mediation: Rhetoric and reality revisited. *Journal of Social Issues, 41*, 161–178. doi:10.1111/j.1540-4560.1985.tb00861.x.

Schank, R. C., & Abelson, R. P. (1977). *Scripts, goals, and understandings*. Hillsdale, NJ: Erlbaum.

Trego, A., Canary, D. J., Alberts, J. K., & Mooney, C. (2010). Mediators' facilitative versus controlling argument strategies and tactics: A qualitative analysis using the conversational argument coding system. *Communication Methods & Measures, 4*, 147–167. doi:10.1080/19312451003680707.

Van de Ven, A. H., & Johnson, P. E. (2006). Knowledge for theory and practice. *Academy of Management Review, 31*, 802–821. doi:10.5465/AMR.2006.22527385.

Vettori, S. (2015). Mandatory mediation: An obstacle to access to justice? *African Human Rights Law Journal, 15*, 355–377. doi:10.17159/1996-2096/2015/v15n2a6.

9 Walking the Challenging Path of Peacebuilding: Reflections of an Engaged Scholar

Benjamin J. Broome

In June 1995, a group of fifteen Greek Cypriots and fifteen Turkish Cypriots organized an "Agora-Bazaar" in the buffer zone that separates the two communities in Cyprus. Named after (respectively) the Greek and Turkish words for "marketplace," this was no ordinary set of booths where vendors were trying to sell vegetables and tourist merchandise. Indeed, something far more important than tomatoes or brass plates was being offered by those behind the temporary stalls. The "sellers" were members of a bicommunal team that had been working during the previous eight months on building a vision for peace in Cyprus, and they had created a set of fifteen bicommunal projects that they believed could jump-start a peace movement. Their goal was nothing less than to move the citizens and political leaders on both sides of the conflict toward a future where Turkish Cypriots and Greek Cypriots could become genuine partners in transforming the decades-old conflict into a multicultural society. Not afraid to dream big, they believed that a united Cyprus could serve as a model of interethnic and interreligious cooperation for the rest of the world.

To accomplish their bold aim, they needed to enlist a strong and influential group of individuals from a broad cross-section of Cypriot society to work with them on projects that promote dialogue and reconciliation. To this end, they invited over 100 people from the two communities to join them for a series of brief presentations about the projects they had created, followed by time to visit various booths set up to provide more information about each of the projects. At each booth was a bicommunal team eager to enlist the involvement of anyone interested in peacebuilding in Cyprus. At the end of the day, twelve of the projects had "sold," meaning bicommunal teams of eight to ten people had expressed an interest in working with the project leaders to design and implement a plan to carry out each project. This successful Agora-Bazaar marked the beginning of a sustained action phase of peacebuilding in Cyprus that continues to this day. Although no political settlement has been reached, hundreds of additional bicommunal projects have been implemented, and thousands of individuals on the island have been able to engage in meaningful dialogue and collaborative action across the dividing line.

In the nine months leading up to the event, and during the eighteen months that followed, I had the privilege of living in Cyprus and working as a third-party facilitator with the group of peacebuilders who staged the Agora-Bazaar described above. And in the nearly twenty-five years since that event, I have returned to Cyprus more than a dozen times to facilitate design workshops, trainings, and seminars, and to provide support to this core group and those who carried forward their efforts in the years that followed. We struggled together, we celebrated together, and we learned together as we encountered failures and successes, obstacles and breakthroughs, disappointments and triumphs. Even as an outsider, my life became intricately and intimately intertwined with the Cyprus conflict in ways I could never have anticipated. Nearly twenty-five years ago, I entered Cyprus with some knowledge of both the region and the conflict, but I quickly learned that my understanding was superficial at best and mistaken in ways I could not have known without such close involvement on the front lines of peacebuilding.

In this chapter, I will provide an account of the group's path to the Agora-Bazaar, sharing with you some of the challenges and questions we confronted as we walked together along the uneven paths of peace and conflict communication. This report is based on my personal experience working with the group that organized the Agora-Bazaar. I've shared aspects of this work previously, where you can find more detail about the methodology and the products of the sessions described in this chapter (see Broome, 1997, 2003; Broome & Murray, 2002). In this narrative, I am attempting to give a "behind-the-scenes" look at the challenges faced by the group and how we dealt with them. I will describe the many twists and turns that inevitably accompany peacebuilding work, offering insights into how we approached numerous decision points and how these played out as we worked through difficulties. The role of conflict transformer/peacebuilder is quite complex in practice, and my hope is that my experience will be helpful for those involved in conflict transformation and peacebuilding, and/or those affected by conflicts. Before telling the story of the Agora-Bazaar, I will provide a brief overview of the theoretical perspectives and group methodologies that underlie my approach to peacebuilding.

Grounding My Approach to Peacebuilding

My involvement in peacebuilding is informed and guided by the work of scholars such as Elise Boulding (2000), Johan Galgung (1969), and John Paul Lederach (1997, 2003). Boulding's emphasis on building a "culture of peace" and Galtung's notion of "positive peace" provide an underlying framework for my view of peacebuilding. I am particularly drawn by Lederach's focus on conflict transformation, in which he emphasizes change processes that go beyond ending violence or signing a peace accord, and instead focus on changing both relationships among the conflict parties and the structures that created and sustain the conflict. Lederach focuses on the big picture, on building sustainable peace that addresses the history and root causes of conflict (see Broome & Collier, 2012). Lederach also proposes what he calls a peacebuilding pyramid, in which he distinguishes between three different levels of leadership involved in attempts to resolve or transform conflict. The top-level leadership consists of political, military, and religious leaders, and this is where the most visible attempts at resolving conflict occur, with attention focused on high-level negotiations to broker a ceasefire or an agreement to end the conflict. At the lower level are those people who work daily with the details of conflict situation, including those involved with community development, education, and health care. In between these two levels are leaders of organizations, community groups, and humanitarian agencies who have connections to both the top and bottom levels of leadership. These leaders are able to view the conflict from both top and bottom perspectives, and because of their ties with each level, they can serve as the go-between to bring ideas upwards and help explain to those who are deeply involved in the daily struggle. Conflict transformation requires attention to all three levels, and peacebuilding requires integration of efforts up and down the pyramid.

Most of the work in which I have been involved during my career has focused on bringing groups together for various forms of *dialogue* (Anderson, Baxter, & Cissna, 2004; Bohm, 1996; Buber, 1958; Isaacs, 1999; Johannesen, 1971; W. B. Pearce & Littlejohn, 1997; Saunders, 2003; Stewart, 1978; Stewart & Zediker, 2000). My approach to dialogue is strongly influenced by Martin Buber's (1957, 1958) concept of the *between* as a guiding metaphor for human communication. For Buber, dialogue is rooted in the space that exists in the relationship between persons and groups. It is this common center of discourse, not the individual psyche of the interactants, that provides the dialogic core of interaction. Buber's emphasis on the sphere of the between and the way in which meaning is co-constituted during dialogue takes the focus away from both individualism and collectivism and places it on the relational. This gives recognition to the *interdependence* of self and other, the *intersubjectivity* of meaning, and the *emergent* nature of reality.

Methodologically, I have learned from scholars such as Herb Kelman (1976), Ron Fisher (1997), Harold Saunders (2011), Barnett Pearce (2004), John Stewart (1978), and William Issacs (1999). However, the approach I adopted in working with the peacebuilding group in Cyprus is based on an interactive design process developed by John Warfield (1976, 1994). Essentially, the process took groups through three stages: (1) identifying obstacles they face their peacebuilding efforts, (2) building a collective vision statement to guide their peacebuilding efforts, and (3) creating an action agenda for accomplishing their vision of peace in Cyprus. In Broome (1997), I described in detail the methodology as applied in Cyprus, and in Broome (2009), I described a concept called *relational empathy*, in which I connect Buber's concept of *between* to the methodology I utilized in Cyprus. The concept of relational empathy emphasizes the co-creation of meaning by participants in an interpersonal or group setting. Characterized by a series of constantly evolving approximations, new understandings can emerge within a group, allowing creative approaches to be developed and innovative ideas to be proposed.

I have gained both knowledge and inspiration from these and many other peacebuilding and dialogue scholars and practitioners. They have helped me understand both the complexities and fragility of peace. They have shown me a way to anticipate potential obstacles, and they've provided me with ways to deal with unanticipated challenges. They've given me tools to help groups engage in meaningful dialogue, and they've allowed me to experiment (carefully and thoughtfully) with ways to adapt these tools to the situational reality of the groups with whom I've worked. Without this theoretical and practical guidance, I would not have been able to work my way past multiple blockages or solve numerous puzzles that presented themselves along the way. Relying on established theories and the practical wisdom of other scholars, I could move through the landscape of peacebuilding with greater confidence, knowing that I was not operating in the dark and that if I stumbled, recovery was possible.

Getting Started

My initial involvement in Cyprus as a third-party facilitator came when I was awarded a Senior Fulbright Fellowship in conflict resolution.[1] This position had been requested of the Cyprus Fulbright Commission by Greek Cypriots and Turkish Cypriots who had participated in various conflict resolution workshops in prior years. These workshops had been held both in Cyprus and abroad (see next paragraph). Now they wanted to gain more training and possibly become trainers themselves, able to offer conflict resolution workshops both within their own communities and to bicommunal groups on the island. But underlying their explicit request for training was an even stronger goal of exploring ways to take the peace process forward. They had waited twenty long years for the political leaders to make progress on reaching an agreement to end the conflict. With little tangible progress on the political level, they were ready to work more actively at the civil society level. Although my Fulbright fellowship was for the purpose of providing conflict resolution training, it was clear that the more pressing need was for assistance in organizing and facilitating bicommunal dialogue groups.

When I began my Fulbright position in August 1994, contact between Turkish-Cypriot and Greek-Cypriot residents was very limited, with the "Green Line" that runs across the island (and through the center of the capital, Nicosia) creating a virtually impenetrable boundary of barbed wire and military checkpoints.[2] This physical division of the two communities made bicommunal contact nearly impossible without the assistance of a third party. Despite the physical separation of the two communities, a peace movement had been slowly developing over many years, with the assistance of several well-known conflict scholars, including John Burton (Burton, 1969), Chris Mitchell (Mitchell, 1981), Phillip Talbot (Talbot, 1977), Lawrence Doob (Doob, 1976), Herbert Kelman (Kelman, 2002), Ronald Fisher (Fisher, 1994, 1997), John McDonald and Louise Diamond (Diamond, 1997; Diamond & McDonald, 1996), and Diana Chigas (Chigas, 2003). Through these periodic workshops, a core group of Cypriots from both communities had engaged in various discussions and conflict resolution trainings, both inside and outside Cyprus. Most of the participants in the group I worked with had been part of one or more of those efforts, with the majority of them becoming involved through the recent seminars in which I had been part of the training team prior to starting my Fulbright residency.[3] Although it didn't necessarily make the work easier, this prior involvement gave me a head start as I began working with the core group that organized the Agora-Bazaar.

Even though I had already met most of the people with whom I would be working, and although many of them were ready to engage in bicommunal dialogue, I devoted my first few weeks to gaining a better understanding of the needs and desires of potential participants. I did this by spending time with individuals to learn more about their views, their needs, and their goals. I visited them in their workplaces and homes, shared meals with them, attended cultural events, and took walks with them through the city and in the countryside. I learned a lot about the complexities of the conflict and, more importantly, I developed personal relationships with many of the group members. Even though we started later than intended with our group work, I found these few weeks of relationship building to be invaluable in plotting a strategy for moving forward. And as we settled on a plan for our bicommunal dialogue sessions, everyone was onboard. Taking so much time to learn the context of the work and to develop personal relationships might not be an approach that most third-party facilitators can afford, but it was key to our surviving several setbacks.

My conversations with individuals during the beginning of my stay helped me understand the diverse motivations, goals, and interpretations held by different individuals about how to move forward with the peacebuilding work. These differences existed not only between community groups but equally *within* each community. Furthermore, other than their participation in the earlier conflict resolution workshops, participants had little experience working together, even in mono-communal settings, much less in a bicommunal setting. Partly because they had taken part in training with the "other side," they were already under attack from the media in both communities. Most importantly, their conversations with me reflected uncertainty about what they faced as peacebuilders or how to overcome the obstacles that stood in the way of peacebuilding.

This diversity of perceptions within and between groups, and the lack of experience working with one another, indicated that the group would benefit from sessions focused on identifying obstacles they faced as peacebuilders. These problem-definition sessions would position them to work on a joint vision for peace in Cyprus. If they could achieve the ambitious goal of constructing a collective vision statement, they would be well prepared for moving to the action stage of peacebuilding. I envisioned taking the group through these three phases, which I knew would require a lot of effort and willingness to tackle difficult topics. I didn't expect it to be a quick process, although the participants were eager to reach the action phase. Thus, one of the first challenges I faced was how to bring the bicommunal group onboard for prolonged and sustained design work. I wasn't sure they were ready to hear that it might take several months to progress through the three phases we had outlined. I also knew there were many unknown variables that could affect our progress, and it was best not to set up a timeline that would inevitably lead to disappointment. Fortunately, we were able to reach general agreement about moving forward carefully and purposefully, and they were willing not to impose a specific time frame for completing our work.

Overcoming Setbacks

Our first setback occurred almost immediately. We could not obtain permission to meet in a bicommunal setting. The buffer zone in Cyprus, which is monitored by United Nations peacekeeping troops, as well as by military/police forces on both sides, serves for the Greek Cypriots as a cease-fire line and for the Turkish Cypriots as a "border" for their self-declared state. At the time, there was a single official crossing, located in Nicosia, where diplomats and others with special permission were able to travel between the two sides. In the buffer zone between the checkpoints on either side is located a former luxury hotel, the "Ledra Palace," where U.N. troops were housed. Although the building was in poor condition and offered nothing more than a sparsely furnished (and rundown) set of meeting rooms, it was the only place where bicommunal meetings could be held, if proper permissions could be obtained from Greek-Cypriot, Turkish-Cypriot, and United Nations authorities. For the United Nations, the approval process consisted primarily of scheduling a room in which to meet. For the Greek Cypriot authorities, the approval process consisted primarily of providing a list of individuals who would be attending. For the Turkish-Cypriot authorities, however, the approval process required obtaining permissions from their foreign affairs office (and the Turkish military), since anyone crossing beyond the checkpoint is leaving what Turkish Cypriots consider to be their territory. Since bicommunal meetings were not looked upon favorably by the Turkish-Cypriot authorities, permissions were usually difficult to obtain.

Our initial plans were derailed when we were not granted permission to meet in a bicommunal setting, and we had to make a painful choice. Should we wait until we could obtain permission, not knowing when that might happen, or was there useful work that could be done in separate mono-communal meetings? The first option was in some ways the most logical. After all, the point of my being in Cyprus as a third party was to facilitate dialogue sessions *between* the two communities. Perhaps meeting in separate groups would just reinforce the division. Personally, I was torn between the need to move forward together as a bicommunal group, and the need to get started while the motivation was strong. I thought that meeting in different communal groups might accentuate the separation, but at the same time I feared that if we delayed until permissions were granted, momentum could be lost.

As it became clear that it could be several weeks before we could meet together as a bicommunal group, I started to wonder if we might actually benefit from meeting separately. Perhaps by engaging in the problem-definition stage in mono-communal groups, we could understand better some of the similarities and differences in how the two communities each see the situation. If we worked separately to identify obstacles to peacebuilding, the products from these mono-communal sessions might help each side learn about what the other side faced in their own community. It was not until after we started our work that I understood an equally important value of working in mono-communal groups—the need to resolve intra-group differences and promote teamwork within each community. The individuals who were part of these groups had not worked together before, and although some of them knew each other well, most were only casually acquainted with each other. Although unanticipated, it turned out to be beneficial for the two groups to spend time separately getting to know one another on a deeper level within their own group before engaging in the difficult task of dialogue across community lines.

In the mono-communal groups, several internal issues emerged in each community—differences in political orientations, various views about the meaning of "peace" with the other side, insufficient level of trust, competition for leadership of the group, and other potentially divisive matters. It's likely that these issues may have remained below the surface if we had been working in a bicommunal setting, and this could have made the dialogue more challenging. Although it is difficult to know how it might have played out had we been able to stay with our original plan of bicommunal meetings, it was easier to focus on issues of substance in the bicommunal group because we had surfaced these concerns first in a mono-communal setting. In fact, based on our learning from this experience, we later followed a similar pattern with other bicommunal groups, first scheduling mono-communal meetings prior to bringing them together in a bicommunal setting.

Dealing with Surprises

Soon after completing the mono-communal sessions, in which each group produced a structure depicting their view of the barriers to peacebuilding in Cyprus, we were able to obtain permissions for meeting together. The agenda for this joint meeting consisted primarily of presentations by each group of their product, with time for questions, observations, and comments. Of course, it was also a time for participants to see each other again after several months without contact, so we allocated a good deal of time for everyone to socialize.

Until the bicommunal meeting took place, neither group knew the results of the other's work, although each group knew that the other was exploring the same topic using the same methodology. I did not share information about one group's products with the other, because I did not want them to be influenced by the thinking of the other group. In any case, I thought it was best for the groups themselves to present their own views to the other rather than have it filtered through the eyes of a third party. There was, however, an assumption in each group that their products would be largely similar, since everyone involved was dedicated to building peace in Cyprus. As the facilitator for both sessions, I could see both similarities and differences in the obstacles they discussed, but I did not give a lot of thought to the implications the differences might have when they presented their products to one another in a joint session.

When the groups met and exchanged products, both groups were surprised by the disparities in outcomes, but the reaction from each group was quite different. The Turkish Cypriots were pleased to see how different the two structures were, while the Greek Cypriots, who had been expecting a great deal of overlap with their Turkish-Cypriot compatriots, were extremely disappointed that the two structures were not more compatible. As is common with minorities in every society, the Turkish Cypriots were aware that each community lived in a different world. The Greek Cypriots, however, did not realize how much the Turkish-Cypriot worldview differed from their own. Watching the reaction of the Greek Cypriots to their presentation, the Turkish Cypriots felt that for the first time the Greek Cypriots were confronted with the reality that the two communities faced quite different circumstances. Discouraged by the results, Greek Cypriots came away with the feeling: "If peacebuilders see the situation so differently, then what hope do we have that the two communities can live together in peace?"

The unexpected response of the Greek Cypriots reinforced for me the value of what we were doing, especially the need for in-depth discussion that helped participants get below the surface of issues. It became clear that most Greek Cypriots, even those who had been through conflict resolution workshops, were not sufficiently aware of the deeper reality of the other side. However, I also realized that it was naïve of me to expect the groups to take a purely academic point of view when dealing with the differences. Such discrepancies in views of peacebuilding called into question (for the Greek Cypriots) the very rationale for their work, while for the Turkish Cypriots, it served to reinforce their side's political position. It took quite a number of consultations with both sides to talk through the effects of the problem definition exchange. Although the results from this initial bicommunal discussion held significant learnings for all of us, I concluded that next time I should probably take specific steps to lessen the shock of differences prior to the groups exchanging results of their mono-communal sessions. Already deeply divided, it might be important to give some comfort by emphasizing the similarities. I would soon have a chance to test that conclusion.

Recovering from Breakdowns

When we completed our work on the problem-definition phase, we were ready to move into the vision phase of our work. Because our permission to meet as a bicommunal group was granted for a single meeting, we once again faced the dilemma of continuing in mono-communal groups or waiting until we could obtain additional permissions for bicommunal meetings. Although it had worked well to start our problem-definition work separately, it seemed inappropriate to work toward a joint vision in separate groups. But once again, we thought we might lose momentum if we stopped meeting. Thus, we decided to continue our work by initially meeting separately, as we had done in the previous stage, and then meet together to exchange results when we were able to obtain permissions.

The task each group took on was to develop a vision statement for the future of peacebuilding efforts in Cyprus. Our hope was that sufficient commonality existed across the two vision statements to start building a joint vision statement. Although we had been surprised by the divergent perceptions between the two groups when we were discussing perceived obstacles, this time we were all expecting to see even greater differences as each group considered goals for the future. After all, conflicting perceptions of the future are often what keep groups in conflict apart. Surprisingly, as these discussions unfolded in separate community sessions, I could see that, contrary to our expectations, there was significant overlap in the two structures. This seemed to be a positive development that would encourage each group in their work for peace.

Whereas in the earlier exchange I had not been involved in presenting the results from each community's problem-definition sessions, this time I thought it would help if I provided a contextual introduction and a summary of the similarities and differences. I prepared a graphic that showed both the overlapping aspects of the two vision statements, as well as the areas where they went in different directions. In the bicommunal meeting, I provided an initial contextual statement about the work, and after the groups had exchanged their vision statements, I presented this graphic, emphasizing the degree to which each structure had much in common. As I talked about the overlapping aspects of each group's vision statement, I detected a look of satisfaction on the faces of the Greek Cypriots, who appeared relieved that even though they had been disappointed by the differences in views of obstacles to peacebuilding, there was sufficient common ground to build a future together. But the Turkish Cypriots appeared concerned about the results. As we pursued our discussion, the enthusiastic response from the Greek Cypriots, eager now to work together to produce a collective vision statement, was contrasted by the lukewarm response from the Turkish Cypriots, hesitant to move to the next step.

During my consultations with the Turkish Cypriots after the exchange of communal vision statements, I learned that the surprising degree of overlap in each community's focus on the future was out-of-sync with the worldview prevalent within the Turkish-Cypriot community. They had been taught from an early age that they could never live with the Greek Cypriots because each held such vastly different views of the future. This was the basis for the argument that separate political entities and geographical zones were necessary in Cyprus. The extreme version of this view was not held by most members of the group, and some Turkish Cypriots were pleased by the degree of commonality. But everyone in the Turkish-Cypriot group was concerned that such a product could be used against them and could further complicate the process of obtaining permissions to hold bicommunal meetings.

Now we faced another serious dilemma. The Greek Cypriots, who had been ready to give up after the earlier exchange of problem structures, were eager to proceed, and the Turkish Cypriots, who had been pleased with results of the first phase, were now ready to stop work on the vision statement. If we tried to move ahead, the Greek Cypriots would be enthusiastic, and the Turkish Cypriots would resist. Complicating the issue was a history of past failed attempts by Turkish-Cypriot and Greek-Cypriot groups to create a common vision statement. Indeed, the lack of a shared view of the future seemed to be at the root of the conflict and the inability to reach a political agreement. Should we just skip this phase and move directly to the action agenda?

In spite of the resistance and the risks, I believed that building a joint vision statement was critical to the success of the group. In the third phase, where we would concentrate on building an agenda for joint projects, the group needed a clear vision of where it wanted to go before trying to start action projects. Many groups fail precisely because they take the wrong actions. Even when well-intended and supported by all, if actions are not taking the group where it needs to go, they will end up disappointed and feel as if they have been wasting their time. In fact, inappropriate actions could cause more damage than good. I realized there were risks involved—we might fail in our task, as other groups had done, or the Turkish Cypriots might resist the work, or the Greek Cypriots might become disillusioned if it did not go smoothly.

Fortunately, the Turkish Cypriots agreed to meet with the Greek Cypriots and share with them their fears about producing a joint vision statement and discuss how to move forward. I was prepared for a rocky start, and indeed there was a lot of discussion within the Turkish-Cypriot group between those who wanted to emphasize the differences against those who wanted to emphasize their commonality with the Greek Cypriots. At one point, two members of the Turkish-Cypriot group, both of whom had positions that could be jeopardized if the political leadership in the north turned against the group, decided they could no longer take part in our work on a collective vision statement. Fortunately, none of the other Turkish Cypriots joined them. This was a bold move on the part of those Turkish Cypriots who remained in the joint group, and their courage was recognized and greatly appreciated by the Greek Cypriots.

After the departure of the two Turkish Cypriots who believed it was not appropriate to continue working toward a joint vision statement, the atmosphere changed noticeably. It moved from a tense, highly charged discussion into a supportive exchange of views. Greek Cypriots acknowledged the concerns of the Turkish Cypriots, who in turn expressed appreciation for their understanding and sensitivity. The group began to view itself more as a single entity working toward a common set of goals, rather than separate community groups with different agendas. Surviving such a strong threat to their very existence gave them a confidence in moving forward. Over the next two months the group met regularly to undertake the delicate job of examining the future of peacebuilding efforts in Cyprus. It progressed smoothly in the beginning, until we hit the next "bump in the road."

Resolving an Impasse

Starting with the shared goals from each community's vision statement, the bicommunal group proposed additional goals they thought would be important to include in their joint vision statement. Unsurprisingly, there was intense discussion about the wording of some of the statements. Some goals from the original community structures, as well as some of the new items, included phrasing that was objectionable to one community or the other. These objections were not mere personal preferences in phrasing; rather, they reflected critical identity issues. It took time in every case to work through the disagreements, but both Turkish Cypriots and Greek Cypriots demonstrated sensitivity to each other's position and showed flexibility as they eventually worked through nearly all of the contested items.[4]

But at one point in the group's work on their vision statement, there was a particularly intricate struggle dealing with wording of one of the items proposed by the Greek Cypriots. The group could not get past the disagreement, and it was not clear how we would be able to proceed. We had reached an impasse. As it became clear that the solution would not likely come from within the group, they decided to ask a few trusted colleagues from outside the group to see if they could find an appropriate wording that might satisfy the concerns of both communities. Since the group had been working every week for nearly two months, the chance to take a break from the intense discussions was welcomed. Fortunately, the outside individuals were able to propose a change in wording that helped the group move forward, although it took more discussion and additional changes by the group before it could be accepted. Their ability to negotiate an acceptable wording for this critical goal was a breakthrough for the group, and it allowed them to move forward with completing a joint vision statement, an accomplishment that had eluded several other attempts by prior groups.

The group was able to overcome this impasse for several reasons. First, by this point, the group bonds were strong, and there was no fear that the existence of the group was threatened by the dispute. In earlier breakdowns, there was doubt on everyone's part about the ability of the group to survive and continue with their work. Second, the group had learned to trust each other, and they knew that one side was not trying to harm the other. They didn't interpret the reluctance of the other side to compromise as an attempt to gain an advantage, but rather as a genuine concern about an identity issue that was important to protect. Third, they had resolved several disagreements successfully, and they were confident that this stalemate could be broken. Earlier in the process, they were facing a long history of failures on the island, and it was easy for them to view their difficulties as simply one more example of the impossibility of progress, even among well-intentioned people. Now, however, they knew that something could be worked out, but they were just stuck and needed help. Fortunately, the assistance they sought was available and came through for them. As a result, they resolved the impasse and were able to complete the collective vision statement.

The importance of achieving a collective vision statement required a great deal of time and effort, but it provided a strong foundation for the group's next steps in the process. With direction and guidance from their joint vision statement, they understood where they wanted to go as a group. As they moved into the action phase, they were well-equipped to make choices that would help them realize the future they envisioned. Perhaps even more importantly, the process of thinking about the future together helped them understand and accept individual and community differences in aims and objectives. As they entered the next phase, where they would consider the merits of various options and proposals for action, individuals would naturally bring somewhat different motivations and purposes. While these differences could cause friction and conflict, the vision statement would be there to help focus the group toward a common set of goals, while preserving the individual differences. They were now well-positioned to enter the final phase of their work with momentum, enthusiasm, and perspective.

Holding on for the Ride

With the collective vision statement complete, the group was eager to start the third phase of their work: design a collaborative action agenda for peace-building in Cyprus. In the earlier phases, I had to struggle with a series of unanticipated challenges that were thrown at us or that emerged within the group. At times, I felt that I had to paddle against a strong current and steer the group away from turbulent waters and rocky shores. Now I found myself needing to hold on tight as the group pushed ahead in fast-moving waters. A simple question, asking them to generate options for making their vision structure a reality, unleashed a torrent of ideas, all of them presented with a confidence that they could make them happen. In a short time, they generated a set of options that ranged across a broad spectrum of activities and projects. Proposals included conducting workshops for educationalists, business leaders, young political leaders, and other groups across society; establishing academic programs and centers that focused on issues related to peace and conflict resolution; empowering women and other segments of society whose voices had been minimized; conducting training workshops in mediation and other types of conflict resolution skills; establishing a bicom-munal radio station, magazine, and other media outlets that could provide an alternative to the nationalist programming that dominated the scene at the time; organizing artistic exchanges for music, poetry, theater, photography, and other forms of artistic expression; setting up language learning programs so that everyone could study Greek or Turkish; forming study groups to focus on governance practices that might have lessons for Cyprus; meeting with politicians from both sides to urge forward thinking and risk taking; bring-ing together religious leaders to talk about peace; rewriting history books to paint a less biased image of the other community; securing better facilities for conducting bicommunal gatherings and for housing administrative work associated with all the projects, and numerous other ambitious projects.

In total, they proposed more than 240 options, which we sorted into 16 categories. In our initial attempt to select a set of activities for implementation during the following year, the group selected fifty-four projects, which of course was quite unrealistic for such a small group to implement. In attempting to move toward a more realistic plan, we formed fifteen bicommunal teams and each team selected a project from the set of fifty-four ideas. Then, we discussed how to involve people outside our group in implementing these ideas, and after considering a number of possibilities, we realized that what we were trying to do was not that different from what vendors are doing every day in the marketplaces of Cyprus, Greece, Turkey, and other countries across the eastern Mediterranean. Hence was born the idea of an Agora-Bazaar!

The Story Continues[5]

The success of the Agora-Bazaar set the stage for a very active period of bicommunal meetings over the next eighteen months. The thirty Turkish Cypriots and Greek Cypriots, who had worked so tirelessly to reach the point where they could bring a set of projects to a wider group of participants, were now strengthened in both numbers and possibilities for peacebuilding. When the Agora-Bazaar ended that June day in 1995, there were approximately 150 people involved in the peacebuilding efforts, and over the next 18 months it expanded to nearly 2,000 people who were attending various meetings and participating in the events that were organized by the project groups. All twelve projects went forward in some form, and other related projects spun off as more people got involved. During the nearly twenty-five years that have followed the Agora-Bazaar, dozens of new groups have formed, most of them with no direct connection to the original twelve projects. Across Cyprus, a surprising number of people have been inspired to meet and work with individuals from the other side.

There have been many setbacks, at times making bicommunal dialogue extremely difficult, but also extremely important. Some setbacks arose from violent events in the buffer zone that increased nationalist rhetoric and led to a prolonged suspension of bicommunal activities (see Broome, Anastasiou, Hadjipavlou, & Kanol, 2012). Impediments frequently arose from political decisions, including a nearly complete shutdown of bicommunal activities by the Turkish-Cypriot authorities when the bicommunal movement became large enough to be seen as a threat to the rhetoric of division that the authorities (at that time) used to justify the existence of a separate state.[6] Perhaps the most serious setback occurred after a U.N.-brokered peace plan was voted down in 2004 by the Greek Cypriots (while overwhelmingly accepted by the Turkish Cypriots), an outcome that effectively brought down the sails of the bicommunal boat for an extended period of time.

But through all the adversity, the urge to have contact and communication with the other community has not diminished. And the people involved in the bicommunal peace movement have persevered, keeping alive the collective vision statement and carrying forward the results of the Agora-Bazaar. Despite the challenges they faced, the small group of thirty peace pioneers who met together during 1994–1995 produced products that directly led to a sustained activity phase of the peace movement in Cyprus that continues to this day.[7]

Reflections

My involvement with the peacebuilding efforts in Cyprus provided many opportunities to observe the group dynamics of both mono-communal and bicommunal settings, and to reflect upon my role as a third-party facilitator. Although I have been constantly learning from my experiences, I hesitate to offer "lessons" for others. The Cyprus conflict is both complex and protracted, and I realize that what I learned might not be transferable to other conflict situations. Nevertheless, I can offer a few observations and reflections that I hope will be interesting and informative, and perhaps useful, for those working in other conflict settings. I will discuss the complexity of developing trust, the nature of sustainable peacebuilding, the constant monitoring of my own cultural biases, and the search for how to best respond appropriately to the cultural context in which I am working.

From the beginning of my stay, I experienced both the importance and the difficulty of *building trust* with participants. Third parties working with intergroup conflicts always face scrutiny, but it is essential that participants have confidence in the ability of the facilitator to work fairly with all sides. Fortunately, the job of establishing trust did not fall completely on my shoulders. I came to Cyprus as a Fulbright Scholar, bringing with me both the prestige and status associated with academic positions, as well as the credibility of the Fulbright Commission, which had a long history of treating both sides fairly and equitably. Second, because I had served as a member of the workshop training team prior to taking up my Fulbright position, participants had the opportunity to know me as a knowledgeable and sincere person, committed to peace. Third, because I had lived in the region previously and had studied the culture, I was able to adapt quickly to my surroundings and feel more comfortable in social situations, with less probability of making a cultural faux pas.

Despite these initial advantages, I realized over time that the critical task of building trust was a more complex endeavor than we usually acknowledge. The positive circumstances related to my position and prior relationship with participants were only the starting point. I found that developing strong interpersonal relationships was key to success, and the only way to cement these ties was to spend quality time with the participants, eating together, taking long walks, traveling around the island, attending local cultural events together, and visiting in their homes. Sometimes the need to be with group members cut into my own professional and family obligations and my personal care time, and the sheer intensity of the group meetings sometimes left me with the need for time alone, rather than continuing discussions outside the workshop setting. Importantly, I came to understand that trust is a multi-level process, and actions that promote it on one level may mitigate it on another. Establishing trust with one side did not always help (and sometimes hindered) in building trust with the other side. Of course, having the trust of the participants with whom I was working closely was not sufficient for establishing trust with officials or within the wider society. This was a very different task, and space does not allow me to adequately discuss this aspect of my experience in this chapter. Trust, I came to understand, is a complex and fragile process that must be constantly nurtured.

In Cyprus, I came to appreciate the framework for *sustainable peacebuilding* developed by Lederach (1997), in which he stresses that interventions in protracted intergroup conflict situations are best viewed as long-term commitments. All too often, and for many understandable reasons, conflict resolution interventions occur in what might be called a "parachute-in" fashion. The third party drops in, sometimes without extensive knowledge of the local situation or culture, offers a packaged training module, and then departs with little or no follow-up. It is easy to understand the reasons for this pattern, although they are not entirely persuasive. While not all third-party assistance requires a continuous physical presence, in situations where citizen peacebuilding is a primary concern and where there is high tension, physical division, and low trust, those receiving third-party assistance need continuous support over a long period in order to build the group's capacity for sustainable peacebuilding.

I realized early in my stay that the facilitator must be perceived as having the best interests of the groups always in mind. If participants had seen me as being in Cyprus primarily for my own academic research purposes, they would have treated me politely but at arm's length, and it's unlikely they would have been willing to participate in the design sessions with strong commitment. After all, I was asking the group to invest in a lengthy process for which the outcome was uncertain. But they trusted me to guide them through a facilitated process that probably appeared risky to them. I was greatly assisted by the residency nature of my assignment—I was not just flying in for a few weeks and leaving the results (good or bad) in the hands of the Cypriots, but I was living side by side with the individuals with whom I worked. It was clear that I was making a commitment to their efforts, devoting a sizable slice of my career and my life to their endeavors. They understood the seriousness of my intentions, and they knew that I would be with them through both the difficult situations and the successes. I realize that very few third-party facilitators have the luxury of stepping away from their academic position and devoting months or years of their career to working in a remote setting.[8] This doesn't mean they won't be able to accomplish meaningful results, but it affects the nature of both the process and the outcomes that are possible.

It is difficult to know how the work in Cyprus would have progressed without the continuous presence of a third party, but most of the bicommunal meetings could not have occurred,[9] and some of the more challenging groups would not have formed. In addition, several external events occurred that severely affected peacebuilding, and I believe it was very important to have someone who could provide a broader perspective on the situation during these times of crisis, and who could offer encouragement to continue the work of peacebuilding in the face of increased nationalist rhetoric. My Greek-Cypriot and Turkish-Cypriot colleagues deserve all the credit for the growth of the peacebuilding work in Cyprus, but looking back I can see that the continuous presence of a third party during an important period of its development played a key role in helping shape the direction of the work and in overcoming several difficult hurdles. Since leaving Cyprus, I have continued to visit the island regularly to work with an expanding group of peacebuilders on their joint projects. Even though I am no longer living in Cyprus, working on a daily basis with my colleagues, I remain involved and available when needed.

Throughout my stay in Cyprus, I found it was critical to *constantly monitor my own biases*, to prevent my cultural predispositions from negatively affecting the task of mediating conflicts. Most of the time when we advocate "neutrality" (which is not possible) or "impartiality" (which is a more reasonable goal), our focus tends to be on the content of the conflict. I believe I was able to maintain an impartial position about the Cyprus conflict; if anything, I could see fully the logic in both the Greek-Cypriot and Turkish-Cypriot positions. However, my own cultural background sometimes led me unconsciously to side with the preferred mode of operation of one group or the other. For example, I found myself more comfortable with the Greek-Cypriot orientation to moving beyond the past and focusing on the future, while I had more difficulty adapting to the Turkish Cypriot's emphasis on past events. On the other side of the coin, I was often more comfortable with the low-key and careful approach of the Turkish Cypriots than with the more sometimes impulsive spontaneity of the Greek Cypriots. These and other cultural biases led me to often advocate a position that was agreeable to one side but resisted by the other. Of course, cultural bias is inevitable, but I'm always seeking to be more aware of and hopefully minimize the interference of my own cultural values in performing effectively as mediator and facilitator.

Finally, I continuously searched for how to *respond appropriately to the cultural context* in which I was working. As my former colleagues Kevin Avruch, Peter Black, and Joseph Scimecca (1991) have noted persuasively, one of the most delicate challenges for the third-party facilitator is operating appropriately within the local cultural context. One of the clearest examples of this challenge was my struggle to find the right balance of imported/indigenous methods of conflict resolution methodologies and processes. I have seen several third-party trainers simply bring in approaches to conflict resolution that they used in U.S. and European settings and apply these without giving much thought to cultural considerations. Sometimes, these are effective and have positive effects. Other colleagues have advocated using only processes that were developed in the local culture, avoiding those developed elsewhere. As a student of intercultural communication, I was well aware of cultural factors, and with previous experience in numerous intercultural settings, I realized the types of adjustments that might be necessary. Nevertheless, the subtleties of working in Cyprus required constant monitoring of my own mode of operating, as well as making appropriate adjustments in the processes and methodologies I employed. I was always concerned about the cultural fit between the eastern Mediterranean culture of the Cypriots and the Western-developed group processes that I was bringing with me. I tried to be careful that the methodologies I employed were not incompatible with the cultural context in which I was working. Failure to do so not only results in poor-quality outcomes, but also can cause damage that may not show up until well after the outsiders are safely back in their own environment (Galtung, 1969).

At the same time, imported processes should not be rejected just because they are from the outside. One of the advantages of a third party is the ability to introduce new methodologies that help break destructive cultural patterns that may be keeping the participants from moving forward. I believe that it is important to engage in mindful application of techniques and principles, doing one's best to implement them with the appropriate degree of cultural sensitivity. In my case, I had to carefully evaluate the entire process at each step of the way in order to determine the cultural fit of anticipated actions, encouraging local participants to adapt or shape the methodologies in ways that better fit their culture.

Clearly, I gained much more than I contributed during my time in Cyprus. My Greek-Cypriot and Turkish-Cypriot colleagues taught me much, and I was privileged to work with them. They helped me to see past many of my own cultural biases, and to constantly examine my goals and intentions. They showed me the true meaning of sustained commitment to peacebuilding and helped me understand what it takes to engage in conflict transformation. I had the luxury of knowing that I would leave Cyprus and go back to a more secure environment, certainly not one without its own issues, but one where resources and possibilities were more plentiful. I will be always indebted to my colleagues and friends in Cyprus for allowing me to join them in the quest for dialogue across the Green Line.

Wrapping Up

As I finish writing this chapter, the news is filled with stories commemorating the fall of the Berlin Wall thirty years ago. Its collapse left Nicosia, the capitol of Cyprus, as the world's last (physically) divided city. It seems grossly inappropriate that this "honor" goes to a city that is part of the European Union. Of course, there are many other divided countries and geographic regions, and some, such as the Korean peninsula, can claim a division that precedes Cyprus. But the bullet-riddled walls of abandoned and now crumbling homes and streets that cut through Nicosia, along with the guard posts and barbed wire strung 180 kilometers across the island, are truly an anomaly among democratic countries around the world. Without the work of the peacebuilding groups, it is possible that there would have been practically no bicommunal dialogue at the civil society level since the war in 1974, something that is almost inconceivable in today's world.

At the political level, it is difficult to predict when (or if) there will be an agreement to end the decades-old division. The Cyprus conflict has defied the best efforts of the international community to mediate an agreement to reunify the island under a federal arrangement. Five UN Secretaries-General and their special envoys have failed to bring the two sides together. Despite the lack of a political settlement, at the civil society level there has been steady and meaningful progress in promoting bicommunal dialogue and collaboration. Fortunately, the thousands of individuals and hundreds of groups that have met and worked together across the buffer zone have kept alive contact and communication that will be crucial in the event of a political settlement. The lives that have been transformed and the relationships that have developed as a result of these bicommunal exchanges will be vital in working and living together in a united Cyprus.[10] And importantly, the bicommunal activities have helped many individuals on the island embrace a hopeful future where the two communities can break with a painful past to create a society where people live in peace.

Notes

1. This was the first time that the Fulbright program had funded a position focused on conflict resolution. The Washington, D.C.-based office overseeing the Fulbright program had been hesitant to approve this fellowship because they feared it pushed the boundaries of the program's stated aim of educational exchange. The appointment was initially approved for a three-month term, acting as a sort of trial run, and soon after arriving, it was extended (see end of this note). It was also a risk for the Cyprus Fulbright Commission, and I credit Daniel Hadjitoffi, who was then the director of the Cyprus Fulbright Commission, for his willingness to advocate for this position, both with his own local board and with the Washington, D.C. office that was responsible for approving local requests. Ambassador Richard Boucher, who was completing his term at the end of my first year in Cyprus, and Ambassador Kenneth Brill, who was appointed to replace Boucher, were both supportive of continuing the Fulbright Scholar position. Their efforts, along with those of their public affairs officers, Marcelle Wabba and Judy Baroody, were instrumental in making possible my second and third terms in Cyprus. Finally, I want to acknowledge the foresight and commitment of the Greek Cypriots and Turkish Cypriots in Cyprus who had advocated for the initial position and who had continued lobbying for it even after facing resistance. Thanks to their efforts, and the support of the Cyprus Fulbright Commission, my position was extended initially to a full academic year, and then later additional funds were made available through the United Nations Office of Project Services (UNOPS) to continue my residency for another eighteen months. This allowed me to continue my residency until the end of December 1996, a total of nearly two and one-half years.
2. For a history of the Cyprus conflict, the following resources are recommended: (Anastasiou, 2008; Attalides, 1979; Bryant, 2004; Fisher, 2001; Hadjipavlou, 2007; Heraclides, 2011; Hitchens, 1997; Joseph, 2009; Ker-Lindsay, 2011; Kizilyurek, 1993, 2010; Koumoulides, 1986; Markides, 1977; Papadakis, 2006; Richmond, 1998; Stearns, 1992; Volkan, 1979).
3. The Cyprus Consortium, which included the Institute for Multi-Track Diplomacy (IMTD) and the Conflict Management Group (CMG), offered a series of conflict resolution training workshops during the spring and summer of 1994, prior to the start of my Fulbright fellowship. They invited me to be part of the training team for three of these workshops.
4. Specifics of constructing the collective vision statement, with several specific examples of the struggle over wording, are described in Broome, 2004.

5. Several of the twelve projects that "sold" at the Agora-Bazaar in June 1995 required a third-party facilitator in order for them to move forward, and I stayed in Cyprus another eighteen months, facilitating bicommunal groups of young business leaders, young political leaders, and university students. I also led study groups examining issues of identity in Cyprus, provided training in the dialogue methods we used to create the collective vision statement and action agenda, and facilitated the initial meetings of a women's group that later became a key force for peace in Cyprus.

6. From January 1997 until the partial lifting of restrictions in April 2003, additional limitations on bicommunal meetings were put in place that make it difficult for the group to implement many of its activities. The lack of permissions for Turkish Cypriots to pass the checkpoint for meetings with Greek Cypriots brought a stop to many of the groups that had been meeting on a regular basis, although a few maintained contacts online (Internet Service Providers, or ISPs, were available in Cyprus starting at the end of 1996) and several groups continued to meet at the mixed village of Pyla, located next to the buffer zone in the British sovereign base area.

7. At the end of my residency in Cyprus, the Fulbright Commission authorized the continuation of the conflict resolution Fulbright position, and the work was carried on in following years by other scholars, including Philip Snyder, John Ungerleighter, and Marco Turk, who were particularly instrumental in helping sustain the bicommunal peace movement in Cyprus during the period 1997–2000.

8. I owe a great deal to my department chair at George Mason University (GMU), Don Boileau, for making it possible for me to be away from August 1994 through December 1996. He understood the value such an experience would bring to both my own career and to the university, and he "protected" me during my time away from GMU.

9. At the time I was In Cyprus, the only way for bicommunal groups to meet in the buffer zone was with the assistance of a third party.

10. See Broome (2005) for an overview of the activities of bicommunal groups and the contributions of these groups to building peace in Cyprus.

References

Anastasiou, H. (2008). *The broken olive branch: Nationalism, ethnic conflict and the quest for peace in Cyprus* (vol. I: The Impasse of Ethnonationalism). Syracuse, NY: Syracuse University Press.

Anderson, R., Baxter, L. A., & Cissna, K. N. (eds.). (2004). *Dialogue: Theorizing difference in communication studies*. Thousand Oaks, CA: Sage.

Attalides, M. A. (1979). *Cyprus: Nationalism and international politics*. Edinburgh: Q Press.

Avruch, K., Black, P. W., & Scimecca, J. A. (eds.). (1991). *Conflict resolution: Crosscultural perspectives*. London: Praeger.

Bohm, D. (1996). *On dialogue*. London: Routledge.

Boulding, E. (2000). *Cultures of peace: The hidden side of history*. New York: Syracuse University Press.

Broome, B. J. (1997). Designing a collective approach to peace: Interactive design and problem-solving workshops with Greek-Cypriot and Turkish-Cypriot communities in Cyprus. *International Negotiation*, *2*(3): 381–407.

Broome, B. J. (2003). Responding to the challenges of third-party facilitation: Reflections of a scholar-practitioner in the Cyprus conflict. *Journal of Intergroup Relations*, *26*(4): 24–43.

Broome, B. J. (2004). Reaching across the dividing line: Building a collective vision for peace in Cyprus. *International Journal of Peace Research*, *41*(2): 191–209. doi:10.1177/0022343304041060.

Broome, B. J. (2005). *Building bridges across the Green Line: A guide to intercultural communication in Cyprus*. Nicosia: United Nations Development Program.

Broome, B. J. (2009). Building relational empathy through an interactive design process. In D. J. D. Sandole, S. Byrne, I. Staroste-Sandole, & J. Senihi (eds.), *Handbook of conflict analysis and resolution* (pp. 184–200). New York: Routledge.

Broome, B. J., Anastasiou, H., Hadjipavlou, M., & Kanol, B. (2012). Opening communication pathways in protracted conflict: From tragedy to dialogue in Cyprus. In L. R. Frey & K. M. Carragee (eds.), *Communication activism: Struggling for social justice amidst difference* (vol. 3, pp. 69–104). Cresskill, NJ: Hampton Press.

Broome, B. J., & Collier, M. J. (2012). Culture, communication, and peacebuilding: A reflexive multi-dimensional contextual framework. *Journal of International and Intercultural Communication*, *5*(4): 245–269. doi:10.1080/17513057.2012.716858.

Broome, B. J., & Murray, J. S. (2002). Improving third-party decisions at choice points: A Cyprus case study. *Negotiation Journal*, *18*(1): 75–98.

Bryant, R. (2004). *Imagining the modern. The cultures of nationalism in Cyprus*. London: I.B. Tauris.

Buber, M. (1957). Elements of the interhuman. *Psychiatry*, *20*, 105–113.

Buber, M. (1958). *I and Thou*, 2nd ed. (R. G. Smith, trans.). New York: Scribner.

Burton, J. W. (1969). *Conflict and communication: The use of controlled communication in international relations*. London: Macmillan.

Chigas, D. (2003). Track II (citizen) diplomacy. In G. Burgess & H. Burgess (eds.), *Beyond intractability*. Boulder, CO: Conflict Research Consortium, University of Colorado, Boulder. Posted: May 2004 http://www.beyondintractability.org/essay/track2_diplomacy/

Diamond, L. (1997). Training in conflict-habituated systems: Lessons from Cyprus. *International Negotiation*, *2*(3): 353–380.

Diamond, L., & McDonald, J. (1996). *Multi-track diplomacy: A systems approach to peace*. West Hartford: Kumarian Press.

Doob, L. W. (1976). A Cyprus workshop: Intervention methodology during a continuing crisis. *Journal of Social Psychology*, *98*, 143–144.

Fisher, R. J. (1994). *Education and peacebuilding in Cyprus: A report on two conflict analysis workshops.* McGill University: Canadian Institute for International Peace and Security.

Fisher, R. J. (1997). *Interactive conflict resolution.* Syracuse: Syracuse University Press.

Fisher, R. J. (2001). Cyprus: The failure of mediation and the escalation of an identity-based conflict to an adversarial impasse. *Journal of Peace Research, 38*(3): 307–326. doi:10.1177/0022343301038003003.

Galtung, J. (1969). Violence, peace, and peace research. *Journal of Peace Research, 6*(3): 167–191.

Hadjipavlou, M. (2007). The Cyprus conflict: Root causes and implications for peacebuilding. *Journal of Peace Research, 44*(3): 349–365. doi:10.1177/0022343307076640.

Heraclides, A. (2011). The Cyprus Gordian knot: An intractable ethnic conflict. *Nationalism & Ethnic Politics, 17*(2): 117–139.

Hitchens, C. (1997). *Hostage to history: Cyprus from the Ottomans to Kissinger.* New York: Noonday Press.

Isaacs, W. N. (1999). *Dialogue and the art of thinking together.* New York: Doubleday.

Johannesen, R. L. (1971). The emerging concept of communication as dialogue. *Quarterly Journal of Speech, 57,* 373–382.

Joseph, J. S. (2009). Cyprus: Domestic ethnopolitical conflict and international politics. *Nationalism & Ethnic Politics, 15*(3/4): 376–397.

Kelman, H. C. (2002). Interactive problem-solving: Informal mediation by the scholar-practitioner. In J. Bercovitch (ed.), *Studies in international mediation* (pp. 167–193). London: Palgrave Macmillan.

Kelman, H. C., & Cohen, S. P. (1976). The problem-solving workshop: A social-psychological contribution to the resolution of international conflicts. *Journal of Peace Research, 13*(2): 79–90.

Ker-Lindsay, J. (2011). *The Cyprus problem: What everyone needs to know.* Oxford: Oxford University Press.

Kizilyurek, N. (1993). *Cyprus beyond the nation.* Nicosia: G. Kasoulides.

Kizilyurek, N. (2010). *Glafkos Clerides: The path of a country.* Cyprus: Cyprus Rimal Publications.

Koumoulides, J. T. A. (ed.) (1986). *Cyprus in transition: 1960–1985.* London: Trigraph.

Lederach, J. P. (1997). *Building peace: Sustainable reconciliation in divided societies.* Washington, DC: United States Institute of Peace.

Lederach, J. P. (2003). *The little book of conflict transformation.* Intercourse, PA: Good Books.

Markides, K. C. (1977). *The rise and fall of the Cyprus republic.* New Haven: Yale University Press.

Mitchell, C. R. (1981). *Peacemaking and the consultant's role.* New York: Nichols Publishing Company.

Papadakis, Y. (2006). *Echoes from the dead zone: Across the Cyprus divide.* London: I.B. Tauris.

Pearce, W. B., & Littlejohn, S. W. (1997). *Moral conflict: When social worlds collide.* Thousand Oaks, CA: Sage.

Pearce, W. B., & Pearce, K. A. (2004). Taking a communication perspective on dialogue. In R. Anderson, L. Baxter, & K. N. Cissna (eds.), *Dialogue: Theorizing differences in communication studies* (pp. 43–48). Thousand Oaks, CA: Sage.

Richmond, O. P. (1998). *Mediating in Cyprus. The Cypriot communities and the United Nations.* London: Frank Cass.

Saunders, H. H. (2003). Sustained dialogue in managing intractable conflict. *Negotiation Journal, 19,* 85–95.

Saunders, H. H. (2011). *Sustained dialogue in conflicts: Transformation and change.* New York: Palgrave.

Stearns, M. (1992). *Entangled allies: U.S. Policy toward Greece, Turkey, and Cyprus.* New York: Council on Foreign Relations Press.

Stewart, J. (1978). Foundations of dialogic communication. *Quarterly Journal of Speech, 64,* 183–201.

Stewart, J., & Zediker, K. (2000). Dialogue as tensional, ethical practice. *Southern Communication Journal, 65*(2/3): 224.

Talbot, P. (1977). The Cyprus seminar. In M. Berman & J. E. Johnson (eds.), *Unofficial diplomats.* New York: Columbia University Press.

Volkan, V. D. (1979). *Cyprus—war and adaptation. A psychoanalytic history of two ethnic groups in conflict.* Charlottesville: University Press of Virginia.

Warfield, J. N. (1976). *Societal systems: Planning, policy, and complexity.* New York: Wiley.

Warfield, J. N. (1994). *A science of generic design: Managing complexity through systems design,* 2nd ed. Salinas, CA: Intersystems.

Part V: Teaching and Learning Peace and Conflict Transformation

10 Dialogic Prudence: Promoting Transformative Conflict through Civil Dialogue®

ROBERT J. RAZZANTE, KATRINA N. HANNA, AND JENNIFER A. LINDE

> I think that hate is not a very productive thing to be feeling. I also feel that, I would never, you know, back somebody who is advocating eugenics or something. But I also think it's important that we maintain our freedom of speech because language is so strong. It can change and it hurts us in some ways. But I feel that in order to have a society where we can live and hear other people's opinions that maybe don't agree with us, but maybe we can live alongside them we should be able to say what we feel.—Dialogue participant

Communication scholars are called to solve problems and manage social dilemmas (Craig, 2018). However, as engaged scholars, we have the responsibility to create a "reflexive bridge" between the academy and our communities when intervening (Putnam & Dempsey, 2015, p. 9). As defined by Connaughton and colleagues (2017), a relationally attentive approach to engaged scholarship centralizes collaboration, inclusivity, and reflexivity when deciding how to intervene. For example, when social catastrophes like the 2017 Charlottesville uprising occur, the authors of this chapter assumed a responsibility to act. However, before acting, we engaged in what we define as, dialogic prudence. In this chapter, we first theoretically situate our project within engaged scholarship generally and critical communication pedagogy specifically. We then offer a case study rooted within the Charlottesville uprising of 2017. In doing so, we define and exemplify dialogic prudence as a method and orientation for engaging communities on provocative social issues through educational contexts. Finally, we offer Civil Dialogue®[1] (hereinafter, CD) as a specific dialogic space for research and pedagogy.

Critical Communication Pedagogy

Engaged scholarship focuses on how communication scholars can use their skills to respond to the needs of communities and organizations of which they are a part (Seibold, 2005). Rather than transferring knowledge to community members, engaged scholars embraces the notion of co-producing knowledge with communities through various ways (Dempsey & Barge, 2014). For example, Putnam and Dempsey (2015) review five faces of engaged scholarship: applied communication research, collaborative learning, activism and social justice, practical theory, and public scholarship. While axiologically aligned with activism and social justice research, our use of CD most closely aligns with critical communication pedagogy (Fassett & Warren, 2007).

Critical communication pedagogy centers the link between communication, culture, and power in educational contexts (Fassett & Warren, 2007). More particularly, a critical communication pedagogical approach offers the space where diverse and competing narratives engage one another for transformative understanding to emerge. Recently, there has been a push to move critical communication pedagogy beyond the confines of an academic classroom (Fassett & Rudick, 2016). As such, we advocate how critical communication pedagogy aligns with the motives of engaged scholarship when held in communities. We also advocate the need for dialogic prudence when designing and implementing educational events around contentious issues. In other words, we use dialogic prudence as a grounding mechanism to raise our awareness of the risks and harms our educational intervention may cause.

In what follows, we offer a description of CD as a dialogic space (Rule, 2004) for educational purposes. We then offer our definition of dialogic prudence by describing its three tenets: provocation, value-rationality, and synergy—each derived from our experience and previous scholarship using the method. More specifically, we offer dialogic prudence as a methodological orientation engaged scholars can adopt when engaging communities in dialogue on provocative social issues. We then use dialogic prudence as a framework to analyze how community members engaged one another through CD. Finally, we conclude with implications for engaged scholars who wish to engage transformative conflict through critical communication pedagogy. By embracing dialogic prudence in critical communication pedagogy, engaged scholars can work with communities to foster transformative conflict.

Civil Dialogue®

Civil Dialogue®, a model distinguished by John Genette, Clark Olson, and Jennifer Linde (2018) features spontaneous face-to-face interaction among students/citizens (not a panel of experts) in an atmosphere that promotes respect and equanimity. Audience members consider a provocative statement, and volunteer participants are called upon to embody their positions in a semi-circle of five chairs on stage—"Agree Strongly," "Agree Somewhat," "Neutral/Undecided," "Disagree Somewhat," and "Disagree Strongly" (see Figure 10.1). It is not a contest; the goal is not to seek advocacy but to reacquaint the public with the notion that citizens can have differing viewpoints or disagree without demonizing the opposition. The core dialogue participants, each of whom have self-selected to take one of the five chairs, are invited to give opening statements, followed by a guided but spontaneous discussion of their viewpoints. Following the core dialogue, audience members are solicited for their questions and input. Such input is encouraged to challenge and extend the core dialogue's conversation. The CD concludes with a summative recap by the dialogue's facilitator. We used this particular model to engage community members on the topic of White supremacy.

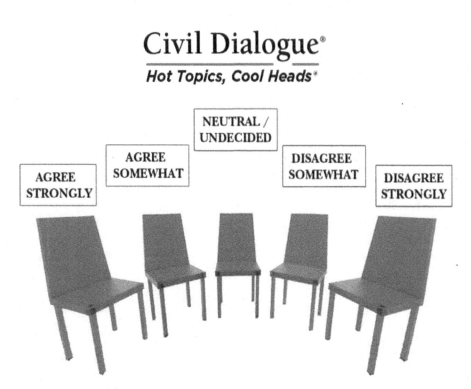

Figure 10.1. Civil Dialogue® Format (Genette, Olson, & Linde, 2018, p. 103).

Charlottesville Uprising

On the night of August 11, 2017, a group of White men and women flooded the University of Virginia's campus with lit tiki-torches. Chants of "White lives matter," "Blood and soil," and "Jews will not replace us" pierced the silence of night. The White faces-turned-fiery-red captured an image of frustration, revenge, and hate. The tiki-lit march culminated around the campus' oxidized bronze statue of Thomas Jefferson. The next morning, flames burst into fury as White nationalists and anti-White nationalist protesters unleashed their animosity toward each other. Fists, clubs, and sprays paint an image of estrangement, anger, and torture. The scene slammed to a halt when a car plowed into a crowd killing Heather Heyer, an anti-White nationalist protester. Medics rushed to the scene, enforcement officers took hold, and protesters left the scene.

Peacebuilding efforts are necessary to engage conflict in transformative ways. In defining peacebuilding and conflict, we draw from Broome and Collier's (2012) notion that "peace requires attention to individuals' orientations, relationships between individuals and groups, and the role of institutions and social systems that discourage violence, promote equity and offer mechanisms for dealing constructively with differences and disagreements" (p. 251). As communication scholars and teachers, we have a responsibility to use our tools to address the social tensions in our classroom and communities through peacebuilding efforts. In response to the Charlottesville uprising in August 2017, CD was used as a peacebuilding method to engage classrooms and communities. In alignment with engaged scholarship and critical communication pedagogy, our use of Civil Dialogue® was not intended to transfer knowledge to students and communities (Barge & Shockely-Zalabak, 2008). Rather, our goal was to use CD as a method to foster understanding through dialogic prudence and therefore co-create transformative conflict through collaborative learning.

In collaboration with the Institute for Civil Dialogue®, the three authors of this chapter co-led a series of CD events in the fall of 2017. Among the three of us, we facilitated seven dialogues all dealing with racial tension. Among the topics covered were, Confederate statues, affirmative action policies, and hate speech. Open to students and the public, we facilitated dialogues across the Phoenix area on various college campuses. Participants were recruited through the Institute for Civil Dialogue's® social media, emails to community leaders who previously hosted CD events, and paper flyers posted on college campuses. The majority of participants were students at a local universities and community colleges (see Table 10.1 for participant's racial demographics).

Table 10.1.   Racial make-up of Civil Dialogue® participants.

Race	Audience	Core Dialogue
White	35	13
Black/African-American	5	6
Asian-American	7	0
Hispanic/Latinx	16	12
Pacific Islander	2	0
Bi-Racial	2	1
Multi-Racial	4	0
Native American	1	1
Other	5	2
Total	**77**	**35**

In what follows, we offer an overarching definition of dialogic prudence by its three tenets: provocation, value-rationality, and synergy. We then offer a more nuanced definition of each tenet before analyzing our case study through the lens of each component. We use our three tenets of dialogic prudence to demonstrate how CD can be used as a method of critical communication pedagogy with the aim of transformative conflict.

Dialogic Prudence

We advocate the need to embrace dialogic prudence when engaging communities around provocative topics and education. Dialogic prudence is both a method and an orientation. As a method, dialogic prudence consists of three main tenets: provocation, value-rationality, and synergy (see Genette et al., 2018). When taken together, each tenet provides a heuristic to consider when addressing contentious social issues. Through provocation, underlying assumptions come to the surface through value-rational narratives (Mumby, 1987; Mills, 1998). Through the process of dialogue, contrasting value-rational narratives contradict and coalesce to offer a more holistic understanding of the contentious social issue. As an orientation, dialogic prudence encourages the acceptance of ambiguity and diversity of thought with the ultimate goal of co-creating understanding. Dialogic prudence is important when the goal is to transform conflict by embracing diversity of thought and inclusivity of emotional expression. In what follows, we further define each tenet and show how they help analyze the CD events.

Provocation

In a CD, a provocative statement is introduced and participants are asked to consider their orientation to it. Provocation operates to stimulate a reaction that will yield dialogue and a passionate interrogation of a challenging topic. In this sense, it operates as a critical-thinking exercise that is inclusive of the use of subjective, emotional positions as a legitimate method of learning. In his use of provocation in college philosophy courses, Mills (1998) notes how techniques that are intended to incite and "awaken students from their dogmatic slumbers" often lead to stronger logical arguments (p. 21). Madison (2005) suggests that provocation allows for an unsettling of the taken-for-granted and can lead us to critical awareness. Provocation operates in classrooms as a critical pedagogical tool that generates passion and commitment to a topic, disrupts passive teaching/learning spaces, and brings forth critical consciousness. Provocation contributes to dialogic prudence in generative ways by provoking participants' curiosity and pushing them to evaluate their position on particular topics. It operates to expose personal truths and allow for collective and transformative problem solving.

Facilitators of provocation are tasked with finding the capacity to successfully embrace the ambiguity of the provocative moment and to move participants through discomfort in productive ways. CD is one such method that is uniquely designed to handle provocation by embracing a multiplicity of perspectives. It is inspired in part by Boal (1995), creator of the Theatre of the Oppressed, Forum Theatre, and Legislative Theatre. This work lays an important foundation for provocative, embodied public scholarship. One of Boal's most salient goals is the notion of balance or protecting the forum itself from being overrun by one polarized view. Jackson (2004) reminds us that Boal's Forum Theatre "was never about a simplification into right and wrong, never in absolute terms of black and white" (p. xix). Boal's use of the joker as facilitator (or "difficultator" in Boal-speak) works to undermine easy judgement of a problem and therefore reinforce complexity without letting that complexity "get in the way of action or frighten us into submission or inactivity" (p. xixi).

Provocation has the capacity to extend beyond the predicted results of curiosity, passion and positionality, and move participants to knowledge generation. Provocation leads to generative dialogue where ideas can be verbally examined and understood. Ong (2000) reminds us that verbalizing is necessary because "thought is nested in speech" (p. 138). "In all human cultures," Ong explains, "the spoken word appears as the closest sensory equivalent of fully developed interior thought" (p. 138). It is through the process of speaking and listening that participants come to understand ideas more fully and benefit from recognizing the knowledge deficiencies that may exist for them. Provocation provides a foundational principle for dialogic prudence in its capacity to stimulate a response, move participants to productive and collaborative dialogue, and generate and extend knowledge.

Provocation: Case Study Analysis

Provocative statements for the CD series on race in higher education were crafted to respond to the tensions felt on college campuses and the communities in which the campuses were located. The uprising in Charlottesville, as well as at racist flyers posted in university buildings, spurred our interest in offering CD as a dialogic space to engage White supremacy. In many ways, provocation was heightened by the rhetoric that surrounded the topic at the time of this series. Since provocation is used to elicit subjective, emotional responses, the crafting of these statements and the facilitator's unpacking of them was complicated. Consistently throughout the series, participants of the core dialogue and audience responded to the provocation with deep honesty and civility.

A dialogue that used the provocative statement "White students are treated unfairly on college campuses," resulted in participants unpacking racial privilege and disrupting the silence that surrounds the experience of minority students in classrooms. Some of the dialogue focused on affirmative action policies as "unfair" to White students, but the majority of the participants were willing to connect the statement to their own experiences. In one exchange between a White-identified man and a Hispanic-identified man, the provocative statement operated to facilitate questions and responses about the ways White bodies rarely experience discomfort in classroom spaces. The exchange was a series of disclosures and questions that disrupted taken-for-granted understandings of how raced bodies interact in classroom spaces. The statement becomes the provocation for a transformative moment for both participants as they navigated the exchange with respect and openness.

As noted before, the facilitator of CD operates as the "difficulator" of the dialogue and moves participants through the discomfort of the provocation. This was the case in several of the series on race and higher education. In a dialogue that used the provocative statement "It is more important to protect freedom of speech than it is to silence hate speech," the participants anchored in the "strongly agree" and "strongly disagree" positions made statements that were clearly oppositional—one claiming directly that hate speech incites violence, and the other suggesting that the revealing of dehumanizing rhetoric is a mechanism of progress. To open the opportunity for these positions to keep pushing at their interpretations of hate speech, the facilitator stepped in with a clarification of the relationship between hate speech and freedom of speech. The participants then shifted the discussion to be about accountability of university policies regarding hate speech, opening their positions slightly to find a mutual focus and allowing a new position that validated both statements, yet generated a new way of understanding them.

To speak about race and racial injustice in public spaces through a process of provocation is challenging. There is always a possibility that, as participants move thought to speech in an open dialogue, racist ideas are revealed. The format of CD has multiple mechanisms in place to address this possibility. The statements in this series were carefully crafted and vetted by Jennifer and Rob to ensure useful provocation without giving a platform for unchallenged racist statements. Throughout the dialogue, the facilitator, participants in the core dialogue, and the audience operate to maintain an honest dialogue and a commitment to having productive exchanges on difficult issues. In a CD debriefing, a participant pointed out the possible limitations of censoring participants after inviting them to be honest, and it is in this ambiguity that we acknowledge the powerful impact that provocation can have on communication and dialogues about race.

Value-Rationality

The concept of value-rationality has roots connected to Aristotle and extends to more contemporary critical thinkers like Max Weber and Jürgen Habermas (via the Frankfurt School). The following thoughts will unpack the roots of value-rationality in relation to dialogue and dialogic prudence specifically. Broadly speaking, the connection between value-rationality and early rhetorical roots can be made through the concept of *phronesis*. For Aristotle, there are three different types of intellectual virtues: *episteme, techne,* and *phronesis* (see Kennedy, 1991). In general, *episteme* concerns universals and the production of consistent knowledge across space and time (Flyvbjerg, 2001). *Techne,* on the other hand, is context-dependent, concrete knowledge aimed to apply "technical knowledge and skills according to pragmatic instrumental rationality" (p. 56). Finally, *phronesis* has been consistently defined as practical wisdom, common sense, or prudence. Put another way, *episteme* seeks to "know why," while *techne* seeks for the technical "know how," leaving *phronesis* to consider the use of practical knowledge. Of the three, *phronesis* is most concerned about ethics in the particular and is, therefore, the underlying assumption for value-rationality.

"Value-rationality," as articulated by Flyvbjerg (2001), is the balancing response to our desire for instrumental rationality, both inside and outside the classroom (p. 4). Drawing from the work of Marx Weber (1978), Flyvbjerg (2001) is summarizing Weber's argument that instrumental rational action is distinct from value-rationality. For Weber, we know these two types of rationality are different by their intentions within an interaction and how it may inform action. On the one hand, instrumental rationality seeks to inform one's behavior through calculability, (i.e., a cost benefit analysis). While, on the other hand, value-rationality relies on "a conscious belief in the unconditional intrinsic value—interpreted in ethical, aesthetic, religious, or other terms—of a specific act purely as such and independent of the outcome" (Weber, 1978, pp. 24–25).

Value-rationality is itself practical and guided by deeply held beliefs about politics and social ethics. As Habermas (1984) explicitly articulates, rationality in general "has less to do with the possession of knowledge than with how speaking and acting subjects *acquire and use knowledge*" (p. 8). Much of Habermas's work demands a critical orientation to how varying forms of knowledge are socially and historically bound and perpetuate certain interests (Roderick, 1986). Indeed, Habermas is quite skeptical about how instrumental rationality is used to determine "all other forms of knowledge" (Ewert, 1991, p. 350). He critiques this type of knowledge (re)production not to reject it entirely, but to reject its assumption as the only acceptable form of knowledge.

Based on this framing from Weber and Habermas, the type of knowledge a value-rationality centers differs from others forms, like instrumental rationality. Rooted within the experiences of the individual and collective, value-rationality is aimed at dialoguing about the risks, problems, and possibilities we face as humans as a means towards action. Thus, as we understand value-rationality within the context of civil dialogue, one individual's way of employing value-rationality will be unique to their experiences, the timing, and the space in which they are communicating. In terms of dialogue, value-rationality is a place from which interlocutors speak to sense-make, not in broad, scientific truths, or to seek a definitive answer to a social issue. Rather, value-rationality is used to share how one rationalizes their version of reality *through* subjective, personal narratives.

Before moving on to our discernment of value-rationality within our dialogues, we must acknowledge that because value-rationality is rooted within *phronesis* and consequently rhetoric, we do not claim that Civil Dialogue® is inherently persuasive. On the one hand, a dialogic perspective on rhetoric requires communicative scholars to be aware of how everyday people engage in rhetorical practices within dialogue. As argued by Genette, Olson, and Linde (2017), CD was created to fill-in a gap within rhetorical scholarship specifically to illustrate how rhetoric is practiced (and negotiated) by people. Based on the impassioned call by Crowley (1992), we advance that a dialogic take on rhetoric calls communicative researchers to locate how "rhetoric is practiced, how language is deployed" (p. 464). Taking up Habermas's critical lens, this means seeing dialogue as one precise communicative act that allows people to "criticize the discursive conditions that cause and maintain unfair and destructive practices" (Crowley, 1992, p. 464). While on the other hand, as noted earlier, the aim for CD is to create space for interlocutors to gather and have a dialogue about a difficult topic without intentionally trying to change other's minds. Therefore, in the assumed sense of what is rhetoric, those in the core dialogue are not there to use "available means of persuasion" (Kennedy, 1991, p. 36). However, this does not mean that a dialogue cannot have rhetorical effects. Simply put, the use of value-rationality within dialogue is not necessarily rhetorical, but its effects may be. We will demonstrate this theorizing between dialogue, communication, rhetoric, and value-rationality below.

Consequently, within a dialogue, the goal is not to "solve" an issue by coming to a consensus. Rather, phronetic dialogue makes sense *with* those in classrooms or communities while being rooted in their particular circumstances (Schwartz & Sharpe, 2010). Phronesis underscores how the ability to speak from one's ethical values emerges from the relationship between the self and society (see Farrell, 1991). Given this, value-rationality invites people to speak through the complexity of multiple truths while "being concerned with one's life ... and with the lives of others" (Smith, 2003, p. 88). Thus, one end goal of a dialogue is not to determine what is true or false but to cultivate an ability to "act wisely" (Miller & Bee, 1972, p. 205). Instead of guiding a dialogue to the point of a cost-benefit analysis (i.e., does fighting racism outweigh the cost of changing structures and laws), we value one's standpoint (i.e., one's experience about receiving daily acts of racism on a college campus). It is through this tenet of dialogic prudence that scholars and practitioners must admit that the dialogue may impact how interlocutors behave after they leave the dialogue. Through practicing value-rationality, they may adopt more "practically wise" and prudent ways of being and communicating in the world. Just as communication does things in the world, dialogue formulates and opens the space for us to self-assess how things are done, and *should* be done, in the world by asking us to speak from a position of value-rationality.

Value-Rationality: Case Study Analysis

Within the larger context of the United States, beliefs and attitudes about race are variant and contentious. An individual's skin color will play a large role in their value-rationality as one's race will shape how they experience the world around them. In one dialogue, the provocative statement invited participants to consider their views on whether or not statues honoring Confederate soldiers should be taken down. One core dialogue participant reflected:

> I believe we need to have more dialogues because we need people to hear about it [the Confederate statues]. It helps people to feel like they're not being bashed for what people say because sometimes people say it's an argument when it's just a dialogue and we were just talking, we were just trying to understand each other.

This reflection directly illuminates the power in shifting the focus from an argument or debate to be won to dialoguing. Doing so, as noted by the participant, encourages people to come from a place of understanding rather than attack. Or as stated by another core dialogue participant during their closing remarks at the end of the same dialogue, "the process of communicating is the important part instead of being right or wrong and being able to understand where they're coming from." This emphasis of moving outside "right" and "wrong" is how people in dialogue are able to tap into their value-rationality. This means more than just "tapping" into one's values. Value-rationality is the groundwork for how one informs their future communicative and embodied actions outside the realm of ruthless calculability and utilitarian beliefs. The "rationality" in value-rationality acknowledges how dialogic exchange is itself transformational, or an intrinsic value within itself, because the sharing of one's experiences and perspective can be just that as well. With CD, one does not need to rationalize their belief. Adopting phronesis over episteme creates the discursive space for the dialogue to flourish. More importantly, phronesis allows for individuals to demonstrate a complex and nuanced approach to a given difficult topic.

The provocative statement of another dialogue was "White students are treated unfairly on college campuses." One young Hispanic man took the "Strongly Agree" chair based on his experience of a teacher telling him that, as a Hispanic, he would have a better chance of getting into college since there are increasing scholarship opportunities. Because he was the last volunteer to offer their reasoning for why they selected the chair they did, his comment became the catalyst for the rest of the dialogue. As the dialogue progressed, most participants in the dialogue began naturally agreeing that college should be a level-playing field where people should get accepted based on their qualifications.

Just as this particular dialogue was winding down in terms of new insight, one participant encouraged their peers to dig deeper by offering the following personal experience,

> I feel that now colleges are more accepting of minorities than the typical White. But I feel like it was race and uh, the majority got a really long head start and then they tripped and now the minorities are catching up and they don't see it as fair . . . .I'm a scholarship student, like, I rely on the federal government to come to school and if it weren't for them I wouldn't be here. So that's kinda how I see it.

This comment, rooted within personal experience, launched the dialogue into a conversation about intersectionality. Instead of talking about race alone, the group began to layer racial injustice with concerns of socioeconomic status. An intersectional turn may not have occurred if this volunteer had not shared his value-rationality. Additionally, comments like this work to create dialogic moments where participants rooted in personal experience rather than abstract thought.

In another dialogue on the same topic, the core dialogue participants spent the majority of the time speaking from their personal experiences. While one young woman acknowledged that she has privilege because she is White, she has endured frustrating working situations with two fellow college students whose first language is not English. One speaker, who spent a good portion of the dialogue grappling with the position he took on the statement, offered this experience,

> So, I was in my FSU 100 class, which is an introduction to engineering, and I was the minority in that class. When 80 percent of the students were not White and there was [sic] people there just kind of different because I was the minority and I definitely feel like it's hard to relate with other people because sometimes they really don't speak English that well. They speak their native language sometimes and, ya . . . . So, that can be one disadvantage. One way you could be treated unfairly—I guess you have people come to the states but they don't speak English as well.

This sharing invited a series of questions from another volunteer. However, instead of questioning him to get him to make some large claim, this individual's questions served to get the first speaker to unpack his experience more. In other words, the questions posed were used to help deepen the core dialogue's understanding of this one young man's experience, not with the aim of condemning or attacking but to sense-make and compare to their own assumptions and experiences. Indeed, as the questioner summarized with his last comment on this particular experience, "That's not saying there's anything wrong with that [being the minority in the room and wishing for others like yourself] but it's something to be recognized and said out loud."

For us, this example illustrates the unique power that speaking from one's personal experience, in order to sense-make, and value-rationality is one of the strengths of dialogic prudence. Instead of just talking about ideas and repeating messages circulated through (social) media, CD opens space for people to speak through value-rationality, bringing their personal, nuanced, and sometimes contradictory experiences and opinions into the forefront. That is where dialogue can happen, not through abstract concepts but through a common agreement to speak beyond the assumption of who is right and wrong in order to get to understanding. With CD, this can be achieved through the power of provocation, guided through the speaking forth from value-rationality.

Synergy

Rooted in Bohm's (2013) systems-approach to dialogue, synergy is the coalescence of individual contributions that create a sum greater than individual contributions alone. When applied to the concept of dialogue, synergy is what happens when meaning emerges from various interlocutors' contributions. That is, the sum meaning co-created among interlocutors, becomes more holistic than meaning attributed by individual members prior to dialogue. Through a systems-based approach, dialogue becomes what individual members contribute. However, paying too much attention on individual contribution can become problematic.

Alvesson and Kärreman (2000) warn that too much focus on an individual's standpoint may obscure larger rhetorical influences such as White supremacy. As such, a tension between individual agency and structural constraint is needed in order to more fully understand the emergence of meaning. Synergy in CD emerges through the tension of understanding the self and other in relation to larger historical and social contexts. To further articulate synergy, we utilize a definition of dialogue that draws from Arnett's (2001) concept of dialogic civility and Deetz and Simpson' (2004) concept of dialogue as radical encounter with otherness. We go into each of these definitions to show how dialogue is a certain form of communication that embraces both individual standpoint and larger rhetorical influence.

Arnett (2001) describes dialogic civility as communication that embraces difference, opens room to learn from difference, creates unforced dialogue, and takes into consideration historical structures that inform difference. In taking up Arnett's (2001) definition of dialogic civility, we address historicity as a starting point for transformative dialogue. CD embraces dialogic civility through its very nature of offering dialogic spaces to critically examine contemporary social issues as they relate to ongoing social, historical, and political topics. As such, in attending to Alvesson and Kärreman's (2000) warning, adopting dialogic civility embraces the relationship between micro-level talk and macro-level influences. Furthermore, dialogic civility opens the door for various experiences of historical events to contradict and coalesce to provide a more holistic understanding of the rhetorical influences at play. However, exposure to difference is not enough for transformative conflict.

Deetz and Simpson (2004) critique certain dialogue theorists for advocating an abstract liberalist approach to difference. That is, by embracing abstract liberalism, differences and power dynamics are ignored in favor of creating common ground. Rather than adopting an abstract liberalist approach to dialogue, Deetz and Simpson advocate a politically responsive constructionist approach. Such an approach encourages self-deconstruction through radical encounters with otherness. A radical encounter with otherness manifests when one experiences another's value-rationality that challenges one's own previous understandings. By sharing one's value-rationality—such as an encounter with White supremacy—members of dialogue become exposed to others' sense of being. In what follows, we analyze how dialogic civility and radical encounters with otherness lead to a synergetic understanding of White supremacy.

Synergy: Case Study Analysis

Each CD begins with a background statement on current racial tension (i.e., Confederate statues, affirmative action, hate speech). The facilitator provides reasons why one be in favor of, against, or undecided/neutral on the provocative topic. Providing such information allows those listening to situate themselves in the topic. Finally, the facilitator reveals the provocative statement; in this case, "Statues commemorating Confederate heroes should be removed." Through envisioning their location to the topic, members of the audience begin to formulate their value-rationality. After a few moments, the facilitator requests five core dialoguers to take one of the seats on stage.

At this point, synergy is non-existent. Five members identify themselves as having value-rationality in response to the provocative statement. As individuals, their value-rationality may be based on what they have heard in the news, read, learned from family, and so forth. However, until taking those larger narratives and placing them in conversation with one another, synergy remains absent. The facilitator joins the core dialogue and requests everyone to share why they chose the chair they did. At this moment, larger narratives emerge. After everyone speaks, the core dialoguers take 10–15 minutes to talk through the provocative statement and how they enter into the discussion. In the case of Charlottesville, participants would share their various value-rationalities.

For example, two Black participants shared why they feel excluded on college campuses when they see statues of White men. One Black male professor expressed a similar sentiment when thinking about his daughter who attends a university founded by a slave-owner. These narratives demonstrate an argument for why Confederate statues should be revisited—whether removed, relocated, or re-signified. However, dialogue remains absent of synergy until other, contradictory, value-rationalities are expressed. One White male participant situated himself in the larger dialogue as a descendent of a southern family that has roots in the Confederacy. His value-rationality was one of honoring his ancestors that gave up their lives for standing up in what they believe—a value associated with life, liberty, and the pursuit of happiness. In removing the statues, that participant would receive a message that his ancestors' valor should be silenced.

With these contradictory value-rationalities, CD becomes synergistic when narratives are embraced for what they are and challenged for reproducing macro-level ideologies that perpetuate discrimination. For example, in response to the varying narratives, a White female audience member asked the question, "Where do we draw the line?" She followed up her question and said how she grew up on a street called "Washington." She was curious as to whether streets with names of slave owners should also be removed. Later in the dialogue, another White female student brought up the importance of K-12 education and its role in educating U.S. citizens on the importance of various U.S. histories. While left unanswered, the first question and second response offer value-rationalities that complicate and nuance participants' value-rationalities. After audience participation concludes, the facilitator rejoins the core dialoguers and asks for each participant to share their biggest takeaway.

After the CD on Confederate statues, those originally in favor of removing the statue came to understand the role of transforming place through re-signification. For example, a Black male student, who was originally in favor of destroying the statue, came to see value in how moving the statue to a museum offers an educational context to explore the contradictions behind certain people. Likewise, the White male student came to understand why the commemoration of Confederates might strike fear in Black U.S. Americans. As demonstrated, synergy inspires transformation, especially when it comes from co-participants.

Radical encounters with otherness occur when one experiences self-deconstruction. Self-deconstruction happens when one (re)examines their previously held assumptions. Through CD, core dialoguers and participants were offered a space where they could embrace ambiguity as a means to break down and re-envision their positionality in relation to provocative social issues. As such, the goal was not to solve the problem of personal and institutional racial discrimination. Rather, the goal was to embrace difference and to learn from differing value-rationalities. Fostering such synergy allows for transformative conflict to occur on all sides of an issue—which may result in challenging discrimination. In addition to radical encounters with otherness, the CD on the Confederate statutes embraced dialogic civility by recognizing difference as the central starting point for conflict transformation (Arnett, 2001). Through perspective taking, participants can cognitively grasp why someone may have a different viewpoint. Such a process maintains implications for how scholars can engage conflicted communities through transformative and educational dialogue.

Implications

Communication studies is a pragmatic discipline that requires phronetic research to address contemporary social issues (Craig, 2018). With a pragmatic orientation, engaged scholars and teachers have a responsibility to engage communities to both develop communication theory and inform practice (Ashcraft, 2002; Keyton et al., 2009, Seibold, 2005). Putnam and Dempsey (2015) offer five faces of engaged scholarship: applied communication research, collaborative learning, activism and social justice, practical theory, and public scholarship. The current chapter most closely aligns with activism and social justice work. Rather than working with communities to *solve* social issues, as does communication activism pedagogy (Frey & Carragee, 2007), a critical communication pedagogy approach (Fassett & Warren, 2007) embraces divergent perspectives with the intention to gain a more holistic understanding of contentious social issues. As such, we advocate the need to situate critical communication pedagogy as another thread of activism and social justice engaged scholarship. Weaving critical communication pedagogy into the conversation of engaged scholarship does two things. First, it provides a theoretical home for critical communication pedagogy when applied outside the classroom (Fassett & Rudick, 2016). Second, it offers language for engaged scholars interested in pedagogy as a site for critical-consciousnesses raising.

Critical communication pedagogy can be conceptualized as another thread of activism and social justice engaged scholarship—especially when the goal of community engagement is to manage dilemmas and not solve problems. With pressure to move beyond the classroom setting (Fassett & Rudick, 2016), critical communication pedagogy can find a home within engaged scholarship. One vital critique of critical communication pedagogy has been that its application has "stopped at the classroom door" (Frey & Palmer, 2014, p. 8). We believe with our combined experiences as facilitators, and co-experiencers of CD, that this method is just one tool communication practitioners and scholars can use to bring critical communication pedagogy into the public. Although one of the central tenets of critical communication pedagogy is social justice, as those interested in engaged communication pedagogy and practices, we cannot assume that every community is interested in social justice or is even at the place to act (Fassett & Warren, 2007). However, as Fassett and Rudick (2016) have later noted, critical communication pedagogy is more interested in "what we might call social justice-ing rather than social justice as an end goal" (p. 592). Since pedagogy has been framed as a space to reflect and transform through praxis (Freire, 1970/2003), we can see how CD fits the call for taking critical communication pedagogy outside of the classroom.

Civil Dialogue® is one method—for research and pedagogy—to engage communities in transformative conflict through critical-consciousness raising. Education is a vital first step before communities decided to adopt a social justice approach to conflict transformation. To act, just in the name of acting, is a troublesome assumption. As Freire (1970/2003) warned, acting without reflection and dialoguing can lead to the application of unquestioned assumptions that may not benefit everyone in a given community. In other words, taking the time to dialogue with your community permits those invested to unpack what social justice and/or equality feels and looks like in addition to what it accomplishes (Fassett & Rudick, 2016). If dialogue is a way of knowing (Freire, 1970/2003), then CD is one method through which people of a given community can come together and theorize about their world. Yet, social change cannot just be about talking, words must be put into action. In this framework, dialogue only occurs when participants' ways of understanding and being are transformed. One clear limitation of CD is that it is not an appropriate method for social justice action at a systemic level. Communication activism pedagogy is more geared toward this end (Frey & Palmer, 2014).

As a method of critical communication pedagogy, Civil Dialogue® embraces dialogic prudence, especially when contentious social issues are recent and rooted within community conflict. The Institute for Civil Dialogue® hosts series of CD events that respond to recent social issues as they emerge. Oftentimes, contentious social issues are rooted within larger discourses of culture, privilege, and oppression (i.e., provocation). As demonstrated in this chapter, we responded to the Charlottesville uprising to engage the larger discourse of White supremacy. As such, as a method for research and pedagogy, CD is one particular tool that exposes macro-level ideological discourses through participants' micro-level narratives (i.e., value-rationality). It is through the sharing of narratives that participants can embrace difference as a central starting point for conflict transformation. While further action may manifest, the goal of CD is to raise participants' awareness of the complexities behind social issues. This learning process can move participants beyond rhetorical sticking points to new understandings for change (i.e., synergy).

Finally, at a macro-level, engaged scholars should embrace dialogic prudence when engaging communities, especially when teaching and learning about provocative social issues. As detailed in this chapter, dialogic prudence is a methodological orientation that embraces provocation, value-rationality, and synergy. By embracing dialogic prudence, engaged scholars can work with community members of varying ideological backgrounds that diverge on contentious social issues. Through provocation, participants' value-rationalities emerge through the use of narrative. Synergy manifests when value-rationalities contradict and coalesce into the emergence of new meanings through dialogue. However dialogic prudence also requires engaged scholars to be prepared for what emerges when provocation elicits value-rationalities. That is, rather than provoking for provocation's sake, dialogic prudence requires an attention to the pragmatic use of provocation to expose ideological narratives for transformation purposes. In turn, CD as a method encourages participants to develop dialogic prudence when interacting with people who hold contrasting beliefs.

Conclusion

Engaged scholarship has much to offer when it comes to collaborative learning between scholars, practitioners, and communities (Putnam & Dempsey, 2015). In this chapter, we situate critical communication pedagogy (Fassett & Warren, 2007) as another face of engaged scholarship (see Putnam & Dempsey, 2015). Whether in the classroom or in the community, pedagogy regarding heated social issues requires dialogic prudence. As a *method*, dialogic prudence embraces provocation, value-rationality, and synergy. CD is one such tool that cultivates dialogic prudence among participants. As an *orientation*, dialogic prudence fosters a phronetic and relational-investment between scholars and practitioners. When framed relationally, engaged scholars can glean insight from the relationally attentive approach to doing engaged scholarship (Connaughton et al., 2017).

The relationally attentive approach to doing engaged scholarship consists of four components, "(a) engaging in ongoing co-construction, (b) embracing the reciprocal relationship between (communicative) choices made when doing engaged collaboration and the impacts achieved from engaged collaboration, (c) fostering conditions for inclusivity, and (d) practicing reflexivity about a relational orientation" (Connaughton et al., 2017, p. 519). A relationally attentive approach generally, and dialogic prudence specifically, is necessary when co-constructing an educational environment where participants can learn through provocation. Dialogic prudence, becomes another helpful framework deciding *how* to create educational spaces where participants can experience provocation, learn from each other's value-rationalities, and experience transformative conflict through synergy. If scholars and practitioners desire education through provocation, they should mutually collaborate and design a pedagogical tool that sustains inclusivity throughout.

When applied to the context of White supremacy, CD was used as a pedagogical tool for communities experiencing racial tension. In establishing a relationally attentive approach to engaged scholarship, dialogic prudence was then used to design provocative statements that excavated participants' underlying assumptions regarding Confederate statues, affirmative action, and hate speech. Without dialogic prudence we run the risk of reinforcing combative conflict. Rather, dialogic prudence fosters an educational environment where provocation can lead to transformation.

Note

1. Civil Dialogue® is a registered trademarked format of the nonprofit organization The Institute for Civil Dialogue (ICD). The concept, format, and technique of Civil Dialogue® (CD) was created by John Genette, Jennifer Linde, and Clark Olson, founding directors of ICD and alumni and faculty of the Hugh Downs School of Human Communication at Arizona State University.

References

Alvesson, M., & Kärreman, D. (2000). Varieties of discourse: On the study of organizations through discourse analysis. *Human Relations*, *53*(9): 1125–1149. doi: 10.1177/0018726700539002.

Arnett, R. C. (2001). Dialogic civility as pragmatic ethical praxis: An interpersonal metaphor for the public domain. *Communication Theory*, *3*(1): 315–338. doi: https://doi.org/10.1111/j.1468-2885.2001.tb00245.x.

Ashcraft, K. L. (2002). Practical ambivalence and troubles in translation. *Management Communication Quarterly*, *16*, 113–117. doi: 10.1177/0893318903253421.

Barge, J. K., & Shockley-Zalabak, P. (2008). Engaged scholarship and the creation of useful organizational knowledge. *Journal of Applied Communication Research*, *36*, 251–265. doi: 10.1080/00909880802172277.

Boal, A. (1995). *The rainbow of desire: The Boal method of theatre and therapy*. London, UK: Routledge.

Bohm, D. (2013). *On dialogue*. New York, NY: Routledge.

Broome, B. J., & Collier, M. J. (2012). Culture, communication, and peacebuilding: A reflexive multi-dimensional contextual framework. *Journal of International and Intercultural Communication*, *5*(4): 245–269. doi: 10.1080/17513057.2012.716868.

Connaughton, S. L., Linabary, J. R., Krishna, A., Kuang, K., Anaele, A., Vibber, K. S., & Jones, C. (2017). Explicating the relationally attentive approach to conducting engaged communication scholarship. *Journal of Applied Communication Research*, *45*(5): 517–536. doi: 10.1080/00909882.2017.1382707.

Craig, R. T. (2018). For a practical discipline. *Journal of Communication*, *68*(2): 289–297. doi: 10.1093/joc/jqx013.

Crowley, S. (1992). Reflections on an argument that won't go away: Or, a turn of the ideological screw. *Quarterly Journal of Speech*, *78*(4): 450–465. doi: 10.1080/00335639209384010.

Deetz, S., & Simpson, J. (2004). Critical organizational dialogue: Open formation and the demand of "otherness." In R. Anderson, L. Baxter, & K. Cissna (eds.), *Dialogue: Theorizing difference in communication studies* (pp. 141–158). Thousand Oaks, CA: Sage.

Dempsey, S. E., & Barge, J. K. (2014). Engaged scholarship and democracy. In L. L. Putnam & D. K. Mumby (eds.), *The SAGE handbook of organizational communication: Advances in theory, research, and methods* (pp. 665–688). Los Angeles, CA: Sage.

Ewert, G. D. (1991). Habermas and education: A comprehensive overview of the influence of Habermas in educational literature. *Review of Educational Research*, *61*(3): 345–378. doi: 10.2307/1170636.

Farrell, T. (1991). Practicing the arts of rhetoric: Tradition and invention. *Philosophy & Rhetoric*, *24*, 183–212. Retrieved from https://www.jstor.org/stable/40237676

Fassett, D., & Rudick, J. (2016). Critical communication pedagogy. In P. Witt (ed.), *Communication and learning: Handbook of communication sciences* (pp. 573–598). Boston, MA: Walter de Gruyter.

Fassett, D., & Warren, J. (2007). *Critical communication pedagogy*. Thousand Oaks, CA: Sage.

Freire, P. (1970/2003). *Pedagogy of the oppressed: 30th anniversary edition*. New York: NY Continuum.

Frey, L. R., & Carragee, K. M. (2007). Introduction: Communication activism as engaged scholarship. In L. R. Frey & K. M. Carragee (eds.), Communication activism (2 vols., pp. 1–64). Cresskill, NJ: Hampton Press.

Frey, L. R., & Palmer, D. L. (eds.). (2014). *Teaching communication activism: Communication education for social justice*. New York, NY: Hampton Press.

Flyvbjerg, B. (2001). *Making social science matter: Why social inquiry fails and how it can succeed again*. Cambridge, UK: Cambridge University Press.

Genette, J., Linde, J. A., & Olson, C. D. (2017). Hot Topics, Cool Heads: A handbook for civil dialogue. Dubuque, IA: Kendall Hunt.

Genette, J., Olson, C., & Linde, J. (2018). *Hot topics, cool heads: A handbook for Civil Dialogue*. Dubuque, IA: Kendall Hunt.

Habermas, J. (1984). *The theory of communicative action: Reason and the rationalization of society*. Boston, MA: Beacon.

Jackson, S. (2004). *Professing performance: Theatre in the academy from philology to performativity*. New York, NY: Cambridge University Press.

Keyton, J., Bisel, R. S., & Ozley, R. (2009). Recasting the link between applied and theory research: Using applied findings to advance communication theory development. *Communication Theory, 19*(2): 146–160. doi: 10.1111/j.1468-2885.2009.01339.x.

Kennedy, G. A. (1991). *Aristotle, On rhetoric: A theory of civic discourse*. New York, NY: Oxford University Press.

Madison, D. S. (2005). *Critical ethnography: method, ethics, and performance*. Thousand Oaks, CA: Sage.

Miller, A. B., & Bee, J. D. (1972). Enthymemes: Body and soul. *Philosophy and Rhetoric, 5*, 201–214. Retrieved from https://www.jstor.org/stable/40236814

Mills, J. (1998). Better teaching through provocation. *College Teaching, 46*(1): 21–25. doi: 10.1080/87567559809596228.

Mumby, D. K. (1987). The political function of narrative in organizations. *Communication Monographs, 54*, 113–127. doi: 10.1080/03637758709390221.

Ong, W. J. (2000). *The presence of the word: Some prolegomena for cultural and religious history*. Binghamton, NY: Global.

Putnam, L. L., & Dempsey, S. E. (2015). The five faces of engaged scholarship: Implications for feminist research. *Women & Language, 38*(1): 11–21. doi: N/A.

Roderick, R. (1986). *Habermas and the foundations of critical theory*. New York, NY: St. Martin's.

Seibold, D. (2005). Bridging theory and practice in organizational communication. In J. L. Simpson & P. Shockley-Zalabak (eds.), *Engaging communication, transforming organizations: Scholarship of engagement in action* (pp. 13–44). Cresskill, NJ: Hampton Press.

Schwartz, B., & Sharpe, K. (2010). *Practical wisdom: The right way to do the right thing.* New York, NY: Riverhead Books.

Smith, D. L. (2003). Intensifying phronesis: Heidegger, Aristotle, and rhetorical culture. *Philosophy and Rhetoric, 36,* 77–102. doi: 10.1353/par.2003.0016.

Weber, M. (1978). *Economy and society.* In G. Roth & C. Wittich (eds.). Berkeley, CA: University of California Press.

11 Teaching Conflict Transformation in the Basic Communication Course: Narrative Reflections by Graduate Teaching Instructors

ALEX J. PATTI, BRUCE CASE, AND CHRISTOPHER V. JORDAN

"It is the voice of life that calls us to come and learn."

—Anonymous

"There is, in fact, no teaching without learning."

—Paulo Freire (1998)

For those of us in the humanities and social sciences who embrace the messy, frustrating, complex, and rewarding activities of teaching, we are conscious of our unique position to cultivate infinite possibilities in the lives of students. Indeed, achieving these possibilities is laden with the often maddening and difficult decisions of instruction and curriculum: how we teach and motivate students; determining what students should to know and be able to do; and what fits the institutional and departmental mission, the course description, and our expertise as instructors. As teachers with a critical/cultural world-view, believing in the move from "what is" to "what could be" (Madison, 2012), we authors lean toward a more social critical-radical teaching philosophy. Therefore, we agree with Slattery's (2013) argument that education can orient students to creating/maintaining a more prosperous, stable, and just world. Injustice, oppression, and inequality are the expressions of unaddressed or unhealthy conflict; therefore, such concerns entail addressing a manifestation or expression of conflict.

In the communication studies discipline, understanding conflict is key to realizing the discipline's full charge, particularly as it seeks to teach students to be more mindful in their ways of being, relating, and communicating (National Communication Association, 2015). Aware of this, we sought to use our position as graduate teaching instructors (GTIs) to try something different in the basic communication courses we taught during the spring 2018 semester: teach the foundations of conflict *transformation* alongside the conventional subject of conflict *management*. We sought to pilot test John Paul Lederach's (2014) concept of conflict transformation as a core concept of communication, nuanced enough to distinguish it from, say, topics in interpersonal communication, yet essential enough to establish relevance in basic course curriculum.

So, how did we get here? In the spring of 2018, we enrolled in a graduate seminar, Communication and Conflict Transformation. All the while, we held full-time GTI appointments, each of us teaching two sections of our department's basic communication course. Inspired by our colleague, Nancy Maingi (2017), who writes about GTIs of the basic course coming to racial and critical consciousness, we embarked on a slightly different journey, one that meditated specifically on conflict pedagogy. Simultaneously teachers and graduate students, we moved back and forth between self-as-teacher and self-as-student. As we occupied multiple roles at the university and in the community, we noticed a significant overlap in our experiences: the desire to incorporate our own graduate learning into what and how we taught our undergraduate students. For us, it was coming to a higher pedagogical awareness. What we learn and teach makes a difference, and the art of teaching and learning are truly inseparable practices. Importantly, as GTIs, we were assured by feeling rather unaffected by what some refer to as the "curse of knowledge" (Camerer, Loewenstein, & Weber, 1989; Grant, 2018)—those so educated and immersed in their fields can be ineffective at teaching novices.

We hope that our experiences, like Maingi's (2017), illuminate the challenges and celebrations of laboring as GTIs. However, we attempt to write with a still wider audience: expert theorists, seasoned practitioners, tenured professors, and laypeople alike. Ultimately, we hope that this chapter reveals possibilities for educators who use their teaching to build peace, focused on, like us, creating safe, value-laden communicative spaces (Foss & Griffin, 1995); who are communication and peace and conflict pedagogues; and any and all other teachers who aspire to mold engaged citizens in pursuit of a more just and peaceful world.

Curriculum Design Process

The pedagogical decisions made in this quasi-case study were dictated by both necessity and relevant literature on pedagogy (Anderson, 2001; Gerbner & Gross, 1976; Jenkins, 2009; Watzlawick, Beavin & Jackson, 1967). In the basic course at our institution, it was required curriculum to teach a unit on conflict management. The course's textbook includes a chapter titled "Managing Conversations and Conflict" (Schwartzman & McCall, 2014), which is required reading for our students. However, using the knowledge of conflict transformation gleaned from our graduate seminar on the subject, we questioned the language of conflict *management* and implied praxis. With this in mind, we turned to Lederach's (2014) case for conflict *transformation* in the foundational book, *The Little Book of Conflict Transformation*:

In order to facilitate a move toward conflict transformation, we designed a common assessment tool and unique lesson plans. During the curriculum design process, we found ourselves frequently pondering over two questions: (1) Does this content belong in basic communication course curriculum? and (2) How much depth and breadth is too much for our students (predominantly general education students) to comprehend in a single-semester general education course? What was born from our efforts was curriculum that sought to strike a balance between depth of content and curricular fit, between rigor and foundational learning, between conflict *management* and conflict *transformation*, ultimately aiming to orient our students toward the latter while considering the tradition of the former.

In line with Wiggins and McTighe's (2005) effective model of teaching, backward design, we each used the same assignment with which to assess student progress toward the following learning outcome: understand and apply the principles of conflict transformation. The assessment tool was a persuasive roundtable group dialogue in which groups of four or five students, separated into opposite camps, were required to first persuade the audience on a chosen topic and then identify, critique, and collaborate on a possible application of a relevant peacebuilding program or organization (United Nations Women, UNICEF, etc.). To establish consistency across each of our lessons and ensure we are providing an adequate scaffolding of knowledge in order to achieve our learning outcome, we each incorporated Schwartzman and McCall's (2014) chapter, "Managing Conversations and Conflict," and Lederach's (2014) (1) definition of conflict transformation and (2) the accompanying four categories of change—personal, relational, structural, and cultural. Lederach (2014) describes the categories as such the *personal* dimension refer to changes affected in and desired for the individual; the *relational* dimension refers to changes in face-to-face relationships; the *structural* dimension refers to changes to underlying social, political, and economic causes of conflict; and the *cultural* dimension refers to consequences of conflict group life, identity, and cultures. Among the many resources offered by our graduate seminar, we found Lederach (2014) to be foundational, easy to comprehend for an undergraduate audience, and easily accessible to students as an ebook through the campus library.

What follows are our reflections on the experience of teaching conflict transformation in the basic communication course. Among the many drafts, notes, and essays, we refined each story to capture the patterns of our experiences. Alex writes about coming to a higher consciousness as a teacher and inspiring students to do the same; Bruce writes generally about the pedagogy of conflict transformation as well as the consequences of teaching "outside the box"; and Chris writes about the multicultural experience of studying abroad and weaving cultural competence into conflict transformation pedagogy. We conclude our essay with a discussion and a set of activities-questions. We do not claim that our reflections are anything other than the beginnings of a deeper conversation, grounded in our experience as teachers, yet with blind spots and gaps and needs for future development.

The Dilemma: Alex Patti

There is a violent storm outside. It is always elsewhere, distant, far away. The wind always comes rattling in first, followed by the rain, accompanied by a light show on the horizon. In all my years, though, I have only seen lightning from a distance. It is always elsewhere, distant, far, far away. My second grade teacher showed the class photos of a tree in her backyard splintered and charred by a lightning strike. I recall the lightning's animalistic burrow in the dirt around the roots of the tree. My dad told me a story of when lightning struck the front yard as he looked out the living room window. I imagine an eleven-year-old boy stumbling backwards away from the glass. These are disembodied stories of storms far, far away.

The reaching pines across the parking lot are lost in the black sky, black rain, rain-slicked black asphalt lot. With small brushstrokes, the streetlights smear yellow around the wet pavement. It is the lightning in the distance that, for a split second, paints the night in bright color. The pines create a serrated horizon. The black comes back.

I turn up the lights inside, and listen to the storm as it loses breath, muffled in the distance. It is dry and warm and safe inside. Outside, only the rain lingers. The real threat to our safety is far away, striking trees I will never see. So I check on my son (still asleep), and I go to bed soon after. When I wake in the morning, the day is breaking and parking lot is nearly dry.

* * *

In my experience, conflict seemed a snug fit with this metaphor. I've lived a charmed life: privileged (white, straight, male, cisgender, abled, from a middle-class family) and insulated from war and violence in my community in the United States. Even with a parent retired from the armed services, for me, war and violent conflict have always felt far, far away. Sure, I've consumed many stories that speak of conflicts, but separated by history, time, and an immense and incomprehensible geographical distance, I felt still no closer to a deeper understanding of these deeply structural and cultural patterns of conflict we were learning about in class. Perhaps in my ignorance, my narrow-mindedness, I initially missed the mark graduate professor was trying to guide us toward. Perhaps my privilege—of never having to directly shoulder the burdens of, say, slavery, a war-torn neighborhood, or a corrupt criminal justice system that would simultaneously deceive and rob me—blinds me to how conflict is manifest in the macro levels of societies, structures/institutions, and cultures.

I confess: I doubted in my ability to understand. But upon close examination and thoughtful reflection, I was able to cull out understandings from everyday observations and my graduate learning. It took considerable effort from both the student and the teacher in me. As you will see, this process of elevating consciousness was difficult for my students, too.

Bookends

It's November 8, 2016, on a college campus in a southern city. There's little doubt that this is a year that will endure as one of the most contentious general elections in contemporary American history. Our return to class on Wednesday is greeted with a mix of deep dolor and ecstatic jubilation. The general tenor on this campus is that of the former. Teachers and students alike walk into classrooms still disturbed by the conflict this election has sowed. For many of my students—freshmen and sophomores—this was their first election, the first chance to exercise that almighty, ever-discussed privilege that underpins our democracy: the vote. Yet, they were witnesses to contentious Democratic and Republican primaries. They watched American democracy enter into a garish spectacle as the top two major party presidential nominees were polarizing in their own right. ("I only voted for Hillary/Trump because it was a vote against Trump/Hillary," is a popular refrain among some of my friends and family members.) This was an awakening to the idea that conflict has the potential to be both destructive and creative. This is a beginning, and I realized there is more.

It's Valentine's Day, 2018. In Florida, a man murders seventeen people and injures several more in a shooting on a high school campus. Habitually, older and younger generations echo: *Another school shooting?* In class, I catch myself watching the door more frequently and deliberately. Even as I deny the morning news' attempts to haunt my day, the "mean world" is catching up to me (Gerbner & Gross, 1971). In the timeframe of writing this chapter, this was the ending. Not so much a terminal event that evidences the adequacy of my knowledge, but a bookend that designates a key moment in my graduate studies. In the year and a half between the 2016 election and the Parkland shooting, I have noticed the hints of a coming to consciousness. My graduate studies in conflict transformation provided me a vocabulary and framework with which to describe it. These are the bookends that inspired my approach to conflict transformation pedagogy for the spring 2018 semester. These events helped strip away my insular perspective. *The lightning is closer now, and I am in the storm.* Indeed, these current events are examples of conflict that call for a nuanced, hands-on approach to peacebuilding and transformation. They cannot be ignored.

Inspired by my graduate learning, I sought to teach conflict transformation as the foundational basis for confronting others and the world at large. To achieve this, in my class lesson on conflict transformation, I lectured on Lederach's (2014) following description:

> Conflict transformation is to envision and respond to the ebb and flow of social conflict as life-giving opportunities for creating constructive change processes that reduce violence, increase justice in direct interaction and social structures, and respond to real-life problems in human relationships. (p. 14)

I used the Syrian civil war as a case study for applying the four change categories—personal, relational, structural, and cultural. It was not an easy task: most students in class were unfamiliar with the details of the Syrian civil war, thus requiring a truncated lecture on the subject. When the three-hour class meeting was finished, we had filled an entire eight-foot-long dry erase board with diagrams, definitions, and ideas for remedying the war. At the request of one student, we identified a pair of peacebuilding organizations with which we could involve ourselves. I left class that night with a renewed sense of hope. Together, we understood the situation more deeply and orchestrated a fine assessment of the conflict, even identifying directions for change.

Did we heal the world? Not at all—which delivers me mixed feelings of guilt and determination. However, I sincerely felt that we all moved closer toward that invocation to lay bare that Levinas (1981) wrote of. We moved out of our warm, insulating ignorance and apathy. What stands out a few weeks later, though, was each group's shallow or absent conflict analysis from their respective roundtable presentations. This component of the assignment was one of the reasons for teaching my lesson. It was as if the lesson had never occurred, or magically disappeared from memory after only a few weeks time. It was tragically frustrating.

Advancing Conflict Transformation Pedagogy in the Basic Communication Course

After assessing the roundtable assignment, it became apparent that my students struggled to connect conflict to their lived experiences. As is evidenced in my opening story and as you will read in Bruce's section, this was not unique. In a written reflection on their group's roundtable presentation, one student wrote: "If we were to do this project again, I would have wanted our group to locate more sources that could help make the topic relate to everyone better." This student expressed confidence in the group's ability to identify and evaluate conflict, but also expressed concerns about identifying a personal connection to a disembodied conflict half a world away. This student's particular topic, big game hunting, did not directly impact any of the audience, making it difficult to stir the audience's apathy. In our in-class debrief of the assignment, however, most of the students expressed the confidence to use conflict transformation as a theoretical lens, even if they had not yet come to a dedicated following of, say, global current events or a fine-tuned awareness of everyday conflicts.

In my experience, patience and persistence is key to elevating students' consciousness. Enhancing student learning requires a clear purpose and adequate scaffolding of knowledge. Maybe my lesson was inadequate in providing a clear foundation of information. Then again, maybe the students who ignored the primary requirement—to identify, critique, and collaborate on an application of a peacebuilding program—were not unmotivated, but were rather overwhelmed by the assignment itself. After all, a 25-minute group presentation during finals week can be rather taxing on even the most organized and cohesive group. So I must remind myself: it took me nearly a year and a half to arrive at a hint of elevated consciousness. *Be patient—it's a process.*

I believe my move toward peace and conflict studies as a communication teacher reflects the possibilities for graduate programs that trust basic communication courses to GTIs, GTIs themselves, and the disciplines of communication and peace and conflict studies. While the theory and application of conflict transformation extend far beyond my lesson, far beyond my learning as a student, I trust that the assessment tool and lesson I used are sound reflections of scholars and practitioners who seek justice, humanity, and peace in their research and service. With this, I have expanded my instructional toolbox and hopefully yours.

Student Empowerment and the "Small Bites" Approach: Bruce Case

As an undergraduate, I took many communication classes that helped me transform actual conflicts in my life. I knew early on that I intended to major in communication studies, and this path has led me through a variety of conflict communication courses, informing me as both a student and a teacher. One message that has always been consistent across these courses: Conflict can create positives from negatives. This was a new idea for me when I first took Conflict Communication as a nineteen-year-old undergraduate, so why would it not be the same for my students? What are the clearest, most effective ways for teaching it? I wrestle with these questions throughout, but I first begin this section with my experience teaching conflict transformation to then move to some suggestions for its pedagogy.

What Can Instructors Do When Teaching Conflict Transformation?

Based on my experience, here is a pair of strategies that helped to enhance student learning: first is to carefully consider class size and, second, practice student empowerment behaviors. First, I had the unique opportunity to teach a class of only twelve students. This allowed for more discussion-based collaboration than I would otherwise have in other classes capped at twenty-five students. With fewer students, I was able to establish a greater personal connection and tailor lessons in a way that better resonated with them. Indeed, this size is conducive to the kind of incremental, experiential learning common for the basic communication course (Lucas, 1999; O'Steen, LeFebvre, & Ott, 2018). One main requisite of our basic course is participation, and the smaller class size seemed to open up increased participation and, arguably, lowered the amount of time it took for students to build community.

This was extremely advantageous when it came to the roundtable dialogue assignment. Students quickly formed small groups that they were comfortable working with, and, because of this, group conflicts among them were minimal. These group members seemed to empathize more instinctually and naturally. Part of this may have been due to the smaller group sizes (three) than I usually utilize (five) for this assignment. Altogether, this allowed my students to focus on analyzing the conflicts that they chose as part of the roundtable dialogue assignment.

The small class size also helped me to engage more consistently in empowerment behaviors. We were able to conduct in-class workshops more frequently, during which I could work one-on-one with students. Once they began researching a topic they cared about, the students' applications of conflict transformation occurred organically. They actively wanted to see and be a part of some hope, some change, and some transformation of the issues that they chose. The best presentations were inspired by a fire of interest and passion. They stopped worrying about the grade and invested in the learning process.

I believe a teacher can inspire these things—with 12 students or with 200. One must inspire them to find a subject that they are passionate about and tell them that their work matters. Help them navigate positionalities that differ from their own and encourage radical perspective taking. I believe the rest of the conflict transformation process will happen organically. In one activity, for example, students self-identified their conflict management style (Kilmann & Thomas, 1975). Then, students role-played scripted examples of interpersonal conflict; however, each script exemplified a conflict management style that differed from their own. This aided in learning how to take the perspective of the other. Whether or not class activities result in a positive transformation, make sure to reinforce the idea that the goal of any conflict lesson is *growth*, not *perfection*. Celebrate every victory—no matter how small. I understand that you may be skeptical about the lack of "rigor" in this process, that it may sound unrealistic or idealistic. I am in no way implying that this is the absolute right way to do things, but it is one effective way of doing them.

It is worth mentioning that one of the biggest challenges of teaching conflict transformation was bridging the age difference between myself and a class comprised primarily of a younger generation of students. Most of my students in spring 2018 were in Generation Z, around eighteen–nineteen years old. Fernández and Fernández (2016) suggest that students in this generation generally do not want to engage in face-to-face interaction and actively try to avoid it in favor of a digital or virtual environment. They also seek instant gratification, which, as many educators know, is often unhelpful in the process of conflict transformation. Furthermore, I have observed my students polarize their ability to accomplish tasks; either they can absolutely do something (as if it comes easy to them) or they absolutely cannot do something (as if they will never be able to). A large number of students that I have taught believe conflict is only argumentation; they misunderstand conflict to only be interpersonal "fights." I believe that this may be for a multitude of reasons—foremost is inexperience in the so-called "real world." For these reasons, I share with my students the following quote by Rothman (2016):

> Most of the time, conflict, especially when it is about values, culture, and identities (which so often is the case), should be engaged as an opportunity for learning: learning about oneself in a conflict, learning about another or others in conflicts, and learning about the interrelationships between self and others. (p. 126)

It's important for students to know that the struggle that comes with conflict is not without reward, and that they possess the power to transform conflict.

The ultimate goal of my teaching philosophy is to "empower my students to exercise their own self-determination, and respect and support the self-determination of others" (Hedeen, 2005, p. 186). In line with Freire's (1970) rejection of the banking model of education, I believe that students are not empty heads that need to be filled with information like coins into a bank. The teacher-student dichotomy, in relation to communication, implies that the student does not have the tools required to learn to communicate. The issue is that students see themselves through this empty-headed perspective. The written reflections that I assign on various course concepts are often met with students concerns about getting a "good grade," or questions along the lines of, "How can I do the bare minimum for this assignment?" Still others worry about writing down what they assume I want to read—the "correct" answer—not what *they* feel. I find myself having to remind them that they are the source of their answers on reflective assignments, and reminding them that the experience and knowledge that they possess is valuable. While this process of "deschooling" is not new or unique, it is pervasive in schools squeezed by a neoliberal education model in that free-market logic of efficiency, productivity, and standards is extended into the education sphere (Mirowski, 2013). And I find this model to be problematic and a hindrance to creative, effective, quality conflict transformation pedagogy.

Advancing Conflict Transformation Pedagogy in the Basic Communication Course

Many students have heard of conflict management/resolution, but we need to make an argument for why conflict transformation is better terminology and a more effective practice. So, how do we go about fitting conflict transformation into the basic course? Do we commit two or three class days— about three hours—covering the conflict chapter in the course textbook?

I find it important to teach conflict resolution and transformation throughout the course, not just during one or two class periods. I call this the "small bites" approach. With this approach, students get a taste of conflict transformation ideas throughout the semester, well before we discuss it more explicitly. When we get to the "main course," the chapter reading on conflict (Schwartzman & McCall, 2014) and the roundtable dialogue assignment, there will already be a sense of familiarity. I argue that conflict is not a concept that can merely be taught by instructing students to write down key terms and definitions, or write down "correct" answers as if every conflict has an easy, correct one. Because of this, one of the first things that I teach my students is that there is not always a clear path to navigating conflicts. They must accept that not every conflict is going to end after one conversation. I strongly believe that an appropriate lesson on conflict and communication begins on day one and continues throughout the course.

Here is an example of what this type of "small bites" approach may look like: Walton (201) suggests that there are three key components of teaching conflict transformation: (1) teaching students to understand and interpret metaphors, and how they shape our construction of conflict situations; (2) helping students embrace broader conceptualizations (paradigms, discourses, metaphors) of conflict; and (3) empowering students to investigate conceptual tensions. These may be advanced goals for a basic course, but not so unachievable if you strategically incorporate these patterns of thinking. It is important to ask the right questions of the students. For example, Walton (2016) used the following questions in his study:

1. In your own words, describe your understanding of conflict.
2. How would you explain the role of communication in conflict situations?
3. For me, conflict is like _____. Please explain. (p. 39)

I used these questions in my course because they are intentionally student-centric—they imply that the student is the root of the knowledge needed to answer the question. The student is thus empowered to answer in the way that they see fit, without worrying about being right or wrong. Framing questions that are aimed at reflection as opposed to perfection can thus enable students to assess their own subjective positions, standpoints, biases, predispositions, and idiosyncrasies. This is crucial to transforming our students' understanding of themselves as communicators with a stake in transforming conflict.

Dissecting and understanding metaphors can be done throughout a course and in small increments. I argue that similar activities, with the right questions, can help students become more skilled in understanding conflict metaphors in their lives. I do this by finding a recent or relevant popular culture reference and discussing it with my class. I have found that popular music videos and movies are a way to help students wrap their heads around complex metaphors. Recently, I facilitated a class discussion about identity and culture using rapper and actor Childish Gambino's "This Is America" music video. We were able to talk about a variety of complex metaphors within the song and video. This included various sights and sounds in the video: lyrics; pauses in the audio; various sound effects, such as gunshots and explosions; stereotypes and caricatures; and many others. This discussion helped students move toward a greater understanding of how larger-scale conflicts—for example, the video's portrayal of a mass shooting—are understood, represented, and performed, as well as how popular media ultimately informs and impacts our perceptions of conflict. The discussion was a success in both of my classes, with high rates of participation and engagement. We talked about oppression, privilege, race, identity, and the "state" of the United States, which led us into a discussion about the roots of conflict, stakeholders, and rationale for a transformational approach.

A Never "Finn-ished" Practice: Chris Jordan

During my time in graduate school, I spent the fall 2017 semester abroad as a graduate student at the University of Jyväskylä in Finland. The purpose of my trip was to improve upon my intercultural knowledge, with the hope that that wisdom would be brought back into my American classrooms. As a lightly seasoned teacher and graduate student at the time, it was an excellent benefit to study abroad while still new to the work; I feel comfortable putting new and experimental activities and practices into play. My time abroad gave me the space to examine how I understood intercultural communication and conflict, and how I was teaching them.

Once classes in Finland began, quite a few pedagogical differences quickly caught my eye. First, there is less of a hierarchical power difference than what we expect to see in the United States. For example, students in Finland regularly call instructors by their first names, and there is more autonomy for students to complete assignments and reach out for help whenever they deem it necessary. When thinking through the differences between Finland and the United States, I have noticed American teachers participate in a higher degree of "hand holding"—we frequently remind students of their tasks, assignments, and other components of their education. In my Finnish classes, it was apparent that students possess a higher degree of autonomy. It is easy to see

how students in American classrooms are not often afforded as much autonomy to develop their own understandings of the world. Finally, and most
obvious, there is a major language difference; interestingly, while English is
Finland's *lingua franca*, there is still a major presence and influence from
Finland's official language, Finnish.

When I returned from Finland at the end of the semester, I brought back
a desire to share my experiences with the students at my institution in the
United States. Differences in language, culture, and approaches to conflict
that I learned firsthand in Finland classrooms inspired me up to bring my
experiences back into the American classrooms I taught in. I was motivated
to help my students become more culturally aware of situations, interactions,
and approaches to conflict that may exist outside the traditional American
classroom and outside of their typical cultural understandings. It should be
mentioned, though, that there is often hesitation in how to approach cultural
differences and conflict, even in a culturally diverse classroom. Before I could
follow through with any new pedagogical practices, I had to first examine and
deeply reflect upon culture and conflicts, and how I understood them prior
to traveling to Finland and upon returning.

One such example was the 2016 American presidential election. Like Alex,
I encountered numerous instances of controversy in my classes during the fall
2016 semester. There were many highs because of the winner. There were
many lows because of the loser. There was an apparent feeling of polarization
in the air. My two classes were no longer a single unit. There were those who
were *for* and those who were *against* the results. There was also a lack of
understanding as to why the "other side" could not understand the position
of their counterpart. I used my trip to Finland to pose a series of questions
about the election: How do we, as Americans, feel about the results? What
do others and we think about the state of our politics? Importantly: How
does our president and government affect other countries? This was deeply
important and something that I had to think long and hard about. Seeing
how conflict is such a bigger issue outside of our own cultural-national understandings is something that, I argue, students should experience. Although
we teach a section on culture as a part of our basic course curriculum, it is up
to me as the instructor to bring relevant and varied intercultural experiences
into the classroom. It is also important to encourage students to learn in
multicultural spaces. Working together, instructor and student can approach
conflict transformation with a multicultural mindset with the goal of bridging
differences and creating sustainable peace.

I brought some key practices back with me: I allowed my students to call
me by my first name—understanding, though, that this is a privilege afforded

to me by my gender; I started to place increased accountability on the students; and I directed the focus of classroom topics and examples to beyond the United States. This last practice was important in setting up the context for my conflict transformation lesson. It helped students to see how they may possess a singular, narrow view on global issues, communication, and conflict processes.

Through the roundtable dialogue assignment, I wanted to access students' ability to understand conflict in other geographic locations while exploring possible multinational/multicultural solutions. This objective of emphasizing a culturally competent approach to conflict transformation fell in line with our course's learning outcomes while ensuring that students were gaining as much relevant, appropriate experience as possible. As you may have noticed from Alex's and Bruce's accounts, each classroom is different and has different challenges. For example, one of my classes was eleven people strong ... on a good day—smaller than both Alex's class and Bruce's smallest class. While this low number may be ideal for upper-level courses and seminars, I had the opposite experience as Bruce: the class experienced a high degree of apprehension. Working with the small class was no easy feat. There were a number of issues that came along with the intimate setting. For example, when students harbored an apathetic position or attitude, I, as an instructor, had to make intentional effort to motivate students to engage in the lesson. In an otherwise larger class, students often volunteer participation, removing me from the role of "hand-holder." And because conflict transformation may seem tedious and complex to students in a general education course, maintaining a high level of interest, energy, and motivation is a key consideration for teachers.

Advancing Conflict Transformation Pedagogy in the Basic Communication Course

My experience varied between the two sections of the basic course in which I taught conflict transformation. The smaller class found it harder to grasp bigger, broader ideas; now, this could have been because they were feeling that more abstract topic areas were harder to understand, or that it was too early in the morning for them to care much about the outside world. The larger class built off of each other with a positive group synergy. When we talked about conflict and conflict transformation, students would readily offer examples and elaborate upon the topics of the day. Having a simple standardized conflict transformation lesson and the freedom to teach how we wanted was important for my teaching process. Overall, the lesson I created was fun and engaging for both myself as the instructor and the students—I say *fun* and *engaging* because it reinforced my learning as a graduate student and as a teacher of communication.

As a component of the assignment, each group had to choose, evaluate, and incorporate at least ten sources. Students initially found this research component difficult. Once we passed this intimidating hurdle, finding information about conflict transformation and peacebuilding programs seemed to be a more welcomed process. I noticed their excitement to share what they had learned from their research. This is when the roundtable dialogue became fun! Each group had an abundance of information and crafted the presentation in a way that was easy for the audience to digest without diminishing the seriousness of the conflict. The solutions and ideas provided were both thoughtful and enlightened. I attribute this to how receptive students were to my multicultural approach. Feedback from students revealed that they enjoyed the opportunity to think in different and culturally competent ways and still engage with the process of conflict transformation. I believe it had a transformative effect on the students and their approach to conflict and communication.

Overall, I consider the lesson and assignment a success, but there is always room for improvement. There are many things that I would do differently. For space, I will mention two. First, I would assign readings on conflict earlier in the semester, which speaks to Bruce's argument for a more sustained, semester-long emphasis. I would also try to find unique, experiential pedagogical strategies to better engage my smaller classes. Together, I think this speaks to the benefits of being an expert in the content—or "expert"-in-training—and being flexible and responsive to students. But most importantly, like the lessons I learned in Finland, broadening our horizons should be a welcome challenge. And we should work alongside our students, especially those who struggle most, to see the importance of intercultural competence and conflict transformation.

Synthesis and Discussion

To pursue healthy relationships, engaged citizenship, and peacebuilding efforts, we believe that teaching conflict transformation theory and practice is crucial. It is apparent that we engage with these efforts in the classroom in a variety of ways. We argue that this speaks to the need for well-rounded teachers and practitioners with a thorough understanding of content and practice—even if this comes, like us, in the early stages of advanced learning. Together, we believe that our reflections shine light on the need for diversity and opportunity for GTIs, the deeply human encounters, the vulnerable, risky action of facing others in the classroom. We are, indeed, "laid bare" to the risky nature of teaching, of being human (Poulos, 2004, p. 148).

We also believe that clearly communicating course materials and the syllabus, instructional materials, and instructional methods can help reduce student apprehension, apathy, and increase motivation. Tuning in to the lives and labor of students may help you to actualize student goals and enhance the rigor of their studies and practice. Perhaps not as salient is the difficulty of demystifying conflict. As Walton (2015) notes and Bruce reflects upon, conflict is seen by many through a narrow lens: negative, oppositional, and competitive. In line with evidence-based teaching (Lucas, 1999), that is why Bruce argues for unfolding a semester-long, experiential teaching process. That is also why we speculate that some of Alex's shortcomings were caused by, in large part, forcing the issue in one class period toward the end of the semester. We argue that, like conflict transformation itself, its pedagogy should be process-based and experiential, perhaps spread across a semester, and the distinction between *transformation* and *management/resolution* clearly communicated if we are to achieve nuance and depth in our teaching of the subject matter.

Each of us are motivated to prepare students with the knowledge and skills required of being a responsible participant in the world, including collaborating on solutions to emerging 21st-century concerns. Embracing the heart of critical/cultural communication studies, pedagogy should not be lost among the myriad ways we utilize the basic communication course as a part of the general education curriculum. We agree with Morreale, Myers, Backlund, and Simonds (2015) when they argue: "the basic communication course is crucial to preparing undergraduate students for competent participation in civic life" (p. 353). And according to Frey and Palmer (2014), communication pedagogy should also include encouraging democratic participation and collaborating on solutions to social problems. As graduate students of a communication studies program with a critical/cultural worldview, we are trained to interrogate the status quo. Therefore, with the desire to prepare students for civic engagement, democratic participation, and collaborative problem solving, we are moved to promote critical thinking skills that, hopefully, inspire our students to cultivate a conflict transformation sensibility.

Conflict is well established as a core communication concept. If Lederach (2014) is right—and we think he is—then a transformation approach provides the most helpful theoretical definition and rich, practical groundwork for future research and application. This makes conflict transformation a core communication concept, deserving of a place in the basic communication course. Altogether, we believe that our case reveals varied truths of teaching and learning. So in the spirit of opening up and helping others, we pose the following activities-questions for you to consider as you teach and practice in varied contexts, with varying audiences:

1. *Write a brief story that conveys your ethical and moral beliefs.* Consider how you have developed these beliefs and how they inform your teaching and peacebuilding. Set your story aside. Then, a few days later, read it through. Have you seen these beliefs in action between when you wrote and read this story? How strictly do you adhere to these beliefs? What do you think your beliefs and practice say about you as a teacher and practitioner?

2. *Reflect on your experience as a peacebuilder and/or teacher.* What is one thing you learned while you were starting out that you find essential to a deeper understanding of conflict transformation? Why and how have you applied this knowledge in your practice? How might you communicate this advice to others?

3. *Write down a list of ten values that inform your peacebuilding or teaching.* From that list, narrow it down to the top five, then to the top three. How are these three values expressed in what and how you communicate in the field and/or the classroom? What can you improve upon in order to communicate and teach in your most authentic voice?

4. *Write or speak generally about a culture you belong to.* What are some cultural practices that influence your conflict management style (avoiding, competing, compromising, collaborating) (Kilmann & Thomas, 1975)? What is the dominant style of your culture, and how are deviations from the style received? How can you help bridge differences in cultures such as the dimensions delineated by Hofstede (1986) so that tenets of conflict transformation can take root?

5. *What are the most challenging considerations when you design curriculum for your class(es)?* Working with these challenges, what new lessons or activities can you try that orient student learning toward conflict transformation, engaged citizenship, and action (Slatterly, 2013; Frey & Palmer, 2014)?

With these questions as a guide, we encourage you to step out into the "unending conversation" (Burke, 1941) of learning, teaching, and peacebuilding.

References

Anderson, L. W., & Krathwohl, D. R. (2001) *A taxonomy for learning, teaching, and assessing: A revision of Bloom's taxonomy for educational objectives.* New York, NY: Longman.

Burke, K. (1941). *The philosophy of literary form.* Berkeley, CA: University of California Press.

Camerer, C., Loewenstein, G., & Weber, M. (1989). The curse of knowledge in economic settings: An experimental analysis. *Journal of Political Economy, 97*(5): 1232–1254.

Fernández, F. J., & Fernández, M. J. (2016). Los docentes de la Generación Z y sus competencias digitales. *Comunicar, 46,* 97–105.

Frey, L. R., & Palmer, D. L. (2014). Introduction: Teaching communication activism. In L. R. Frey, & D. L. Palmer (eds.), *Teaching communication activism: Communication education for social justice* (pp. 1–42). New York, NY: Hampton Press.

Foss, S. K., & Griffin, C. L. (1995). Beyond persuasion: A proposal for an invitational rhetoric. *Communication Monographs, 62*(1): 2–18.

Freire, P. (1970). *Pedagogy of the oppressed.* New York, NY: Herder & Herder.

Freire, P. (1998). *Pedagogy of freedom: Ethics, democracy, and civic courage.* Lanham, MD: Rowman & Littlefield.

Gerbner, G., & Gross, L. (1976). Living with television: The violence profile. *Journal of Communication, 26*(2): 172–199.

Grant, A. (2018). Those who can do, can't teach. *The New York Times.* Retrieved from https://nyti.ms/2P5QedB

Hedeen, T. (2005). Dialogue and democracy, community and capacity: Lessons for conflict resolution education from Montessori, Dewey, and Freire. *Conflict Resolution Quarterly, 23,* 185–202.

Hofstede, G. (1986). Cultural differences in teaching and learning. *International Journal of Intercultural Relations, 10*(3): 301–320.

Jenkins, S., & Fredianelli, T. (2009). Bonfire [Performed by Third Eye Blind]. On *Ursa major* [CD]. San Francisco, CA: Mega Collider.

Kilmann, R. H., & Thomas, K. W. (1975). Interpersonal conflict handling behavior as reflections of Jungian personality dimensions. *Psychological Reports, 37,* 971–980.

Lederach, J. P. (2014). *The little book of conflict transformation.* New York, NY: Good Books.

Levinas, E. (1981). *Otherwise than being: Or beyond essence.* (A. Lingis, trans.). Pittsburgh, PA: Duquesne University Press.

Lucas, S. E. (1999). Teaching public speaking. In A. L. Vangelisti, J. A. Daly, & G. W. Friedrich (eds.), *Teaching communication: Theory, research, and methods* (2nd ed., pp. 75–84). Mahwah, NJ: Lawrence Erlbaum.

Madison, S. (2012). *Critical ethnography: Method, ethics, and performance,* 2nd ed. Thousand Oaks, CA: Sage.

Maingi, N. (2017). Culturally responsive graduate teaching instructors: Lessons on facilitating dialogues on racial, ethnic, and cultural injustices. *Kaleidoscope: A Graduate Journal of Qualitative Communication Research, 16,* 19–41.

Mirowski, P. (2013). *Never let a serious crisis go to waste: How neoliberalism survived the financial meltdown.* New York, NY: Verso.

Morreale, S. P., Myers, S. A., Backlund, P. M., & Simonds, C. J. (2015). Study IX of the basic communication course at two- and four-year U.S. colleges and universities: A re-examination of our discipline's "front porch." *Communication Education, 65*(3): 338–355.

National Communication Association. (2015). *What should a graduate with a communication degree know, understand, and be able to do.* Retrieved from www.natcom. org/uploadedFiles/Teaching_and_Learning/1%20What%20Should%20a%20 Graduate%20with%20a %20Communication%20Degree.pdf

O'Steen, D., LeFebvre, L., & Ott, B. (2018). Class size for the basic communication course: A recommendation for the dean. *Basic Communication Course Annual, 30,* 212–216.

Poulos, C. N. (2004). Spirited teaching: A pedagogy of courage. In D. Denton, & W. Ashton (eds.), *Spirituality, action, and pedagogy: Teaching from the heart* (147–158). New York, NY: Peter Lang.

Rothman, J. (2016). Reflexive pedagogy: teaching and learning in peace and conflict studies. *Conflict Resolution Quarterly, 32*(2): 109–128.

Schwartzman, R. (2014). *Fundamentals of oral communication,* 3rd ed. Dubuque, IA: Kendall Hunt Publishing.

Schwartzman, R., & McCall, J. D. (2014). Managing conversations and conflicts. In R. Schwartzman, *Fundamentals of oral communication* (3rd ed., pp. 373–399). Dubuque, IA: Kendall Hunt Publishing.

Slatterly, P. (2013). *Curriculum development in the postmodern era: Teaching and learning in an age of accountability,* 3rd ed. New York, NY: Routledge.

Walton, J. D. (2015). The effects of a critical transformative pedagogy on students' understandings of conflict metaphors. *Journal of the Communication, Speech & Theatre Association of North Dakota, 28,* 36–47.

Watzlawick, P., Beavin, J., & Jackson, D. (1967). *Pragmatics of human communication.* New York, NY: W. W. Norton.

Wiggins, G. P., & McTighe, J. (2005). *Understanding by design,* 2nd ed. Alexandria, VA: Association for Supervision and Curriculum Development.

Conclusion: Response and Prologue to Further Work

GEORGE CHENEY, STACEY L. CONNAUGHTON, AND PETER M. KELLETT

In reflecting further on the chapters of this volume, we are inspired to revisit their insights here in a manner that complements the claim that we made in our introductory chapter, that conflict transformation and peacebuilding work is constituted by *both* promise *and* reality. The organizing scheme we chose for our conclusion is dialectics. Dialectic, of course, has many meanings in social inquiry and in communicative practices. Dialectic can be investigated at every level of society from clashes of major ideas (as in Hegel's, 2004, writings) to historical trends and forces (as Marx's, 1974, writings) to the examination of tensions inherent in the various domains of human affairs. For example, Billig and his colleagues (1988) uncover and assess key dilemmas in human social organization—between equality and expertise, teaching and learning, prejudice and tolerance. In sociological theory, a long-standing and overarching dialectic is between individual agency and social-structural forces (Giddens, 1984). For theories about democracy, dialectic is very important because of how, for example, participatory structures and processes can ironically come to undermine democracy itself: as when a participative system in an organization is installed top-down, or when a dictator is voted into power and even maintained (Stohl & Cheney, 2001). In the field of communication, Baxter and Norwood (2016) and others have employed a dialectical perspective to analyze relationships, for example, considering the tension between openness and self-protection in interaction and with respect to ongoing identity formation. Particularly relevant to this volume and book series, Cheney (2008) has encouraged us to consider dialectics related to ethics when doing engaged scholarship (i.e., privilege and equality).

Here, our use of dialectic is heuristic in that we aim to capture key tensions that are inherent in the challenging transformational work involved in addressing and sometimes moving beyond a conflict. In this way, we are not interested in delineating fine differences between what are called tensions, contradictions, and paradoxes (Putnam, Fairhurst, & Banghart, 2016), but rather we are inspired by the work of these chapter authors to name and employ six dialectical tensions in order to help us position the authors' various contributions and propel further thought, research, and engaged work. Like the contributors to this volume, we are not positing end points or definitive conclusions but instead are encouraging all of us, and you, to probe and explore further.

Under each of the following dialectics, we highlight several chapters in order to offer examples and to illustrate as vividly as possible how certain tensions may be recognized and addressed in however contingent and open-ended ways. The reader is encouraged to think of still other examples from other writings and experiences that help to illustrate and interrogate these tensions. Through this heuristic and reflective work, we the editors and contributors to the volume hope to inspire still other creative approaches to engaging with conflicts in our lives, in engaged scholarship, and in the larger society.

Seemingly Intractable Problems<->Unexpected Windows of Opportunity and Leverage Points for Positive Change

For several different reasons, conflicts can be deemed intractable (in a dialectical sense "stable" or "closed"). First, the history of conflict in a region, community, organization, or family may have been witnessed so long that all parties (engaged or other) may have given up on the possibility of any sort of resolution. In other words, the assumption of non-resolution becomes assumed and ossified. Second, there may be a structural or third-party barrier to attempting to transform the situation. This could be because a powerful institution is invested in the maintenance of the conflict. Third, emotions may be running so high with the mere mention of the conflict, or associated differences, that no attempt at intervention or even a quiet bringing together of diverse groups seems possible. In fact, this can be applied to some societal divisions with respect to globalization today. Fourth, of course, it is common to see conflicts as tied to fundamental value differences, to clashing cosmological orientations, and to apparently irreconcilable personal beliefs. This is in one sense a realistic view, yet, where does it leave us? Finally, intractability can sometimes be a convenient label for giving up on any hope of or effort toward transformation.

Several chapters in this volume deal directly with experiences in regions where conflict has been long-standing and, at times, seemingly endless. If there is a theme running through these chapters, it is sustained and sensitive attention to local contexts and possibilities for positive social change (in a dialectical sense "open" or "changing"). Here we highlight three such chapters.

In Chapter 3, Mwangi uses a case study in Kenya to illustrate a larger point about engagement of local actors and local knowledge, contrasting them with state-driven initiatives. He writes:

> As a direct critique of the liberal peacebuilding models as applied to counter-terrorism discourses, this study argues for the value of local agency in peacebuilding. The value of local level initiatives is itself a shift in security governance mechanisms. While not discounting the role of the state in security provision and broadly too in peacebuilding, this study examines the value of local level initiatives and their potential in the security governance framework (Solomon, 2017). Local level initiatives are applied in this study to mean the involvement of non-state actors in security provision in contexts where the state is weak or absent. (p. 70)

In the European context, Broome (Chapter 9) chronicles and interprets his long-standing engagement with different groups on the island of Cyprus. The need for a painstaking, longitudinal approach is captured by his summary of initial conversations:

> My conversations with individuals during the beginning of my stay helped me understand the diverse motivations, goals, and interpretations held by different individuals about how to move forward with the peacebuilding work. These differences existed not only between community groups, but equally *within* each community. Furthermore, other than their participation in the earlier conflict resolution workshops, they had little experience working together, even in mono-communal settings, much less in a bicommunal setting. Partly because they had taken part in training with the "other side," they were already under attack from the media in both communities. Most importantly, their conversations with me reflected uncertainty about what they faced as peacebuilders or how to overcome the obstacles that stood in the way of peacebuilding. (p. 206).

In today's world, there is now enough experience with the Internet, and in particular social media, to temper the prior heralding of a global village. The image is still quite apt, but at least three unanticipated aspects of Internet traffic were not well foreseen: first, that the capacity for rapid response would also have its dark side in terms of fueling anger and stereotypes; second, that it would become increasingly difficult to discern and grasp the truth, in even a contingent way; and third, that the same technologies that afford time-space transcendence may also be used to silo virtual interactions, attitudes, and worldviews. In these ways, "intractability" takes on unforeseen dimensions via technology.

Drew and Thornburg (Chapter 7) address the matter of emotion, selective use/exposure, and unforeseen ways that the Internet has fueled and fostered conflict. In this way, their treatment of the potential for engaged conflict transformation is urgent across the world.

Especially important is their call for counter-measures in the media:

> This is to say that for every instance of hate speech encountered in the social media landscape, there should be at least a tenfold counter response, and one that is developed in direct collaboration with those most victimized by hate speech. This counter response should celebrate and psychologically boost global society's most abandoned by the unforgiving inequities associated with neoliberal globalization, war, racism, climate change and economic poverty. For example, Kruglanski et al. (2014) assert that one possible counter-strategy towards coping with violent extremism is in fact to broadcast the experience of those individuals who at one point may have flirted with extremist thought but who later decided not to become terrorists and are subsequently leading productive and meaningful lives. They argue that this allows for a counter-narrative to be more widely established and harnesses the same forces that lead to the attraction to extremism in the first place. (pp. 181).

Living with History<->Moving to New Spaces/Places

Consideration of vexing, sometimes intractable problems and the emotions surrounding them points us toward understanding how trauma figures into efforts at conflict transformation. Research on trauma and its relationships to conflict has broadened in recent years to consider much more seriously how traumas continue to be manifest in groups and societies, as well as individuals, over time (see, e.g., Derezotes, 2013). The issues, then, are wider than grievances and redress but also take into account emotional dynamics, identity, and security (in several senses). The trade-offs are not often fully appreciated, but the issues have resurfaced at a national (e.g., United States) level with discussions of reparations.

In Chapter 4, Zvaita and Yusuf, whose analysis also deals with seemingly intractable conflicts in Africa, focus attention on cultural and the transmission and cultivation of ways of preventing and handling conflict. As they write about culture and its multiple levels:

> Culture plays a crucial role in shaping the behaviour of people and promoting peace among people. Therefore, it does not come as a surprise that local

approaches for managing disputes around the world (particularly in Africa) become central. Thus, the need to pull together these experiences and use them in educating the young people in fostering culture as a symbol of peace arises. Without a doubt, cultural attitudes and values provide the foundation for the social norms by which people live (Murithi, 2009). Through cultural socialisation, the young ones are taught to respect, forgive, share, protect and preserve traditional values that have been bequeathed to them by their ancestors. This explains why conflicts are easily and often resolved within the family and community settings without necessarily going to the higher authorities for mediation. Further still, the culture of sharing with those who are less privilege (poor) is inculcated into the young ones. The concept of sharing is what is referred to as "Ubuntu." (p. 104)

In a very different cultural and situational context, Waldron and colleagues directly address how to disrupt cycles of revenge and teach both forgiveness and reconciliation. A major lesson of this chapter is about the researchers' listening, but we would also underscore how what they learned is applicable to many other situations and gives us hope about the broader possibilities for training in forgiveness. Indeed, they remind us that forgiveness and hope are at the heart of peacebuilding processes themselves when they write: "peacebuilding is a process whereby harmful conduct is acknowledged by those who commit it, merciful responses are chosen over vengeful ones, and the parties agree to pursue relationships that are just, mutually respectful, and safe" (Waldron, Kelley, & Kloeber, 2018, p. 2).

Participatory Engagement<->Other Forms of Facilitation and Intervention

Here we would like to highlight participatory engagement, which is another theme evident across many chapters in this volume. Being appropriately self-conscious and reflexive about our methods and at the same time open to new ones is key to effective conflict transformation work on a variety of levels.

In this vein, we should underscore Black's treatment of "ordinary democracy" in Athens, Ohio, during discussions of school facilities planning. She writes:

This means that within a community, people ought to have a voice in decisions that affect their lives. Different perspectives should be voiced, listened to, and fairly considered. Silencing or marginalizing people is ethically problematic for a democracy, and public dialogue and deliberation theorists advocate for processes and institutions that acknowledge and clearly address difference. (Chapter 2, p. 44)

In discussing their locally driven peacebuilding work in Liberia, Ptacek and colleagues (Chapter 1) summarize the four components of Connaughton et al.'s (2017) RAA (Relationally Attentive Approach), all of which are grounded in participatory engagement:

(a) *Engaging in ongoing co-construction*: This key aspect of the RAA surrounds the idea of decision-making and communicative choices made while doing peacebuilding work with and between local peacebuilders to collaboratively identify problem areas, activities, and impacts which are rooted in dialogue.

(b) *Embracing reciprocity between choices made in engaged scholarship and impacts*: In this aspect, the researchers and local peacebuilders practice engagement by prioritizing relationships, opting for communicative choices that build reciprocal relationships through engaged collaboration.

(c) *Fostering conditions for inclusivity*: Another form of doing engaged scholarship proposed by RAA is to foster an inclusive mindset among both researchers and local peacebuilders. This act of striving for inclusivity ensures that practitioners transform their behavior to acknowledge various relations, positionalities, and multiple voices on the field.

(d) *Practicing reflexivity*: This aspect alludes to the need for local peacebuilders and researchers to develop critical thinking and questioning of their communicative choices while in the field and keeping relationships and the intended impacts of (in this case) their peacebuilding efforts (as agreed to with their collaborators) as the central goal during collaborations.

Design/Planning<->Flexibility and Adaptability in Intervention

Engaged scholarship, whether in communication or in other fields such as sociology, anthropology, and education, is accustomed to the idea of adaptability and flexibility. Still, too many efforts, even under rubrics like dialogue, deliberation, and mutual understanding, begin with certain frameworks in mind and are not necessarily agile enough to respond to challenges to the framework or to lessons from "unexpected" but profound local knowledge. Thus, it is crucial to focus on the creative tension between careful preparation and planning *and* remaining open to lessons grounded in local experience that will inevitably arise through deep engagement.

In a way, every chapter in this volume manifests this understanding. Here we would like to highlight a few of them. Paul's chapter (6, this volume) explores possibilities for restorative justice, using community dialogues in Kansas. We quote the study at length here because of the vivid way the process of engagement is explained and because of how Paul communicates openness and humility with respect to the research intervention:

> Guided by literature and support from the National Issues Forum and the Kettering Foundation, we followed similar processes for all four sites in terms of community entrance, conversation framing, and conversation hosting. First, Nietfeld would make contact and meet with community stakeholders to introduce the project, get a feel for their work, and invite them to a "framing meeting." This would typically take several weeks to meet with various stakeholders from law enforcement, the court system, schools, mental health organizations, and other community agencies. Second, we conducted a framing meeting in which we facilitated conversation among stakeholders to introduce one another, discuss goals related to juvenile justice, identify issues affecting the accomplishment of those goals in their communities, and identify other stakeholders participants felt should take part in the upcoming community conversation. This was as much a "feeling out" meeting as it was a framing meeting, as all of us were trying to make sense of one another and the work to be done. We tried to demonstrate our desire to support ongoing efforts rather than be outsiders parachuting in with a sense of us "knowing what's best." We were not always successful with all groups, as we experienced difficulty with a contingent of law enforcement officials in one area who were uncertain what to make of us. This was more the exception than the rule, however, as we found that most stakeholders appreciated being able to amplify their work in their communities. (p. 146).

In their chapter (5, this volume) on preventative and restorative approaches to dialogue and justice, Waldron et al. richly capture this tension and the capacity for creative transcendence, particularly in taking seriously the techniques that work for and are advocated by children—in this case members of Boys' and Girls' clubs. They explain how allowing children's *own conceptions of successful apology and forgiveness* can inform such applied research:

> Learning activities that involved performance and active engagement were largely successful. For example, kids enjoyed concocting "lame apologies," such as "I am sorry your feelings were hurt, but that's too bad." Perhaps they had heard many of these. In our closing interview with the children, Max, a quiet boy from Club C, described the "crafting a good apology" lesson as his favorite part of the curriculum. He liked how the "roots" (of the forgiveness tree) made him remember to be strong and shared that he had recently apologized to a friend. (p. 133).

Expressive Dialogue<->Mutual Presence and Silence

As has been well established in the communication literature (e.g., Carbaugh, 1999) but still not always taken to heart, silence is undervalued in interactional contexts and especially in conflict management situations. In a sense, the communication discipline lost something important in its curricula when courses on listening gradually disappeared, in part because they were not effectively tethered to other parts of the curriculum.

At least four lessons with respect to silence are important to highlight here. First, deep appreciative of silence runs cross-grain to some extent with the communication discipline's traditional emphases on persuasion, argument, articulated rather than tacit meaning, and direct expression. Second, dominant, individualistic "Western" cultures privilege individual messaging, even in an age where many messages are disconnected from their sources. Third, analysis of multiple levels of society can be brought to bear on re-appreciating silence: for example, in considering what its roles in contexts as diverse as popular culture, social media, and international negotiations could be. Fourth and finally, cross-cultural analysis can be very instructive in terms of helping us, in our roles as researchers and as citizens, to embrace silence.

For example, as explained in the Ptacek et al. chapter (1, this volume), the Purdue Peace Project (PPP) approach is grounded in dialogue while simultaneously navigating presence (being with) and silence (the U.S.-based team members backgrounding themselves). Indeed, one component of the RAA to doing engaged scholarship is "deferring" which "refers to our choices to rely on our local collaborators to help us understand what is appropriate and to communicate to community members when needed" (p. 8). Adopting this communicative strategy meant that the PPP researchers found it necessary to simultaneously be present with local collaborators and silence themselves to the extent that was ever possible. As their chapter described, everyday Liberians seized opportunities to lead peacebuilding efforts.

In Hullman's chapter (8, this volume), we find a different but an equally important approach to silence: that is in the ways that quiet reflection on one's own work and life path, including missteps and barriers, can deepen understanding in ways that enable the researcher-practitioner to better engage and assist other people. In this way, listening to oneself can offer grounds for listening to others. The author observes:

> During my first years as a mediator, I continued to analyze my own communication skills through a mediation-training lens. I concluded that I took too much responsibility for other peoples' conflicts and for solving them. My own relationships, I had self-diagnosed, were conflict avoidant... I was able to identify

my strengths and weaknesses because of the continuous training and feedback. I began to develop confidence in my newfound skill set. It is a goal for training programs to build confidence in their participants (Denzin & Lincoln, 2001), although confidence came later for me after practice had begun to create competence... I saw that mediation offered a way to empower people to create their own ideas of justice and seeing how people did this in real conflicts could only deepen my skills as someone who taught related courses. (p. 190)

Experiential Learning<->Reading, Discussion, and Reflection

In certain ways, all the chapters of this volume concern experiential learning, and at the same time put experiential learning in conversation with formal and informal forms of research. Two of the chapters address pedagogy explicitly. Together they capture very important points about conflict transformation.

Razzante et al. (in Chapter 10) explain and apply their method of civil dialogue, which may be seen as a member of a family of perspectives and techniques. Especially insightful and potent in this approach is the concept of dialogic prudence. As they explain:

> We advocate the need to embrace dialogic prudence when engaging communities around provocative topics and education. Dialogic prudence is both a method and an orientation. As a method, dialogic prudence consists of three main tenets: provocation, value-rationality, and synergy (see Genette et al., 2018). When taken together, each tenet provides a heuristic to consider when addressing contentious social issues. Through provocation, underlying assumptions come to the surface through value-rational narratives (Mumby, 1987; Mills, 1998). Through the process of dialogue, contrasting value-rational narratives contradict and coalesce to offer a more holistic understanding of the contentious social issue. As an orientation, dialogic prudence encourages the acceptance of ambiguity and diversity of thought with the ultimate goal of co-creating understanding. (p. 233).

Patti et al. (in Chapter 11) use their own multiple voices to address ways that conflict management and dialogue can be part of areas of the curriculum where we would not ordinarily expect to see them—that is, through deliberate but varied means of integration within the basic communication course. They conclude their three sets of reflections with this practical synthesis:

- *Reflect on your experience as a peacebuilder and/or teacher.* What is one thing you learned while you were starting out that you find essential to a deeper understanding of conflict transformation? ... How might you communicate this advice to others?
- *Write down a list of ten values that inform your peacebuilding or teaching.* How are these three values expressed in what and how you

communicate in the field and/or the classroom? What can you improve upon in order to communicate and teach in your most authentic voice?
- *Write or speak generally about a culture you belong to.* What are some cultural practices that influence your conflict management style (avoiding, competing, compromising, collaborating) (Kilmann & Thomas, 1975)? What is the dominant style of your culture, and how are deviations from the style received? How can you help bridge differences in cultures . . . so that tenets of conflict transformation can take root?
- *What are the most challenging considerations when you design curriculum for your class(es)?* Working with these challenges, what new lessons or activities can you try that orient student learning toward conflict transformation, engaged citizenship, and action? (Slatterly, 2013; Frey & Palmer, 2014, p. 23)

Closing

Communication scholars are well-positioned to theorize, research, and do conflict transformation and peacebuilding work for several reasons. For one, we are attuned to how the nature of words and symbols constitute reality and relationships among individuals and groups. In addition, we are attentive to how the communicative can unite and divide, be constructive and destructive, build and conquer. We understand that the work of communication, just like the work of conflict transformation and peacebuilding, takes place at the micro, meso, and macro levels. Moreover, the meta-theoretical diversity of communication scholars enables us to bring to light the structural, cultural, relational, and social drivers of conflict and their influences on (un)sustainable conflict transformation and peace. The complexities of researching *and* doing conflict transformation and peacebuilding cannot be understood, managed, and negotiated unless communication itself is taken seriously. Communication scholars must be at the table.

We, therefore, conclude this chapter and this inaugural volume in this book series with a call for more communication researchers to engage in theory-driven practice (engaged scholarship) in this domain and beyond. The prevalence of conflict and violence at the local, state, national, and global levels necessitates our minds and action. The complexities of said conflict and violence demands our expertise and our dedication. The wickedness of the root causes and manifestations of conflict and violence require innovative, multi-disciplinary, multi-sector solutions which must be designed and nurtured in a genuinely inclusive manner. All of this requires deep listening, multi-cultural and multi-sector teaming, and civil discourse. As communication scholars, we must champion and lead efforts to (re)build our democracy and encourage (engaged) scholars worldwide to work step-by-step, engaged project-by-engaged project, to help create the conditions through which conflict can be transformed and lasting peace achieved. We invite you all to continue this journey with us.

References

Baxter, L. A., & Norwood, K. M. (2016). Relational dialectics theory. In C. R. Berger & M. Roloff (eds.). *The international encyclopedia of interpersonal communication* (1st ed., pp. 1–9). New York: John Wiley. doi:10.1002/9781118540190.wbeic0019.

Billig, M., Condor, S., Edwards, D., Gane, M., Middleton, D., & Radley, A. (1988). *Ideological dilemmas.* London: Sage.

Carbaugh, D. (1999). "Just listen": "Listening" and landscape among the Blackfeet. *Western Journal of Communication, 63*(3): 250–270. doi: 10.1080/10570319909374641.

Cheney, G. (2008). Encountering the ethics of engaged scholarship. *Journal of Applied Communication Research, 36*(3): 281–288. doi: 10.1080/00909880802172293.

Connaughton, S. L., Linabary, J. R., Krishna, A., Kuang, K., Anaele, A., Vibber, K. S., Yakova, L., & Jones, C. (2017). Explicating a relationally attentive approach to conducting engaged communication scholarship. *Journal of Applied Communication Research, 45*, 517–536. doi:10.1080/00909882.2017.1382707.

Denzin, N. K., & Lincoln, Y.S. (2001). *The qualitative inquiry reader.* Thousand Oaks, CA: Sage.

Derezotes, D. (2013). *Transforming historical trauma through dialogue.* Los Angeles: Sage.

Frey, L. R., & Palmer, D. L. (2014). Introduction: Teaching communication activism. In L. R. Frey, & D. L. Palmer (eds.), *Teaching communication activism: Communication education for social justice* (pp. 1–42). New York, NY: Hampton Press.

Genette, J., Olson, C., & Linde, J. (2018). *Hot topics, cool heads: A handbook for Civil Dialogue.* Dubuque, IA: Kendall Hunt.

Giddens, A. (1984). *The constitution of society: Outline of the theory of structuration.* Berkeley: University of California Press.

Hegel, G. W. F. (1899/2004). *The philosophy of history* (J. Sibree, trans.). Mineola, NY: Dover Classics.

Kilmann, R. H., & Thomas, K. W. (1975). Interpersonal conflict handling behavior as reflections of Jungian personality dimensions. *Psychological Reports, 37*, 971–980.

Kruglanski, A. W., Gelfand, M. J., Bélanger, J. J., Sheveland, A., Hetiarachchi, M., & Gunaratna, R. (2014). The psychology of radicalization and deradicalization: How significance quest impacts violent extremism. *Political Psychology, 35*, 69–93.

Marx, K. (1887/1974). *Das capital.* (ed. F. Engels) (S. Moore and E. Aveling, trans. from 3rd German edition). London: Lawrence and Wishart. (Original work published 1887).

Mills, J. (1998). Better teaching through provocation. *College Teaching, 46*(1): 21–25. doi: 10.1080/87567559809596228.

Mumby, D. K. (1987). The political function of narrative in organizations. *Communication Monographs, 54,* 113–127. doi: 10.1080/03637758709390221.

Murithi, T. (2009). An African perspective on peace education: Ubuntu lessons in reconciliation. *International Review of Education, 55,* 221–233.

Putnam, L. L., *Fairhurst,* G. T., & Banghart, S. (2016). Contradictions, dialectics, and paradoxes in organizations: A constitutive approach. The Academy of Management Annals, 65–171. doi: 10.1080/19416520.2016.1162421.

Slatterly, P. (2013). *Curriculum development in the postmodern era: Teaching and learning in an age of accountability,* 3rd ed. New York, NY: Routledge.

Solomon, H. (2017). Beyond the state: Reconceptualising African security in the 21st century. *African Security Review, 26*(1): 62–76.

Stohl, C., & Cheney, G. (2001). Participatory processes/paradoxical practices: Communication and the dilemmas of organizational democracy. *Management Communication Quarterly, 14*(3): 349–407.

About the Editors

Peter M. Kellett (Ph.D., Southern Illinois University at Carbondale) is a professor of communication studies at the University of North Carolina at Greensboro. His scholarly work focuses on narrative approaches to analyzing and transforming relational conflict to create more just and fair relationships. He is also active in narrative scholarship relating to health communication, as well as disability.

Stacey L. Connaughton (Ph.D., the University of Texas at Austin) is an associate professor in the Brian Lamb School of Communication at Purdue University. Her research examines leadership and identification in geographically distributed contexts, particularly as these issues relate to virtual teams/organizations, political parties, and peacebuilding. Dr. Connaughton is the director of the Purdue Policy Research Institute at Purdue's Discovery Park, and she serves as director of the Purdue Peace Project (PPP). As Director of PPP, Dr. Connaughton led the relationship building, project development, and monitoring and evaluation for locally led political violence prevention initiatives in Ghana, Liberia, and Nigeria. Dr. Connaughton is the recipient of Purdue's 2017 Faculty Engaged Scholar Award, and Purdue's 2018 Trailblazer Award—an award given to a midcareer tenured faculty member for innovation and impact in research.

George Cheney (Ph.D., Purdue University) is a professor of communication at the University of Colorado, Colorado Springs. His teaching and research interests include identity in organizations, professional ethics, quality of worklife, globalization and localization, alternative ways of organizing, peace, and sustainability. Working solo or collaboratively, he has published ten books and over 100 articles, chapters, and reviews. George is a committed practitioner of service learning and has served on several non-profit boards or in a consulting capacity with them. He is a regular contributor of op eds to newspapers. Currently, he is at work on a series of articles about how cooperative structures can serve goals of economic justice, social transformation, and environmental sustainability.

About the Contributors

Cynthia J. Becker (M.A., Arizona State University) is an adjunct faculty in the Maricopa County Community College system. As an instructor, her passion is empowering students with the skills necessary to improve their communication competency, emotional intelligence, and critical thinking, toward the goal of improving their personal, academic, professional, and social worlds.

Laura W. Black (Ph.D., University of Washington) is an associate professor in the School of Communication Studies at Ohio University. Her research examines group interaction in public dialogue and deliberation events with a specific focus on facilitation practices and the communication of difference. She serves as the editor of the *Journal of Public Deliberation* and was part of the founding officers of the Public Dialogue and Deliberation division of the National Communication Association. Her research has appeared in numerous book chapters and journals such as *Communication Theory, Small Group Research, Journal of Applied Communication Research*, and the *Western Journal of Communication*.

Benjamin J. Broome (Ph.D., University of Kansas) is a professor and director of doctoral studies in the High Downs School of Human Communication. Benjamin Broome is an intercultural communication scholar whose work centers on the theory and practice of sustainable dialogue and its role in peacebuilding. His research is focused on finding ways to help groups, organizations, and communities respond to conflict through dialogue rather than violence.

Bruce Case (M.A., the University of North Carolina at Greensboro) is interested in rhetoric, discourse, and conflict transformation with a focus on contemporary U.S. anti-immigration rhetoric.

John Drew (MFA, Parsons New School for Design) is an assistant professor of digital media studies, Adelphi University. He is a filmmaker and digital media scholar whose films and research focus on the intersection of neoliberalism, technology and economic disparity, particularly as they relate to the global north/south divide.

John Mwangi Githigaro is a lecturer in peace and conflict studies at the St. Paul's University, Limuru (Kenya). He holds a Ph.D. in International Relations from the United States International University Africa (USIU-A) Nairobi, Kenya. His research interests revolve around peace and security studies, refugee studies, and media portrayals of terrorism with a specific focus on the Horn of Africa. He was a Nextgen Social Science Research Council New York (SSRC) fellow (2016–2019).

Katrina N. Hanna (M.A., Communication Studies, Kansas State University) is a doctoral student and graduate teaching associate at the Hugh Downs School of Human Communication. Her primary area of research is within rhetorical criticism and rhetorical field methods specifically. Kat uses these theories and methods to explore rhetorics specific to education, race, and neoliberalism.

Gwen A. Hullman (Ph.D., Kent State University) is an associate professor and chair, Department of Communication Studies, Ashland University. She is a scholar of message design as it applies to conflict, health, and interpersonal communication. Research focuses on message design, conversational goals, and associated outcomes for relationships, individuals, and communities.

Christopher V. Jordan (M.A., the University of North Carolina at Greensboro) is an assistant director for Academic Advising in the College of Arts and Sciences at UNCG, and a lecturer in the Department of Communication Studies at UNCG. He completed his M.A. capstone project on using humor as cultural adaptation in Finnish society. He has presented a variety of workshops on intercultural communication.

Daniel Kamal (M.Sc., Universiti Putra Malaysia) is a Ph.D. candidate in the Brian Lamb School of Communication at Purdue University. Daniel's research interests revolve around the promotion of preventive health behaviors through social media platforms, which place emphasis on the role of individuals as agents of health promotion. Specifically, he is currently examining how social media could potentially be used to promote regular exercise behavior among audiences. He investigates phenomenon related to this area of interest primarily with quantitative methods (e.g., experiments).

Douglas L. Kelley (Ph.D., University of Arizona) is a professor of communication studies and Lincoln professor of relationship ethics at Arizona State University. His research and teaching focus on intimacy and love between relational partners and how they can respond humanely to hurt and struggle. He is recipient of the 2017 Bernard Brommel Award for Family Communication and author or co-author of five books, including *A Communicative Approach to Conflict, Forgiveness, and Reconciliation: Reimagining Our Relationships* (2019), *Just Relationships: Living Out Social Justice* (2017), *Moral Talk Across the Lifespan* (2015), *Marital Communication* (2012), and the award-winning *Communicating Forgiveness* (2008).

Dayna N. Kloeber, M.A. is a doctoral student in the Hugh Downs School of Human Communication. Dayna's research focuses on how the communication of forgiveness helps advance the theoretical distinctions between forgiveness and reconciliation. She has co-authored a number of journal articles, book chapters, and most recently a book titled, *A Communicative Approach to Conflict, Forgiveness, and Reconciliation: Reimagining Our Relationships.* Dayna also created *The Forgiveness Tree Ceremony,* and together with colleagues and co-authors Vincent Waldron and Douglas Kelley, they bring forgiveness education into communities with *The Forgiveness Tree Project* initiative.

Jasmine R. Linabary (Ph.D., Purdue University), an assistant professor in the Department of Communication and Theatre at Emporia State University, Emporia, Kansas, USA. Her research focuses on organizing, new media, and social change, with particular interests in feminist and participatory methodologies. Her recent research has centered on issues of safety and inclusive participation in digital and physical spaces. She is the former associate director of research and operations for the Purdue Peace Project, an initiative dedicated to locally led peacebuilding housed at Purdue University.

Jennifer A. Linde (M.A., Arizona State University) is a senior lecturer in the Hugh Downs School of Human Communication at Arizona State University and artistic director of the Empty Space (Theatre). She has participated in the design and development of Civil Dialogue at Arizona State University since its inception in 2004. Linde engages Civil Dialogue as a pedagogical tool in performance studies classes and facilitates Civil Dialogue events in public and educational contexts.

Vonn R. Magnin (MPA, Arizona State University) is director of Impact & Outreach Programs at Boys & Girls Clubs of Metro Phoenix. Vonn has more than twenty years in the youth development field working in non-profit organizations, government, and public schools. His work emphasizes both violence and substance-abuse prevention, and social-emotional learning.

Alex J. Patti (M.A., the University of North Carolina at Greensboro) is a lecturer in communication studies at UNCG. He is interested in the intersections of communication, education, and lived experiences. Using qualitative methods, mainly (auto)ethnography, he engages primarily with creating deeper understandings of interpersonal communication and communication pedagogy.

Gregory D. Paul (Ph.D., Texas A&M University) is an associate professor and department head in the Department of Communication Studies at Kansas State University. His research is rooted in an interest in developing systems that promote healing, growth, and dialogue. Much of his research explores restorative justice, focusing on its communicative dimensions and the factors that promote its growth.

Jonathan Pettigrew (Ph.D., Penn State University), an associate professor in the Hugh Downs School of Human Communication at Arizona State University. Pettigrew's scholarship is dedicated to working alongside community members to produce novel health intervention materials that serve youth, families, schools, and society. He has led research that includes developing culturally appropriate intervention programs, studying how interventions are implemented, and analyzing program outcomes.

Jennifer K. Ptacek (Ph.D., Purdue University) is an assistant professor in the Department of Communication at University of Dayton. Jennifer's research examines intersections of health and organizational communication, specifically in contexts of relationships in healthcare workplaces, stress and social support among healthcare workers, and organizational identification and its influence within career trajectories. She is a former research assistant for the Purdue Peace Project, which is a political violence prevention initiative with locally driven projects in West Africa, Latin America, and the United States. Her published work has appeared in outlets including *Journal of Applied Communication Research* and *Communication Yearbook*.

Meghana Rawat (M.A., Purdue University) is a Ph.D. student in the Brian Lamb School of Communication at Purdue University. Her research focuses on using a network theory approach to examine how health organizations at the grassroots and donor-level collaborate. Specifically, she is interested in discovering communicatively constituted relationship patterns which impact project sustainability. She has been a research assistant with the Purdue Peace Project and is interested in engaged scholarly work.

Robert J. Razzante (M.Ed., Ohio University) is a Ph.D. student in the Hugh Downs School of Human Communication at Arizona State University. Among Rob's topics of study are workplace well-being, communicating for inclusivity, and dialogue. At the core of his interests lies a desire to engage communities and organizations to develop pragmatic ways to address complex social problems.

Tonia Smith, Bachelor of Arts, Longwood University, Branch Manager, Tonia has worked with the Boys & Girls Clubs since 2008 in a variety of capacities, including serving as a teen director and education coordinator, giving special attention to teen services. Her professional background includes National Training Certifications from Boys & Girls Clubs of America in Strength-Based Strategies and Learning Coaching.

Devin Thornburg (Ph.D., New York University) is a professor in the Ruth S. Ammon School of Education at Adelphi University. Dr. Thornburg's scholarly work and teaching focuses on psychology, culture, language, and learning, always within the frameworks of social justice and human rights. For the past several years, his scholarly work has focused on the experience of immigrant students in educational settings as well as those who educate them. His latest book is on trust in learning, with research collected from ten countries in three continents.

Vincent R. Waldron (Ph.D., Ohio State University) is a professor of communication Studies and Lincoln Professor of Relationship Ethics at Arizona State University. His research and teaching focus on relational resilience, forgiveness, and the communication practices that make relationships good, in the moral sense of that word. He is author or co-author of eight books, including, *The Middle Years of Marriage: Change, Challenge, and Growth* (2017); *Negotiating Workplace Relationships* (2018), and *A Communicative Approach to Conflict, Forgiveness, and Reconciliation: Reimagining Our Relationships* (2019). His articles have appeared recently in such outlets as *Journal of Applied Communication Research* and *Journal of Family Communication*.

Ibrahim Yusuf is a lecturer in the Department of Political Science, Federal University Lokoja, Nigeria. He is currently a Ph.D. candidate in political science at the University of KwaZulu-Natal, Durban, South Africa. His M.A. and B.A. degrees in political science from the Ahmadu Bello University Zaria, Nigeria. He also holds a Post Graduate Diploma (PGD) in Education from the National Teachers' Institute, Nigeria. Mr. Ibrahim has published in both local and international journals. His research interest revolves around peace and conflict studies, terrorism, security, migration democracy and election violence, and international relations.

Gilbert Tinashe Zvaita is a Ph.D. candidate at the International Center of Nonviolence at Durban University of Technology in South Africa. He is also a research scholar for Good Governance Africa a Pan-African non-profit institution. He holds a master's in social sciences and a BSS (Hons) in Conflict Transformation & Peace Studies (*Cum Laude*) from the University of KwaZulu-Natal. Gilbert is a peacebuilding researcher with interests in African peacebuilding, politics, governance, nonviolence, elections, and democracy. His current research is an action research focusing on promoting youth participation in peacebuilding.

Index